French Theater since 1968

Twayne's World Authors Series
French Literature

David O'Connell

Georgia State University

TWAS 852

French Theater since 1968

Bettina L. Knapp

Hunter College

Twayne Publishers
An Imprint of Simon & Schuster Macmillan
New York

Prentice Hall International
London Mexico City New Delhi Singapore Sydney Toronto

French Theater since 1968
Bettina L. Knapp

Twayne Publishers
An Imprint of Simon & Schuster Macmillan
866 Third Avenue
New York, New York 10022

Library of Congress Cataloging-in-Publication Data

Knapp, Bettina Liebowitz, 1926–
    French theater since 1968 / Bettina L. Knapp
        p.   cm. — (Twayne's world authors series ; TWAS 852)
    Includes bibliographical references and index.
    ISBN 0–8057–8297–4
    1. French drama—20th century—History and criticism.   I. Title.
II. Series.
PQ556.K55   1995
842'.91409—dc20   94–24099
                                                                            CIP

10 9 8 7 6 5 4 3 2 1

Printed in the United States of America.

To the late Roger Blin,
Mentor and Inspiration

Contents

Preface

The goal of the students and militant New Leftists of the May Movement of 1968 was to abolish what they considered the French government's repression and its nurturing of a bureaucratic consumer society. Chief among their multiple targets were a highly competitive educational system, ever-encroaching technocracy, sexual repression, and the Vietnam War.

Violence erupted on 3 May, when the police entered the sacred precincts of the Sorbonne to quiet the chaos brought about by "troublemakers." The rebels erected barricades, wrote tracts, and formed action and decision-making committees that encouraged free-flowing discussions, arguments, and confrontations. Slogans garnished the walls of the Sorbonne and the Latin Quarter. A piano brought into the courtyard of the university to play music and especially jazz encouraged a spirit of festivity, optimism, and hope in the future—within a framework of learning. Passions ran high; such "rationalists" as Hegel, Marx, Freud, Barthes, and Lacan were worshiped and deified, for they introduced—so the protestors thought—a fresh purpose and new awareness of the life experience.

Deep dissatisfaction with Charles de Gaulle's government and the need for self-expression motivated the organization of increasingly militant marches. The young leftists did not, however, ally themselves with the "established" and "staid" French Communist party, which still blamed *all* of humanity's ills on economic factors. Violence exploded as militants overturned and destroyed cars and damaged buildings as well as personal property. A general strike was called on 13 May, following the government's removal of the barricades. Students sided with striking workers and their families in an attempt to redress an unjust economic balance in their society. Some factories were occupied. The ensuing tumult acted as a catalyst for more demonstrations. Spontaneous rather than organizational maneuvers, collective instead of individual action, unfolded in an atmosphere of euphoria.

The comportment of the militants who occupied the Odéon Theater on 16 May—essentially a symbolic act decrying bourgeois culture dispensed through state-run institutions—reminded Jean-Louis Barrault, its director, of a street fair. All sorts of entertainment was offered;

debates were long and passionate, tirades and harangues were delivered by such directors as Jean Jacques Lebel and Julian Beck of the Living Theater; "real" workers told of how they had been exploited, some calling for revolution as they shouted into the microphones. Others contented themselves with another form of rebellion—making love in the Odéon's boxes. They all attempted to sell their political, economic, and aesthetic wares. That Barrault sided with the rebels earned him his dismissal by André Malraux, the minister of culture. The official reason for his removal was his unwillingness, despite orders, to cut off electricity during the occupation.

Finally, by June's end, outward calm was restored. Was the birth of a counterculture in the offing? Did the committed intellectuals seek to destroy a society whose theaters were politicized and whose focus was "bourgeois"? Or were they themselves living out a "happening"—a "guerrilla theater" piece? Were the marches, riots, and fiery speeches a valid way of breaking with tradition in the arts? Were not the goals, functions, and forms of creativity, particularly with regard to the performing arts, being called into question? Could collective theatrical enterprises, where improvisation and individual expression were fostered, where the needs of a popular culture, in terms of language as well as of performance, were met, not be the answer?

The May 1968 anti-establishment movement demanded a reevaluation of the philosophical, psychological, and aesthetic aspects of the theatrical experience. The impact of youth's outcry on directors and playwrights and the changes effected in the decades following are some of the thematics that this study explores.

Although new directives, both aesthetic and social, altered the focus of French theater after 1968, Antonin Artaud (1896–1948) remained a powerful force among directors and playwrights in the 1950s and thereafter. A visionary and mystic, Artaud saw the theater as had the people of antiquity: a ritual capable of rousing a numinous or religious experience within the spectator. Based on myths, symbols, and gestures, the play, as defined by Artaud in the Theater of Cruelty, becomes a weapon to whip up people's irrational forces, so that a collective theatrical event can be turned into a personal and living experience. Artaud had predicted in the early 1930s that his ideas, overtly or covertly, would infiltrate theater in the years to come. He was right.

In the 1950s and 1960s the plays of Beckett, Genet, and Ionesco came to be identified with New Theater, Theater of the Absurd, and Derisive Theater or Anti-Theater. *Waiting for Godot* and *Endgame, Les*

Bonnes (*The Maids*) and *Le Balcon* (*The Balcony*), *La Cantatrice chauve* (*The Bald Soprano*) and *Les Chaises* (*The Chairs*) replaced popular psychological drama and the well-made play of *Théâtre-engagé* fame. In the Existentialist Theater of Sartre, Camus, and to a great extent Anouilh, dialogue and events were vehicles for characters either to accept or reject their lot on earth, either to function in a God-less universe as their own masters or to blind themselves into leading unauthentic existences, becoming what Sartre called *salauds*.

Beckett, Genet, and Ionesco did not offer audiences a theater of concepts that entailed philosophical discussions revolving around the human condition. They presented their ideas within a framework of myth, metaphor, metonymy, symbols, and concrete stage images. By abandoning a discursive presentation of ideas, and by devaluating such theatrical conventions as empathy, plots, psychologically oriented characters, and lucid thought patterns conveyed in dialogue—Beckett, Genet, and Ionesco abolished traditional theatrical forms. The sense of metaphysical anguish and underlying feelings of malaise that are implicit in their works were rooted to a great extent in the suffering endured during World War II and the disenchantment that followed. Values such as purity, truth, and beauty, once looked upon by society as supreme, had been shattered. Dramatists, instead of analyzing feelings of hopelessness or anguish with regard to the human condition, *showed* them. The play *became* the action.

Adamov, Arrabal, Audiberti, Billetdoux, Cousin, Dubillard, Duras, Michel, Obaldia, Pinget, Schéhadé, Tardieu, Vauthier, Vian, Weingarten, Yacine, and others, each in his own way, followed suit. As dramatists broke new ground, so directors broke away from established aesthetics to focus on audacious, provocative interpretations of the dramatist's vision. Studding the horizon were such names as Barrault, Blin, Bourseiller, Mauclair, Planchon, Serreau, Reybaz, Vitaly, Vilar, Wilson, Brook, Grotowsky, Beck, Malina, Chaikin, Wilson, Ronconi, Strehler, Stein, and Gruber.

Structuralism, deconstruction, and semiotics also infiltrated French theater, thanks to the writings of Saussure, Lévi-Strauss, Barthes, Lacan, Foucault, Althusser, Derrida, Deleuze, Lyotard, and a long list of others. Rather than trumpeting a call to action, they used an intellectual methodology and vocabulary as tools to explicate writings: *signs, signifier, signified, metaphor, metonymy, oxymoron, linguistics, psychoanalysis, aporia, code words*. To dismember or deconstruct a text opened it up, these innovators believed, to multiple readings, in the manner of a Bataille, Robbe-Grillet, Duras,

Godard, and Pornoir Plays, film scripts, and scenarios became frag
mented, thereby underscoring their multidimensional and frequently
conflictual meanings. Roland Barthes, the author of the influential
Writing Degree Zero, was also involved in the founding of the Théâtre
Populaire in 1953. He encouraged a dual approach to theater discourse:
textual and *stage* writing, the latter being a manifestation of the director's
and the performers' readings of the play/text.

French directors and playwrights, bursting with new ideas as well as
with confidence in their own worth, formulated fresh criteria, probed
new forms, and experimented with different approaches to the performing arts. In this study I explore these multiple subjects, basing my judgments on personal interviews and correspondence with directors and
playwrights, on theoretical and creative works, reviews, and performances I have attended. Reasons of space have compelled me to omit
the names of many fine directors and playwrights, but I hope that these
omissions will be redressed in a future work.

Acknowledgments

My deepest gratitude to the French directors and playwrights who made available to me so many of their personal documents; and especially Lucien and Micheline Attoun, Liliane Atlan, André Benedetto, Andrée Chedid, Patrice Chéreau, Enzo Cormann, Eugène Durif, Colette Fayard, Armand Gatti, Olivier Gosse, Gérard Gelas, Jacques Lassalle, Georges Lavaudant, Jorge Lavelli, Paul Léaud, Daniel Lemahieu, Eduardo Manet, Marcel Maréchal, Daniel Mesguich, Ariane Mnouchkine, Valère Novarina, Eric Pelsy-Johann, Roger Planchon, José Valverde, Michel Vinaver, Jeanine Worms.

I should like to thank the librarians at Hunter College for their invaluable help. They not only helped me search for innumerable works but thrilled me by unearthing many unsuspected treasures—and always with a smile! In particular, my appreciation goes to Suzanne Siegel, Norman Clarius, Barbara Foster, Danise Hoover, Elliott Kaback, and Patricia Woodard.

Special thanks go to Béatrice Ellis of the French Cultural Services of New York for her kind help in furnishing me with pertinent information; to Allen Weiss for his insights into the works of Valère Novarina and for allowing me to use sections of his excellent translations.

Chapter One
Directors/Directives Galore

The 1970s, 1980s, and early 1990s gave birth to a plethora of directors and a variety of approaches to mises-en-scène in France. Some directors applying a new brand of realism gave a militant political orientation to their productions. Others were more involved in creating works of art or in combining realism and fantasy. Collective productions stressed improvisation, mime, masks, and marionettes. Many directors rejected the text per se, inviting the actor to take center stage. Since eclecticism was in vogue as well, nonconformist approaches were de rigueur. Intellectual stagings underscored what directors labeled deconstructionist theater: a stage piece in which scenic fragmentation was practiced in a context where *sign* was of uppermost importance. Sophisticated, baroque, and imagistic productions cohabited with simple and ascetic stage works. Aficionados of dramatic art were offered complex or ultrasimplified lighting and sound techniques. Whatever suited the individual director's penchant was acceptable.

Activist/Politically or Socially Oriented Theater

A graduate of the prestigious Ecole Normale Supérieure, Bruno Bayen (b. 1950) combined intellectual university activities with a career in theater. His early syncretistic ideology suggested an aesthetically utopian point of view—a wholehearted belief in the May 1968 slogans. By conciliating Marx and Freud, he felt, a successful struggle could then be waged against "bourgeois" or "capitalistic" oppression, as during the French Revolution.

In a 1974 production of Frank Wedekind's *Danse macabre* (*Death and the Devil*), with a translation by Bayen and Bernard Lortholary, society is revealed to be morally bankrupt and responsible for the ills plaguing families. Adults not only mismanage their lives but misunderstand their children's needs as well. As for women, upon whom Wedekind focused relentlessly, they are avatars of the Eternal Feminine: earth spirits, whores, amoral consumers of men—driven by continuous sex urges.

Bayen's direction of *Danse macabre*, with its complicated plot revolving around the white slave trade, pimps, and prostitutes, stressed Wedekind's revulsion for the bourgeois institution of marriage. A woman's virginity prior to marriage, for example, is grotesquely mocked as the bride's mother, preparing her daughter's trousseau, makes a slit in her drawers just at the right place. The dynamism injected into some of the outdated mores of Wedekind's day, which Bayen fleshes out, emphasizes the absurdity of such tribal customs.

Bayen had hung two large photographs of bearded men onstage, one of Marx and the other of Freud, thereby suggesting rebellion against the status quo and hinting at the theme of the play: conventional puritanism as opposed to the desires of the unconscious. In consort were the lilting sounds of Strauss waltzes and the ever-present but repressed shadows of sadomasochistic sexual urges and their fulfillment. The violence smouldering within the protagonists' psyches bursts forth in provocative, sometimes shocking, and symbolic portrayals. The contrived cleavage between Wedekind's direct discourse (acted in a naturalistic manner) and Bayen's stylized dramatization of his subjective and reflexive world worked wonders.

In 1976 Goethe's *Torquato Tasso* was successfully adapted by Bayen, who also played the poet Tasso, author of *Jerusalem Delivered*. As the play opens, Tasso has just received a laurel crown for his work, which he presents in homage to his benefactor, the Duke Alphonso d'Este of Ferrara. After suffering humiliation at the hands of the courtier Antonio and undefended by his patron, Tasso asks permission to leave for Rome. The Duke acquiesces but refuses to return the poet's copy of *Jerusalem*—his only wealth.

Singled out for praise by the critics was the play's scenography, featuring three distinct locales onstage: a park with real trees; a garden with a fountain, authentic patches of grass, and three chickens pecking away; and an interior, with table, desk, and chairs. The ceremony honoring Tasso, featuring the Duke and the Princess, his sister, was set outdoors, against a Watteau-like natural background. The scenic backdrop of farmland, as opposed to sophisticated Italian gardens, stressed the divisiveness existing between the artist and the courtier classes, as well as the growing violence among the rich and the poor. Bayen denounced the plight of the artist who, in order to survive, had to appeal to the goodwill of wealthy families. His state of servile dependency was emphasized by the gestures, tonal qualities, and displacements of the actor playing Tasso. Nor were Tasso's bitter disappointments in love and his feelings for the Princess omitted. What was most interesting in Bayen's production was the manner in which he contrasted Tasso's greatness as a poet and his utter wretchedness as a human being. Still, his portrayal of Tasso was criticized by some for the "the serpentine perversity" he injected into the role.[1]

Bayen's *Hernando Colón* (1992), a text dramatizing the life of Christopher Colombus's bastard son, posed many problems. Because of the play's complexity, critics advised spectators to read the text before attending the performance. Nor did the lengthy monologues alleviate the play's intricacy. Spanning five centuries, the action begins in Seville, where Columbus's bastard son is living opposite the Carthusian convent that was his father's last home. It concludes with the construction on the same site of the 1992 World's Fair in celebration of his father's discovery of the New World. Bayen's work consists in part of a kind of monologue by Hernando Colón, who has just completed an anonymous biography of the "Old Admiral." While narrating the events concerning his famous father's life, this unrecognized bastard son offers playgoers insights into the explorer's work: he was a man who, although increasing the size of the world, had reduced it; and by dividing it, had unified it. Deeply poignant is the sorrow felt by the young man virtually imprisoned in his room and his writing, and living only through the memory of a father whose giant steps led to the reshaping of the world. The sets, underscoring the bastard's sequestered existence, featured a small stage extended by a spiral staircase. Although yearning to sail the seven seas, this rejected, unrecognized, and unloved young man, who participates in neither the celebrations of a venerated figure nor his father's life, accomplishes his travels only via the *word*.

Author, actor, and poet André Benedetto (b. 1934) is also director of the Théâtre des Carmes (formerly the New Avignon Company), which he founded in 1961. A Marxist, Benedetto is deeply committed to effecting a radical change in politics, society, and theater. In 1966 he called for a guerrilla approach to the performing arts in order to achieve his goal. He organized outdoor collective spectacles to entertain and educate the masses—productions reminiscent to some extent of the religious mysteries performed during the Middle Ages. Benedetto invited entire communities to participate in "happenings," favoring striking railroad workers in 1971, for example, or opposing the Vietnam War in 1972.

Like Armand Gatti, Benedetto, deeply involved in reforming stage language, invited those who felt alienated from life's mainstream to join forces with him. To this end he chose to "break" grammatical rules and syntax in the manner of the dadaists, surrealists, and even the deconstructionists. Puns, alliterations, word associations, and groupings of homonyms created cumulative rhythmic effects that activated a listener's body rhythms. Alliances between sound and stage action also worked well for Benedetto: for example, language was made to erupt like a volley of bullets in scenes in which a couple make love. By fracturing traditional speech and linguistic patterns, he hope to generate new forms accessible to all.

Important as well was Benedetto's "inventory technique"—that is, continuously varied descriptions of detailed stage arrangements throughout the drama. Such a repetitive device facilitated the understanding of stage events that might otherwise have been overlooked. The inventory technique offered other advantages: the continuous recasting of information, with minor changes each time, not only served to transform the spectators' perspective but, by presenting them with a multiplicity of hypotheses, to encourage them *to think* for themselves. Benedetto's system of peppering his text with anecdotes was also operational: it changed a *syntagmatic* to a *paradigmatic* order. This new optic released viewers from adherence to chronology even while emphasizing the potentials of each occurrence and encouraging individual probing of each situation.

In *Emballage* (1970; *Wrapping*) Benedetto fleshed out a consumer society's obsession with commodities, demonstrating how such a focus became instrumental in sowing dissension among groups and classes. A worker, for example, strains and struggles in his job to earn enough money to buy a fish. When possibility becomes reality, the same worker yearns for an automobile. Instead of living fully, humans spend their time acquiring more and more material things.

Benedetto was also involved in the Occitan movement, which fostered the acceptance and enrichment of Provençal culture and its liberation from domination by northern capitalistic groups. His play *La Madonne des Ordures* (1973; *Our Lady of the Garbage Heap*), a kind of subversion of the Stations of the Cross, was written and sung in Occitan. Because a peasant family has been robbed of its possessions by the French Agricultural Credit Bank, an Occitan mother is forced to leave her home to wander with her two small children in search of food and shelter. Stopping at one site after another, each one calling up fearfully conflictual historical events, she takes on the dimensions of an allegorical figure preluding future disasters.

Some of Benedetto's recent successes have been Fernando Pessoa's *The Anarchist Banker,* first presented in Lisbon in 1988; *Nuits au Maquis* (1990; *Nights in the Maquis*), based on the testimony of World War II

French Resistance fighters in the Avignon region; *Squatt Connection* (1990), a love story lived out in a drug situation; *Louise et le Yéti* (1993), a fascinating play about the terrifying Himalayan "snowman" whose imprints were supposedly first discovered in 1921 during an expedition to Mount Everest; *Elémens de politesse gourmande* (1993; *Elemens of Greedy Courtesy*); *Nous les Européens* (1993; *We the Europeans*); and *Molly Bloom,* based on Joyce's *Ulysses.*

Benedetto's linguistically revolutionary approach to writing and directing relies heavily on syntactical and literary devices—rhythms, repetitions, vocalizations, intonations, chantings, symbols, and allegory—as well as on ceremonial dances and ritual, to generate a mythical dimension. His visceralization of words injects fire and blood into what might otherwise have been arid and dull scenic sequences.

Jean Jourdheuil (b. 1944) met Jean-Pierre Vincent (b. 1942) in July 1968. Two months later the two men formed a working team with the goal of introducing new elements to what they considered a regressive situation in theater. Although their association was flexible, Vincent acted as director and Jourdheuil as *dramaturge*—a function existing until now only in Germany.

> The [dramaturge] participates in all stages of the work in progress. In that he formulates his judgments critically, while also suggesting solutions to practical problems, he becomes both Critic and Theoretician. The dramaturge's function does not consist in unveiling hidden meanings intrinsic to a text; these must be ferreted out and conveyed when working on the mise-en-scène. The dramaturge seeks to break up a text's metaphysical expressivity: by the time a production is ready for performance the play should be divested of a *focal point.* What constitutes Old Theater, in our view, is a production that revolves around a center, a focal point: to allow such a situation to exist is to impose an inherent meaning on a text or a mise-en-scène, thus enabling the spectator to identify or to recognize him- or herself in it. The phenomenon of protagonist identification is merely another example—an inflated one—of the phenomenon of recognition.
>
> The dramaturge's work consists in analyzing the processes which bring relationships into being: between the actors' play, the mise-en-scène, music, and decor; and connections between the people involved and the meanings the piece is intended to represent. The analytical work accomplished with regard to these factors will encourage the spectator to exercise his own critical faculties during the performance.
>
> The function of the dramaturge is justified, in our opinion, only in a materialistically [in the Marxist-Leninist sense] oriented theater.[2]

Jourdheuil and Vincent's approach to theater, and particularly to Brecht's works, was polemical and utilitarian. Brecht's plays, they reasoned, would fascinate the very group the German playwright was deriding: the class-conscious, narrow-minded petit bourgeois, determined at all costs to retain their little privileges, the people who in Brecht's opinion were responsible for bringing Hitler to power. To this end Jourdheuil and Vincent chose to produce, among others, one of Brecht's early works, *The Wedding*, in 1968. The time: the 1920s; the theme: a wedding feast. The get-together serves to snatch off the carefully constructed masks of the merrymakers, revealing their perverse inner worlds. Made privy to family behavioral patterns, bourgeois audiences faced at the same time their own empty values and ideologies.

Vincent and Jourdheuil's second production of *The Wedding*, in 1973, was far more acidulous than the first. It emphasized the burlesque elements inspired by Karl Valentin, a Munich comic much admired by Brecht. The performers, like sardonic puppets manipulated by a "sadistic demiurge," highlighted the carefully hidden unsympathetic and destructive personality traits of the wedding guests, thus underscoring the impotence of a declining and degenerate class. Expert use of repetition and gags à la Laurel and Hardy helped fragment and "decompose" the actions, thus obliterating the "focal point" mentioned by Jourdheuil, while also creating a condition of malaise among the spectators (Godard, 13).

Theoretical as well as practical concerns motivated Jourdheuil and Vincent's choice of stage music. Used neither as mere accompaniment to performance nor only to create atmosphere, music played a role in enhancing a play's ideology. Musical effects in *The Wedding* served to exaggerate certain situations, pointing up the outrages and redundancies of bourgeois family life. For example, as the petit bourgeoisie gather around the table to recite the Benediction, after which food and wine are offered in silence, spectators hear the blaring tones of Wagner's overture from *Tannhäuser*, signaling from the very outset, as in the opera, the dichotomy between pious and righteous acts and the sins of the flesh. Begun in a spirit of calm and purity, the play concludes in bestiality: the married couple is left standing in a shambles of broken furniture. Not only have the guests yielded to their unregenerate urges, but the groom, having at first repressed his aggressive instinctual impulses, now pursues his wife, throwing himself on her blindly, to the strains of Wagner's *Ride of the Valkyries.*

For Georg Büchner's *Woyzeck (1973)* Jourdheuil and Vincent attempted to avoid the cut-and-dried Brechtian approach to theater that they saw in the works of Planchon and Strehler. Greater freedom was accorded to form, including the inversion of scenes, which, they felt, better suited the protagonist's uncertain mental condition. The resulting disorientation stressed the power of the irrational world on Woyzeck. Decors and increasingly subtle lighting effects reinforced the ambiguities of his personality. Lunar rays cutting through smokey cloud formations set against a night sky enhanced the play's obsessive qualities. Satirical effects were achieved by stereotyped picture postcard sets featuring a purple garden with terraced hills, steps, balustrades, and two sphinxes. Mood swings implicit in the acting invited spectators actually to *feel* Woyzeck's suffering and the humiliating effects of his oncoming madness.

Financial difficulties, perhaps ideological ones as well, led to the breakup of the Vincent-Jourdheuil partnership. The former accepted the directorship in 1975 of the National Theater of Strasbourg (TNS), with two other permanent directors, Dominique Muller, and André Engel. Increasingly did Vincent consider the productions of Peter Stein (the director of Berlin's Schaubühne theater) vital, lucid, and perceptive. Underscored in Stein's direction of Ibsen's *Peer Gynt,* Goethe's *Torquato Tasso,* and Kleist's *The Prince of Homburg* was a sense of parody and critical irony, a balance of suspense and adventure, ambiguity and complexity within the confines of a simple set. Although his use of stylized gestures, cut-and-dried speech patterns, and the intellectual stances adopted by his performers yielded an impression of hardness, they also invited a whole inner world to take root. Vincent also admired Stein's acidulous denunciations of society's wrongs.

Patterning his new endeavors on German civic theater, Vincent appointed Jacques Blanc, Bernard Chartreux, Michel Deutsch, and Dominique Muller as dramaturges. He inaugurated his directorship at the TNS with the adaptation of Zola's novel *Germinal* in 1975. After the dramaturges had thoroughly studied Zola's work, it was decided that because of the novel's thematics—a confrontation between capital and workers—the events would be depicted through the eyes of Zola, "a philanthropico-medical bourgeois." But whereas Zola looked on the poor, with their alcoholism, adultery, and violence, as *one* big problem, Vincent and his dramaturges emphasized multiple and fragmented approaches to it. And while Zola's view was subjective, they thought theirs—"the imaginary world of the bourgeois as projected onto the working class"—was more objective (Godard, 190; Temkine, 2: 243).

The curtains rose on an empty stage space. The cast entered in silence. Zola was dressed in black. He mumbled his words, as did other performers onstage, with the result that some of the text was virtually inaudible. The second part of the drama also began in silence: actors carried chairs into the acting space and then set up a long table. Most of the action, however, took place offstage, and only fragments were perceivable by the spectators. A shock effect, however, was produced in full view of the audience: a trapdoor opened, from which hell-like flames emerged. The socially oriented side of *Germinal* was contained in the scene in which a woman scrubbed the stage floor, then prepared tubs of hot water in which the coal miners bathed. *Germinal* received mixed reviews.

Molière's *Le Misanthrope* (1977), a milestone for Vincent, was a TNS production that featured a stunning yet ultrasimple set consisting of six tabourets placed against a superbly decorated wall hung with seventeenth-century paintings set in richly ornamented gold frames. The protagonist, a paranoiac in this production, acted in a hyperrealistic manner against the virtually empty, abstract stage space, making his conflicted personality that much more apparent. To emphasize the lack of relatedness between the characters, Vincent grouped them together in a corner of the stage and had each one enter and exit in such a way as to cross in front of the others, who observed them. False laughter, purposefully interspersed, emphasized their hypocritical relationships, accentuated their sense of alienation, and helped deconstruct their weakly formed personalities. The effective use of silences, in addition to the decidedly slow pace of the drama, called attention to the great mystery that is the human psyche.

Bernard Chartreux's *Violences à Vichy* (1980), also staged by the TNS, is an ensemble of texts and commentaries dealing with the supposedly well-known events of 1940–45, which are really not so well known anymore owing to the "memory/forgetfulness" syndrome of history around which the play revolves. The author, unwilling to burden the minds of the spectators, limited the vast literature on the subject to news items, descriptions, photographs, philosophical dialogues, and names. The play had a twofold goal: it aimed at "the ear and the eye, separately, in a kind of dyslexic 'montage.'" The imaginations and thought processes of the spectators were to be triggered by the dichotomy or void existing between the heard and the seen.[3] The complex text, essentially pedagogical, reigned supreme.

In 1983 Vincent was appointed to the much-coveted position of director of Paris's Comédie-Française. (Jacques Lassalle replaced him at the TNS.) During his three-year stint he produced both contemporary and classical works; perhaps his overzealousness for the former was instrumental in the nonrenewal of his contract. Nevertheless, he continues to provide audiences with superb arrays of theatrical works, and in 1990 he became director of the Théâtre des Amandiers at Nanterre, one of the most prestigious cultural enterprises in France.

Jourdheuil, meanwhile, pursued his career as dramaturge—always meticulous, and no less so in his approach to Alfred de Vigny's *Chatterton* (TNS, 1976). He went as far as to have the original manuscript radiographed, hoping that by returning to the source he would discover the author's original intent, pauses, and moods. He also felt that this classical/romantic bourgeois play, outdated for many, could be made to appeal to modern audiences. After all, the theme—a poet who considers himself a failure and commits suicide—is not so unusual. That Jourdheuil gave virtually free rein to the actors to invent/construct/seize/fix their characters, even while relating them to the other protagonists, made for the production's novelty.

Innovative as well was Jourdheuil's idea of transforming the eighteenth-century drawing room called for in *Chatterton* into a "mental landscape" or an "imaginary space." René Allio's scenography captured the director's intent: it featured a mirror-paneled room with doors that opened (thanks to a system of pulleys) as if by magic onto smaller and smaller mirrored rooms. Each entrance or exit of the actors invited audiences to peer into what came to symbolize inward and outward worlds. Rather than traditional furniture, the stage space featured massive rectangular tables reminiscent of tombstones. The effect of this "cemetery apartment" diminished the importance of the story line but stressed ideological relationships among the characters.

The hero of *Maximilien Robespierre* (1978), scripted by Jourdheuil and Chartreux and directed by Bernard Sobel, is unlike the historical figure offered by other dramatists. He comes across as a meditative individual whose ideas have been fathered by Rousseau's idealistic concepts and whose life, like that of his mentor's, was lived within his own solitude.

Jean-Jacques Rousseau (1978), also written in collaboration with Chartreux, and directed by Jourdheuil, was a one-man show featuring Gérard Desarthe. It consisted of a collage of Rousseau's *Rêveries* and his "Letter to d'Alembert on Theater," particularly the section devoted to Molière's *Le Misanthrope*. These two works revealed Rousseau's growing sense of isolation and despair as well as his desire to escape from society's castigations. His disclosures allowed the authors to subtitle their strangely analytical and deeply feeling portrait "Tragedy-Reverie."

The sets were arresting: a tent set up on an island of books stressed Rousseau's pervasive sense of insularity. The hero emerged from his tent with 20 or so little potted trees, a bust of himself, pots and pans, a gun heater, a package of letters, a writing quill, coffee, sugar, and a bowl of cherries. The strangeness of this heteroclite vision created a sense of uneasiness in the spectators. Was Rousseau living in a kind of no-man's-land? Or had illusionist theater taken over? When, for example, Rousseau withdrew into his tent, the backstage area became visible to the spectators, adding to the ambiguities involved in the life of this elusive eighteenth-century genius. The provocative sets and dialogue triggered ideas and questions among the spectators. Was Rousseau a marginal intellectual? a tragic reformer in today's world?[4]

One of the most important directors to pioneer the new social and historical theater in France in the 1950s, Roger Planchon (b. 1931), like Brecht, rejected the rhetoric of deceptive realism. Refusing illusionism, he sought to penetrate all types of hidden political, religious, and frequently national realities. His broad-spectrum approach made him equally at home in classical and modern repertoires: he directed plays by Adamov, Brecht, Corneille, Gatti, Ghelderode, Goldoni, Gogol, Ionesco, Marivaux, Molière, Racine, Shakespeare, Vinaver, Wenzel, and others. Himself a playwright, Planchon often focused on peasant life in France's rural communities, where particularly violent events had taken place.

A man of action, both ideologically and artistically, Planchon did not simply intellectualize a play he was preparing for production. What was of import to him was the evolution of situations, their translation onstage, and their interrelationship. Once the play's events were clearly defined, Planchon blocked them out onstage, allowing the written word to take on visual and auditory dimensions. Sound effects were concrete, designed to affect characters and audiences as well as events. Emphasis on physical and palpable acts—for example, a woman giving birth or people making love—was one of Planchon's cardinal rules. Lighting reinforced the drama, while improvisation, mime, and film created earthy reality.

One of Planchon's most fascinating and innovative productions was Molière's *Tartuffe*. Although he initially produced it in 1962, its mise-en-scène was drastically reworked in 1974. Planchon explained:

> *Tartuffe* has been interpreted many ways. After Molière's death, directors saw Tartuffe as an evil atheist and saw the play as an attack on the Catholic Church. Then Coquelin of the Comédie-Française came along and presented

Tartuffe as a very pious man. This, of course, corresponded to Coquelin's violent anti-clericalism. For Coquelin, Tartuffe was the perfect example of the good Christian who wanted to kill and devour everything and everybody. Jouvet felt that Tartuffe had a dual-personality: a Christian saint on the one hand, and a "man" with all the sensual drives on the other.

Our interpretation was different. We were not interested in whether or not the play was pro- or anti-Catholic. We were interested in the psychological aspects of the work. I found Orgon's attitude to Tartuffe very strange. Actually, Tartuffe is not the aggressive one. Orgon gives everything to Tartuffe who, of course, accepts it all. It was not Tartuffe's idea to marry Marianne—it was Orgon who suggested his daughter marry Tartuffe. Orgon was the one who wants to disinherit his own children and make Tartuffe his heir. It is Orgon who gives Tartuffe the strongbox (Tartuffe has no idea it even exists). Perhaps one could argue that Tartuffe leads Orgon on; but in terms of strict morality—and I am a moralist—the one who acts is the guilty man. Orgon was an important man, a friend of the King. He met Tartuffe in church, brought him home, fed him, clothed him, etc. For the past three hundred years these actions have not been understood. Critics have called Orgon stupid—but a man's actions cannot be explained away that easily. Orgon is not stupid, but profoundly homosexual. It is obvious that he doesn't know it—the play would fall apart if he were conscious of it, if he simply tried to sleep with Tartuffe. Our production focused on this relationship between the two men. Understandably, we have not made Orgon effeminate; he does not go around kissing Tartuffe. . . . We bring out his homosexuality in other ways. Do you recall Orgon's last words to Tartuffe? "Ah! Le voilà traître!"—the language of passion. Racine's language. And Dorine, Orgon's servant, tells her master that he has more affection for Tartuffe than he would for a mistress. All this is very striking. The play does not change over the centuries, but our understanding of it does.[5]

Certain parts of René Allio's original sets were retained by Hubert Montloup, the scenographer for the 1974 production. The first, featuring baroque paintings of nearly nude swooning saints surrounding a deposition from the Cross, added an element of sexual ambiguity to the proceedings. At the conclusion of each scene, one section of the panel paintings seemed to simply fly up, so that at the play's end a backdrop of stone walls was visible, creating a hard, prisonlike atmosphere. The second series of sets, while still using the paintings that were raised after each sequence, depicted various rooms in Orgon's palatial home in the process of being refurbished. Scaffolding, ladders, marble sculptures, an equestrian statue, and religious paintings, partly hidden under tarpaulins,

created a disquieting atmosphere. Gestures as sign, subtle body movements, and facial expressions conveying nuanced interraction between
Tartuffe and Orgon underscored a high degree of physicality. The feeling
of intimacy Tartuffe enjoyed within the family circle was achieved by
clever costume design: attire was formal in the earlier production, casual
clothes were used in the later one. Characters entering Orgon's home
would immediately remove their street clothes and remain in shirt
sleeves, dressing gowns, petticoats, nightdresses. Other homey touches
included snacks during discussions of Orgon's veneration for Tartuffe, or
the folding of sheets in the laundry room by Dorine, the soubrette, and
Marianne, the daughter of the house. The mise-en-scène created a distinct feeling of timelessness of stage happenings, while, on another level,
the interaction between the protagonists made in-roads on social, psychological, and cultural domains.

   *La Contestation et la mise en pièces de la plus illustre des tragédies françaises,
"Le Cid"* (1969; *The Arguments about and Tearing to Pieces of the Most
Illustrious of French Tragedies, "The Cid"* [by Pierre Corneille]) is a humorous satire based on the cultural chaos, the contradictory theories, and the
unanswerable questions arising from the 1968 riots. Its long title was
meant as a parody of the extreme length of Peter Weiss's *Marat/Sade.*
Planchon's *Le Cid* was his way of dealing with what he considered to be
the impasse reached by French theater at the time. A collage, it included extracts from Corneille's prefaces to his play and contemporary texts
from fashion magazines and newspaper articles interwoven with discussions of social issues and popular theories on drama and art.

   Among the characters featured in Planchon's *Le Cid* is Fafurle, an
average person endowed with both common sense and prejudices. His
two wives symbolize the dual sides of a man's needs: one is elegant and
beautiful but unintelligent; the other is a sloppy, dowdy woman who
lives in a dreamworld of romances. The performers acting in *Le Cid*—a
play-within-a-play—include a literature professor and his students; the
theater director and his helpers; and a group named Horrible
Gluttonous Enzymes, led by Bip-Bip, a female student. Events are set in
motion when a car driven by Fafurle crashes through the sets and interrupted the rehearsals of *The Cid*. The complicated and frequently hilarious situations in Planchon's collage elicited belly laughs, particularly
when the 12-syllable alexandrines of *The Cid*—known to so many in the
audience—were purposefully distorted by the actors. Interruptions by
one of Fafurle's wives, who takes umbrage at some of the anti-feminist
lines, also stimulated audience reaction. A satiric innuendo was injected

into the plot when one of Fafurle's wives insists that the drama be provided with a happy ending. Don Gomas, therefore, is not killed, as in Corneille's play, but only slightly wounded, and Rodrigue and Chimène are reunited over a plate of paella. Later the pregnant Chimène brandishes a banner bearing the words "Thanks Paul VI."

Planchon's *Le Cid* was an amazing construct, a spectacle in which no one was spared, a puzzle put together with inventiveness, verve, wit, and talent. His ultraimaginative burlesque, with its brilliantly humorous "deconstruction" of Corneille's *Le Cid,* emphasized the poststructuralist void and the vacuity of 1968's ideals. Planchon's parody was his way of cleansing both contemporary and classical ideologies and traditions.

The action in Planchon's peasant plays, most of which are set in isolated villages in or near the Ardèche, where his grandparents had lived, is comparable to the goriest of naturalistic novels by Zola. Based on a case that shocked all of France, *L'Infâme* (1969; *The Villain*) dramatizes the true story of Father Desnoyers (of Uruffe in Lorraine), who in 1956 killed his nine-months'-pregnant mistress, cut out the unborn infant, christened, killed, and then disfigured it for fear that the child resembled him. Rather than focus on the crime, Planchon fleshed out the murderer's environment and the Church hierarchy's reaction to Father Desnoyers's deeds by differentiating the speech of the villagers from that of the clergy. The former, very earthy and frequently poetic in its expressions of love of nature and its outbursts of spirituality, gives the impression of *authenticity.* The utterances of the clergy, replete with ready-made quotations, are not only banal but, far worse, reveal the hypocritical ways of men of the cloth who are ready to explain away the priest's horrendous act just to save face. The play concludes with the murderer's rehabilitation after the bishop convinces the peasantry to allow the enactment of a communal expiation ritual. He then utters another of his ready-made maxims: "If they beat their breast, it is because they recognize the sinner in themselves." Was the bishop leading his flock to understand the "mystery of everyone's culpability"?[6]

Planchon's goal was not to attack the Church, as evidenced by his creation of the character of an old parish priest who practiced only charity and goodness. The murderer, Planchon explained, was driven to his act because he could deal with neither the pressures of his vocation nor those of his faith. Needless to say, *L'Infâme* elicited a variety of reactions: it was banned by the mayor of Nancy out of respect for Desnoyers's relatives living in the area; others condemned it without even having read it; still others admired Planchon's courage in presenting the facts of the event.

Planchon has continued to evolve as director and playwright. His interest in history and politics and their social, economic, and psychological ramifications—has not flagged. Tragedy and fear marked the life of Bernard Sobel (b. 1936) after his father's deportation to a concentration camp. Alienated and a stranger to all cultures and nationalities, he came to New York at the age of 19 on a Ford Foundation scholarship, and another grant took him to Germany, where he worked for four years with the Berliner Ensemble. A year spent with Jean Vilar at the Théâtre National Populaire (TNP) added to his educational storehouse.

Sobel's production of Brecht's *Man Is Man* (1970) was, understandably, sober and macabre, to the point of being farcical. The exceedingly slow pace injected into the play gave the impression not of nonevolving characters but rather of scientifically constructed behavioral patterns. Sobel's approach to Brecht's *Roundheads and Peakheads* (1973), focusing on the rise of Nazism in Germany and denouncing racism, persecution, and the struggle between rich and poor, was not presented didactically. On the contrary, Sobel went out of his way to liven up what might otherwise have been arid dialogue. Although critics felt that a shortened text would have added to the play's tension, they commented most positively on the production's visual aspects: the costumes, masks, and sets that were instrumental in animating and enriching the scenic space.

Jakob Lenz (1751–92), the Sturm und Drang dramatist whose revolutionary realism and strong stand on liberty had attracted many a modern French director, inspired Sobel to produce *The Teacher* in 1975. Rather than using Brecht's adaptation, which denounced the weak-willed, well-meaning protagonist—a teacher on whom the bourgeoisie not only counted but also projected its values—he turned to Lenz's original play for direction. Lenz had castigated such relationships, considering them unhealthy because they prolonged states of dependency and servitude. The melodramatic piece, which includes the teacher's seduction of one of his pupils as well as intense mother-daughter rivalries, also enveighs against hypocrisy and the base values of eighteenth-century Prussia's disintegrating institutions. Sobel's interpretation, more expressionistic than realistic, attempted through distortion of personality traits to convey his deep-seated feelings of rebellion against the status quo. Sobel was praised for toning down the play's melodramatic effects and for ironizing its brutalities.

Sobel's mise-en-scène for his 1976 production of Christopher Marlowe's *The Jew of Malta* was considered monumental by many a critic.

The stage, made to look like the Globe Theater, was symmetrically constructed on two superimposed levels. It included a grand staircase and a throne room above, from which the governor of Malta, a Renaissance potentate, issues his decrees. Barabas, a Jewish merchant, counts his riches in the small room hidden by a curtain beneath the staircase; here he expresses as well, in flights of poetry common to Marlovian heroes, his desire for power. Dignified at first, following unjust persecution by what Marlowe considered hypocritical Christians, Barabas disintegrates, becoming paranoiac and then the incarnation of evil. At the play's conclusion, the ruined and rejected Jew, tearing off the beard that has given him his dignity, dons a huge false hooked nose, thus conforming to history's stereotype. That he takes it off only to replace it moments later signifies that he is playing the role assigned to him by Christians (Temkine, 2: 212–14).

What most marked Sobel's productions was his open-mindedness and unappeased curiosity when choosing playwrights whose works fascinated him, no matter what their origins. Whether directing Molière's *Dom Juan* in German, or Elizabethan theater, or Gotthold F. Lessing or Aleksandr N. Ostrovsky, he served each in his own creative manner. The refinement of his stage imagery; the sensitivity, finesse, and acute understanding of a text's subtleties; and his inherent artistry are impressive. That he was and is editor of *Théâtre/Public,* the only publication focusing on modern drama in France in print uninterruptedly since 1974, also speaks highly of his perseverance, work habits, and vision.

Multidimensional, Aesthetic, Metaphorical Approaches

The ceremonial mise-en-scènes by Victor Garcìa (1934–82) were lyrical in quality and sacrilegious in intent. From the very outset of his Parisian stay, this Argentinian-born director demonstrated the courage of his convictions and the depth of his artistic sense. In Ramón Valle-Inclán's *The Paper Rose* (1964), for example, a melodrama for marionettes, Garcìa used live actors to convey what he felt to be the thrust of the playwright's "existential revolt against centuries of Catholicism; a destruction of fixed values." To emphasize the slave treatment of Spanish women at the hands of men and their enforced withdrawal into a closed domain, he had them wear specially made headpieces that looked as though they had been sculpted of stone, and rendered the woman's gaze "imprisoned by a membrane."[7]

That his 1970 production of Jean Genet's *Les Bonnes* (*The Maids*) was in Spanish did not detract from what some critics considered a most extraordinary moment in theater. Not until García's mise-en-scène had Genet's play been given such tragic dimension: the power of the ritualistic, ceremonial, and violent interaction between the two maids and Madame transcends any language barriers.

The importance accorded to gesture as sign—the lifting of a finger, the extension of an arm—and to vocal tonalities as expressions of rage or sexual passion enabled spectators to dig deep into the protagonists' feeling world. Never, however, could judgment be validated, for each of Genet's identityless creatures existed as a reflection of the other, each becoming what the other makes her out to be, in addition to what each thinks about herself. The more one sister projects her complex behavior patterns onto the other, the greater the reality of her illusory world becomes, and the more pronounced the shattering of her psyche. Any realistic interpretation of the false interrelationships upon which the play was constructed is impossible.

The semicircular room constructed for *Les Bonnes,* with its pivoting panels and several false doors, added to Genet's underlying theme of deception. The sisters, attempting to escape from the bedroom's miasmic atmosphere within which they are psychologically imprisoned, are forever cast back into this sacrificial space with its immense altarlike bed. It was on this magnificent piece of furniture that they lay and frolicked, performing their sacrilegious ceremonies. Madame—a sensual, lustful, and materialistic woman—returning unexpectedly to interrupt their ritual play, might have become the recipient of the sisters' poison had it not been for her lover's chance phone call requesting her immediate departure. Alone, once again, the sisters pursue their blasphemous rituals until the climactic moment: the *ekstasis* in death.

The costumes worn by the actresses enacting their passionate, violent, derisive rituals were in themselves symbolic. The seediness of their black uniforms represents their lowly origins; Madame's red and white dresses for gala occasions, which the sisters try on, stand for crime and its purification. The cothurni worn by Madame, who manipulates them with ease, gives the sisters' stance an unnatural and distorted look, particularly when they claw the ground or drag themselves about in slow or rapid beats (Temkine, 2: 48).

In 1973 the Argentinian director staged the numinous happenings in Federico García Lorca's *Yerma,* which focused on fertility. Yerma, barren after several years of marriage, is also anguished because her husband does not love her. Maternity would have given her dignity and compensated for her loveless marriage. What is surprising, given the regressive Spanish society of the time, is her husband's indifference to paternity: he does not disdain his wife because of her infertility. The cause of his anger is his jealousy of her: he obliges his sisters to chaperon her at all times, thus depriving her of liberty and a sense of her own worth. The variety of moods in the play—from flamboyant to death-dealing—were subtly orchestrated in Garcìa's production. Pleasure is played out during a Black Mass celebrated around a nude man. Bitterness accompanies the arrival of the sisters at Yerma's home, while beatitude marks the scene in which a young mother takes her newborn in her arms. Garcìa's mise-en-scène presents not only Yerma's intense anguish and frustration but that of the Spanish people as a whole.

Another Garcìa production, Valle-Inclán's *Divine Words*, an expressionist drama staged in 1976, attacks Spain's regressive customs and institutions. Ranging from satire and irony to tragedy and black comedy, it is grotesque to the extreme. The play focuses on a deformed child, born to a mother with advanced syphillis, who looks more like a monster than a human being. The care of this "treasure" falls on one of its aunts, Mari-Gaila, the wife of the town's sexton. Beautiful and sensual to the extreme, she enjoys spending her time at fairs. On one occasion she meets a traveling acrobat, Compère Miau, who eyes her not only for her body but for the deformed child's potential for earning money as an exhibition. While Miau and Mari-Gaila make love, beggars spot the child and, with harrowing perversity, feed him so much liquor that he dies. To save funeral expenses, the beggars decide to bury him near a pigsty, where the corpse is mauled by the animals. Mari-Gaila is returned nude to her husband amidst the jeers of the villagers, who castigate her for her adultery. The sexton does not punish his wife for her infidelity; instead, he has incestuous relations with his daughter. He succeeds in calming the populace by pronouncing in Latin "He that is without sin among you, let him first cast a stone at her" (John 8:7). These "divine words" silence the people, who have now submitted to a higher truth that they have never understood nor would ever understand.

The scenography for *Divine Words* consisted of eight large mobile objects resembling beveled organ pipes mounted on a gallowslike contraption. Long trumpets, perhaps like those at Jericho, were attached to the structure, and the entire mechanism was hand-manipulated so that the pipes and trumpets lay horizontally or stood perpendicularly; they could be agitated like reeds in a stiff wind or remain perfectly stationary.

The music varied to include sounds imitating birds singing and bees humming, tones mimicking an old harmonium, and scratchy notes accompanying the child's rolling in his wagon. Dances, some phallus-oriented, were included to enliven and lighten the excoriatingly morbid atmosphere. The neutral-colored costumes of ocher, brown, and gray lent an earthly mood to the events. The sexton and an old blind man wore rough fabrics, while the other men were nude-torsoed. Lighting also played a significant role in *Divine Words:* as, for example, circular luminosities projected around Mari-Gaila and the child, evoking a Pietà scene.

Garcìa died prematurely of AIDS, depriving the world of the performing arts of a remarkable visionary.

An intellectual, an aesthetician, and a man conversant with the writings of Derrida and Lacan, Daniel Mesguich (b. 1952) is a director, actor, teacher, and writer. His approach to theater and opera—Racine, Calderón, Marivaux, Shakespeare, Claudel, Wagner, Prokofiev, and others—is provocative, contentious, innovative, and iconoclastic.

He created his Theater of Mirrors in 1974, basing it on illusion and an ephemeral interplay of continuous images and their reflections. Since such replication of images altered contexts throughout a performance, the human personality and the situations in which it was involved could never be apprehended in their entirety. Stage happenings, like fleeting memories, could be appreciated and understood only fragmentally. Stage life, then, had to be approached relationally, as if individuals or groups were passing through a hall of mirrors. These continuously altering presences became signs—aspects of life's fluctuating shadowy or brilliantly lit representations.[8]

Mesguich observed that *Hamlet* can be viewed as *text* and as *metaphor.* Dual sets were used in his 1977 production of the play: to the left of the open stage a smaller platform had been built featuring a theater curtained in red (theater-within-a-theater; a play-within-a-play). Performance took place on both stages, and to emphasize the complexities of a personality Mesguich frequently asked two performers to play a single role. As Ophelia was drowning, for example, she not only saw the other Ophelia descending from the red-curtained stage but also heard her repeating her text to her.

For Mesguich, the staging of a classic text is the staging of two texts—the text and its history. It is the accumulation of everything that has been said or written about the work since its inception. As such, directors, actors, scenographers, and costume designers must deal not merely with, say, *Hamlet* as text, but the individual as seen by Shakespeare, Mallarmé,

Joyce, and others. The protagonist becomes a *sign* of the times—all times, because theater is "Immanent and Transcendent" (Mesguich, 19). Not only did Mesguich deconstruct *Hamlet,* but everything about his production was referential, with his clue stemming from Shakespeare's own "to be or not to be":

> For me, the greatest theoretician . . . is William Shakespeare (who obviously read Lacan since I have staged him after having read what Lacan had said about him), who read Marx, Nietzsche, Freud and Hegel, Brecht and Artaud as well, and who wrote an *active* little theoretical treatise (therein lies his originality) called *Hamlet*. . . . I'm saying that *Hamlet* is a theory, that at a certain degree of . . . ebullience, theory, rid of rhetoric and dogmatism, becomes theatre.[9]

In Mesguich's theoretical work *The Book to Come Is a Theater* (with Gervais Robin, 1977) he considers the stage a Mallarméan blank page. Actors are hieroglyphs who move about in keeping with certain *signs* or *designs,* which are then interpreted by the director. Only with the entrance of an actor onstage does tension begin: his or her physical presence creates a void between the written text and its sounding.

Antoine Vitez had taught Mesguich that realism in theater required the accenting of "unnaturalness" rather than the replication of the empirical world onstage. Vitez's rejection of "identification" and his emphasis on language, voice, diction, and gesture enabled him to achieve authenticity in his work. Mesguich also repudiated an actor/role identification. Rather than an impersonator, the performer is actor first, the *speaker of a text*—that is, he or she relates *directly* to language and meaning, tones, tensions, and so forth. Thus is "theatrical *real*ism" born onstage—the first syllable, *real,* referring to the ambiguities involved in the basic definition of theater as artifice (Champagne, 89).

Mesguich was attracted to Shakespeare's *Titus Andronicus* (1989) for its violence and for "the absolute but sublimated horror embedded in its language and its culture—a kind of 'meta-horror.'" In his 1989 adaptation, Mesguich retained only two-thirds of the original text, to allow time for the actor to weigh each word, and thus enable contemporary audiences to relate to the sounds, meanings, and associations. Mesguich's translation of Titus's "to this your son is mark'd and die he must" (1.1) as *"votre fils marqué par cet holocauste"* did not necessarily allude to Auschwitz but the future extermination of Titus's family. The spectators, aware of the play's conclusion (the protagonist, Titus, was not) and cognizant of the genocide that had occurred in the twentieth century—knowledge that formed their

tions of history, easily identified the notion of extermination with both the concentration camp experience and that of Titus's family.[10]

The curtains rise for *Titus Andronicus* on an empty stage. A Man (added to the original text) in black suit and bowler hat—not wearing the familiar Roman toga—strolls, holding two white pigeons. In good Beckett tradition, he says, "The end is nigh, perhaps the end is nigh / In a few seconds it will all begin again." The curtains fall heavily and noisily (the first of 28 times during the drama), emphasizing the shocking events to come but also, perhaps, the turning of the pages of Shakespeare's text. The Man's comments, relating ancient Roman times to the horrific fate awaiting modern audiences, also have a jarring effect.

Other characters enter the stage space, either alone or accompanied. Some walk as if inebriated, speaking single lines, perhaps in order to introduce themselves to the spectators. Titus Andronicus, father of 25 sons, of whom fewer than four are left, is old and nearly senile. A Jewish patriarch wearing a prayer shawl enters the stage space. He is barely able to sustain the pain of the slaying of every single Hebrew at Masada (C.E. 66–73). The beautiful, whorelike Queen of the Goths, surrounded by her terrified and degenerate sons, and the black Moor's laughter and charm, which mask his malignance, underscore the corrupt atmosphere in *Titus Andronicus*. Brutality is emphasized as one of the white pigeons is crushed between the pages of a heavy tome. Rape, incest, and violence are not enacted onstage; they are referred to in words, icons, and metaphors. For example, the Prisoners' motley belongings—children's clothing and shoes—are analogous to those of the concentration camp victims in Nazi Germany.

The short and rapidly paced scenes of love and tenderness played out onstage relieve the ever-deepening sense of doom and destruction in Shakespeare's tragedy. They also add to the complexity of the metaphors injected into the stage happenings, inviting spectators to probe ever more deeply into the variety of meanings and innuendoes stirred by each of the images. At the play's conclusion, the Moor, having been taken prisoner, occupies center stage "suspended by arms and legs, head down, held by huge chains that cross the entire space." Titus is stabbed to death.

Mesguich's single set for *Titus Andronicus* was very effective. Because of its mobility, perpetual transformation was achieved, thus adding to the play's multiplicity. The scenography revealed neither the site nor the period of the play's action. No Roman square, room in a palace, or hunting ground was to be seen. Instead, audiences faced a baroque library containing heavy bookcases filled with old and new volumes. Additional tomes were scattered over the proscenium, serving not merely as decor but participating in the play's action: they were used for steps, cutting through stage space, and to fall jarringly from high places, creating clouds of dust on the stage during their trajectories, thereby blurring the spectators' vision (Baal, 114). In Mesguich's view, books stood as symbols for Shakespeare's library, for the many works written on his plays, and for the billions of volumes produced in our machine age.

There was rotting greenery in two rectangular glass tanks onstage, along with two paradoxically decomposing yet living corpses of two young boys who had been killed. The mirror effect allowed their living selves to watch their dead selves, as well as the action as a whole from another vantage point. The rot was a sign of rampant evil corroding the city of Rome: a putrescent, degenerate world of which Titus Andronicus was a part.

The "upending" of one of the walls that turned the back of the stage into the ceiling of the theater, "rising up (toward the back) and narrowing to form an oval opening looking out onto the sky, and through which the actors [made] some of their entrances," added "signs" and "significations" to an already complex work (Baal, 114).

A last coup occurred at the play's conclusion, when the books in the library were set on fire, bringing to mind the burning of the library at Alexandria as well as the book burnings in Nazi Germany. Might not Mesguich also have been referring to Wagner's *Die Götterdämmerung,* and to the burning of Valhalla and the Teutonic Gods? Or was Mesguich suggesting the end of our world?

Inspired exclusively neither by Marx nor by Brecht, as were so many of his contemporaries, Georges Lavaudant (b. 1947) claimed as his mentors Beckett, Faulkner, Burroughs, Borges, Duras, Pinget, Le Clézio, the *Nouveau Roman,* the films of Jean-Luc Godard, jazz, and rock music.

Collages aroused Lavaudant's interest. In *La Mémoire de l'iceberg* (1974; *Memory of the Iceberg*), a detective story performed in the most outrageous and extravagant of styles, he included excerpts from the works of such writers as Marx, Borges, and Lucien Goldmann. A play-within-a-play, *La Mémoire* focuses on a shady detective in search of a man who has vanished. Could it have been his double? The stage, representing a highway edged with grass on either side, not only lends a sense of perspective to the visual image but becomes a *sign* for the continuously expanding field of the search. Many surprises await the audience, as consciousness (memory) and the unconscious (iceberg) vie for dominance in the play-within-the-play.

La Mémoire illustrates what has been alluded to as Lavaudant's Théâtre Froid (Cold Theater). Given his inclination toward aggressiveness, tumult, and excitement, it is surprising that he strove in his mise-en-scènes and in his direction to cool off, to objectify, and to distance stage happenings from the emotional world. Lavaudant was not interested in reconstruction of classics but in drawing on the works of authors he admired to write his own texts. His stage techniques were influenced by Robbe-Grillet's specially styled detective novels, as well as by George Bataille's violently perverse texts. As for the visual element in theater, he owed much to Robert Wilson's *Deaf-man's Glance* (1971)—a play made up of starkly programmed images designed to affect onlookers subliminally. Here, too, was the image/object perceived as a sign, experienced by each spectator on multiple levels, both in harmony with, and antipodal to, the text/language.

Lavaudant's 1976 production of Pierre Bourgeade's *Palazzo Mentale*, with sets by Jean-Pierre Vergier, was considered superb by many critics. A montage of texts by such great authors as Dante (in Italian), Virgil, Kafka, Proust, and Borges evoked images of real or imagined fantastic cities. Although the production offered an exciting universe of metaphors, the play's plot, by contrast, is relatively pedestrian: it concerns a man searching for a woman as he himself is being followed by a detective.

For Lavaudant's production red curtains parted to reveal a three-story palazzo, in front of which stood 16 performers aligned like mannequins. The men, dressed in black suits or tuxedoes, and the women, in long white gowns, remained immobile during the overture played by four musicians standing on a platform that had risen from the orchestra pit only to be redescended moments later.

The palazzo, situated center stage, seemed to be set in a park, with trees, but was enveloped in a fog that added a poetic though frightening note to the play. As different windows in the palazzo lighted up, audiences saw directly into the rooms. Furnishings became visible, and the secret sexual practices of the various partners as well: a jockey tied a red silk scarf around his neck, a man urinated into a basin, a woman sensually removed one bit of clothing only to don another. The "Kafka or flying machine" onstage rose above the sets, sprinkling the entire space with fireworks and inciting the Spheroc, a jazz/rock group, to play a musical interlude (Champagne, 96).

Was the man in search of the woman Orpheus? in search of Eurydice? Were audiences descending to the sixth circle of Dante's Hell in this six-act play? Many critics considered the production to be a fantasy lived out by a 30-year-old lad (Lavaudant) who was fascinated by the films of Fritz Lang, Erich von Stroheim, and others, and by remarkable authors whose works helped animate his imagination. Lavaudant's commitments to stage images were evident in his 1984 production of *Richard III*. By adding a new, energetic, and contemporary note to the play, he felt his work fleshed out Shakespeare's inner meanings. Some critics, however, considered his emotional approach not only "irreverent" but a travesty of the work. In Brecht's *Baal* (1988) Lavaudant used actors as fetishes, thus underscoring the infrarational side of the work. The protagonist of Chekhov's *Platonov* (1990) was described by Lavaudant as an anti-hero in the modern definition of the word: a "talkative, pleasant drunk, a provoker of scandals, a courter of women who is courted by them, a man who deceives his wife, feels remorse, interrogates himself as to the meaning of life, and like a provincial Hamlet, dies as if by chance."[11] In 1992 Lavaudant mounted Jean-Christophe Bailly's *Pandora,* dealing with a mythological enigma embedded in naïveté and cruelty—a work that requires spectators to ferret out those insalubrious realms lying behind the apparent sweet beauty of the Tuscan hills and the quietude of its people. Lavaudant's *Terra Incognita* (1992) is neither a diary of his trips to Mexico nor a real play in the conventional sense of the term. Rather, it is a disparate and frequently contradictory collage made up of an array of texts, monologues, love songs, and mysterious dances, all revolving around fictional Indians in Mexico. Some critics admired the play as they would a staged dream, for its fantasy as well as for its ambiguity. Others found the folkloric sequences interesting but overly long, the acting zombielike, and the Indian initiation ceremony à la Carlos Castaneda—replete with a naked young man imbibing hallucinogenic drugs seen through a smokey haze—banal in today's world. Still, Lavaudant's productions were viewed as provocative, innovative, and intriguing.

Eclecticism on Stage

Gérard Gelas (b. 1947), the founder of Le Chêne Noir (1967) in Avignon, was uninterested in didactic plays and refused to produce works explaining or debating social, economic, or political issues. Those who sought to reform the world, he often stated, should devote their lives to doing so but should not use theater as a tool to achieve their ends. An actor, he noted, "needs silence," time to contemplate, to

institutions. He also rejected well-made plays with their psychologically oriented dialogue. He sought to extend the frontiers of traditional discourse
and pave the way for increasing expression.

In the stage tableaux of the anti-establishment Gelas a fantasy domain
alternates with a dehumanized and depersonalized world of slogans.
Such is his way of struggling against the deadening power of multiply-
ing, oppressive, monoloithic societies. Nowhere is Gelas's class consciousness more evident than in *Operation* (1970), in which people under
the control of the media are fed stereotypic visualizations. Verbal, visual,
and rhythmic beats, as well as violent stage images, accentuate the madness of spoon-fed solutions to the characters' insoluble problems. Gelas's
devices are designed to help spectators see through the pettiness and
miasmic confusion of those who would dominate others. Overt and subtly hidden differences in phonemes are also articulated: words such as
heroism, the people, and *bourgeois* are bandied about, as one class is pitted
against another by slogan creators.

Like Brecht, to a certain extent, Gelas assails his audiences in order to
force them to *think* for themselves and not merely repeat—and, worse,
believe—everything they hear. One of the most effective ways of achiev-
ing his goal is by concentrating verbally, mechanically, and technically
on the power of sound. He aims his tonalities, as one does a laser beam,
directly onto foe or friend. The energy generated by such aggressive
sonants, with frequently nerve-wracking effects, serves not only to
involve the public but also to help the actor, as Artaud suggested, to find
the right bodily expression to convey a feeling or a thought. Authentic
body language may also modify preconceived notions in the actor. To
unblock the performer and permit him/her to shed society's facile psy-
chic imprints may be achieved not by such frantic activity as having an
actor move about in all directions onstage, or roll on the ground in
anguish as death approaches, but by helping the performer to "rediscov-
er inertia." Conversely, just as one cannot imitate positions in yoga without *knowing* the spiritual elements involved, so the Western actor's
attitude, riddled with complexes of all types, must also be discarded if
deeper perceptions and hence more authentic movements are to be experienced. Only by clearing the ground of stultifying age-old behavioral
patterns can improvisation take on meaning and yield the performer's
best. To cut through appearances, to shred superficial approaches to reality, and to do away with spectator/actor identification may enable the
viewer better to experience the character's (actually noncharacter's)
reality.

Gelas's first reading of Fernando Arrabal's *La Vierge rouge* (*The Red Virgin*) struck him because of the cruelty of its thematics as well as the expansiveness of its poetry. Upon learning that Arrabal's plot was not fiction but based on reality, the incidents having taken place in Spain in the 1930s, he decided to adapt it for theater. Arrabal's is the tale of Aurora Rodriguez, a woman of high society—a flaming feminist—who is obsessed with the idea of having a daughter "without a father," whom she would be able to educate as she saw fit. Thus would she take vengeance on those men who had destroyed the lives of so many women. After availing herself of the services of an unknown genitor, she gives birth to Hildegarde (the name means "garden of knowledge"), a strange creature with prodigious learning ability. At 15 Hildegarde speaks many languages; is a brilliant scientist, mathematician, and alchemist; and corresponds with the celebrated of her day. Her mother, disapproving of Hildegarde's political and social associations and fearing she would become the servant of men, murders the 16-year-old girl, for which she is imprisoned.

Gelas's 1992 adaptation, *Pucelle pour un gorille* (*A Virgin for a Gorilla*), begins with Aurora's release from prison, 20 years after the murder of her daughter. One day a poster advertising *The Terrible Life of Hildegarde* attracts her attention. Minutes later she is captured by an itinerant circus manager, who has identified her as her daughter's killer: he plans to make money by exhibiting her. The circus stages a production of her daughter's life story, and Aurora witnesses a grotesque reconstruction of her own adventurous existence. She identifies so closely with the false Aurora onstage that she suddenly intervenes and tries to rectify the dichotomies between actual events and the performers' fictionalized version. By the play's finale she is so powerfully caught up in the action that when the murder is to be performed onstage she stabs an actress—not the one portraying the daughter but the one portraying herself, the false Aurora.

Gelas's baroque mise-en-scène, brilliantly interwoven with song, dance, clowning, acrobatics, and music, brought a dream (or nightmare) world into being. Emphasis on the mother's need to create a perfect creature took on a psychoanalytic twist, suggesting that it was her way of fulfilling her own repressed desires: "My daughter will be everything that I can no longer be." Only to the lesbian with whom she lived could this man-hating woman relate.

The sets *à tiroir* fleshed out various levels of understanding of this play in which love was inevitably linked to death. Iconoclastic ceremonial rituals, acerbic in their humor, gave shape to madness and derision. Variety in rhythms, tonal intensities, and sumptuous and sordid stage images produced arresting scenes, such as the birth of Hildegarde—as she erupted, her flamboyant red hair resting on a blood-red rug. Such fulgurating sequences anticipate the play's pathetic conclusion.

Authenticity and artistry, combined with the emotional and the moral, reign in Gelas's approach to theater: "I cannot dissociate my practice of theater with the search, in one way or another, for a humanistic ideal which so frequently fails to maintain itself in materialistic societies such as ours."[12]

Marcel Maréchal (b. 1937) is an explosive and tempestuous but also an exacting and ordered actor and director. This outgoing man of the theater is meditative and solitary as well. As a youth, he had been attracted to theater by its magic, its ritualistic impress, and its performers' body movements. He opted for roles that would allow him to clown, improvise, and reveal his romantic and satirical fantasies. In his productions of works by Arrabal, Audiberti, Beckett, Brecht, Büchner, Claudel, Goldoni, Guignol, Guilloux, Ionesco, Limbour, Molière, Novarina, Obaldia, Ruzzante, Shakespeare, Vauthier, Weiss, and others his stage images range from the hyperrealistic to the surrealistic to the dadaistic.

Maréchal produced Jacques Audiberti's Le Cavalier seul (The Lonely Cavalier, produced frequently from 1963 to 1983) on Roger Blin's suggestion. Blin knew that Maréchal was a man of courage and also had the knowledge needed to stage this play that went "against the grain."[13]

Le Cavalier seul, a work of epic dimension, focuses on the Crusades. The interplay between monstrous and sublime powers—the Devil and God—that move humans to act was treated by Maréchal derisively and at times acrimoniously. Although mystical elements were highlighted, much of the presentation featured acrobatics, jokes, obscenities, and even a clownlike Christ.[14]

The time: the eleventh century. The places: Languedoc, Byzantium, Jerusalem. The theme: Evil (the Church) versus Good (Christ). The protagonist, Mirtus, a young peasant and great ladies' man, is a Brechtian anti-hero type. Having been led by a priest to believe that the holy war was being waged in order to redeem souls, Mirtus makes his way on horseback from Languedoc to the Holy Land. Inspired by such rhetoric as "the conqueror is the honor of Christian peoples, in the midst of whom the Pontiff sparkles like a nail in the crucified limb," our hero goes forth strong in heart.

The first to arrive in Byzantium, Mirtus is greeted by an "old crazy man," who is none other than the autocratic ruler Theopompe III (Greek *theo*, God; *pompe*, "escort, procession, pomp") and his shriveled wife, the Empress Zoé. The two offer him virtually their entire empire. Maréchal, as the bloated Theopompe, ensconced in a heavily decorated golden alb, performed with a remarkable blend of excessive parody and sober thoughtfulness. His conical miter resembled the garb of the Tin Man of the *Wizard of Oz,* or a beer stein, rather than the headdress of a prelate. His entourage included paleographers, doctors, theologians, courtisans, and adolescents. Nor did Audiberti spare his listeners an interesting vocabulary revolving around "silky and swishing pederasts" (Sandier, 33). Maréchal's poetic eloquence was so extreme that it took on farcical, melodramatic, and parodic stature. Audiberti's undomesticated language allowed Maréchal to savor the pleasure of manipulating words as signs, symbols, and vocalizations.

The Crusaders, as Audiberti noted, this "Occidental pigsty" made up of dirty villains, followed Mirtus's lead with gusto, "like prolongations of manure hitched to his steed." These fomenters of wars, massacres, mutilations, and fires all acted in the name of "their sinister God," who "unremittingly spied on men and women in bed, in the name of priests who bless dogs unleashed on deer" (Sandier, 34).

Mirtus's fervor is such that he braves all obstacles to reach the Holy Sepulcher. Blessed by fate—or God, or the Church—he arrives in Jerusalem where the Calif offers him the command of the entire Saracen army and, an even more alluring gift, his beautiful Fatima's bed. Suddenly Mirtus's faith and sense of morality—that of "operational Christianity"—begins to waver. He becomes increasingly fascinated by the Middle East: its odors of roses and sandal wood, its flutists who ensnare him with their melodious strains (Sandier, 34).

Maréchal's brilliant direction perfectly integrates past happenings with the epiphany to come: a man wearing a crown of thorns suddenly appears to Mirtus. Speaking in a strange fashion, he asks the cavalier to federate the East and the South—Byzantium, Baghdad, and Cairo—in order to prevent the Crusading hordes from reaching and destroying Jerusalem. Although "illuminated by Christ's presence," this "courageous" armored knight is unwilling to offer his life in exchange for grace. Mirtus, the great—passive—hero, watches the hordes of Crusaders enter Jerusalem to perform their ritual bloodbaths. He leaves the area with his compatriots, and with a "chariot filled with hosts" he ruthlessly spills the blood of the pagans for the greater glory of God and of the Pontiff (Sandier, 34).

The fortuitous meeting of Jean Vauthier (1910–92) with Maréchal in 1960, and the author's reading to him of *Capitaine Bada*, gave birth to one of the contemporary theater's rare masterpieces. Primarily a poet, Vauthier, like the Bada of his play, could not hope to be understood by ordinary people, who never look beyond surfaces. Even though the poet, through creative powers and insights, can ultimately contribute to the culture of society, he or she is usually doomed to suffer hurt and loneliness—a Crucifixion.

Vauthier had told Maréchal that to act the role of Bada required enormous stamina, agility, imagination, and versatility. Maréchal himself took the part and had to learn how to handle silences, breaks, and echoes; how to propel sound through colliding background noises or stridencies pointing up the character's conflicted feelings. While in traditional plays scenes build up to a climax during which the actor exerts his maximum effort, followed by zones of repose, in *Capitaine Bada* the paroxystic frenzies were nearly continuous. In order to render such outbursts properly and to create an atmosphere of authentic madness, Maréchal's energy was consumed, leaving him increasingly exhausted as the drama progressed—to the point of being unsteady on his feet. He assaulted his audiences, trumpeted harsh animal sounds as well as screams, whines, laughter, and brutally exciting explosions. He frequently took a puppetlike stance—stiff, wooden in his movements, gesticulating wildly—or, like a fetish, a statue, or a sacred marionette, he contained within himself all the violence and sadomasochism inherent in his role.

At first glance, *Capitaine Bada* (performed frequently from 1966 to 1988) dramatizes a fight to the death between the clownish Bada and his wife, Alice. On another level, the battle is an inner one, waged by two warring principles within Bada himself: anger and aggression lived out during the writing process, and attempts to transform the elusive, amorphous dreamworld into the concrete letter/word.

Bada feels bound and impeded in every way by his tender yet mocking wife, who is, he believes, the source of his torture. As in Strindberg's *Dance of Death,* audiences are not made privy to the heaven-on-earth world of the perfect couple. We are in the presence of a combative Adam (Bada) and Eve (Alice)—animals that, despite their love, tear and devour each other.

What provokes the initial onslaught between the two? Alice wants to make love; Bada does not, but finally yields. In the two succeeding acts

Bada pursues the unconsenting Alice; in the last act he has lost interest in his attempt to transform into poetic discourse the continuous struggle he has waged during his married life.

The feminine power in *Capitaine Bada,* Vauthier remarked, does not understand the masculine force; and Bada, in turn, does not make the necessary effort to try to comprehend Alice's needs. As an obstacle to the fulfillment of her husband's dream, she is a negative power, becoming positive only when sublimated. Bada, that "old and terrible child . . . that fabulous piece of wreckage," a poet in search of some absolute, some perfection to which he can give form, some love for which he quests, derides his Alice, blames her for what he is incapable of perfecting. Is this not another way of conveying his love for her? A doubter and a madman, like Don Quixote, Bada was questing for the unreachable dream.

Jacques Lassalle (b. 1936) pursues an active and varied career as director, teacher, and playwright—*Un Couple pour l'hiver* (1974; *A Couple for the Winter*), *Un Dimanche indécis dans la vie d'Anna* (1979; *An Indecisive Sunday in Anna's Life*), *Avis de recherche* (1982; *Search Notice*).

Although an intellectual, Lassalle is wary of scholars who lay down definitive rules concerning theater or any other discipline. He always alters his approach to suit the text at hand and in keeping with his own evolution as an artist. He creates his mise-en-scènes by jotting down his insights in brief, rapid, and fragmentary phrases rather than in long and tedious dissertations. So precise and, paradoxically, malleable are his ideas throughout rehearsals that changes are often forthcoming even after opening night. To direct, for Lassalle, is to *mettre en crise*—to live crises each step of the way. Such moments may arise while regulating entrances and exits, thus effecting transitions, or changing rhythmic patterns in order to respond more authentically to the play's heartbeat. They may also be felt during dialogic interchanges, inviting spectators to experience the forces at stake more completely, thereby stirring their imagination. Lassalle's humility toward an art that he has practiced so brilliantly for so many years was made evident when he referred to himself as an eternal student.[15]

In his capacity as teacher, Lassalle trains actors in the use of masks, body movements, and vocal tones to elicit moods of enchantment or melancholia, farce or fright, purity or lust. His instructions to scenographers and costume designers are invitations to produce a feast of colors and of architectural wonder onstage.

Of the classics, Lassalle is particularly drawn to Molière's universality, humor, understanding of human nature, satire and acerbity, and expert use of farce and burlesque. Marivaux excites him for his language, his characters' mood swings, timidity, and jealousy, and the play wright's variety of imbroglios and quid pro quos, all centering on the art and the game of love. Goldoni's range of humor and his spirit of satire and artfulness also fascinate Lassalle.

Büchner's *Woyzeck* and *Leonce and Lena* appeal to Lassalle for the dramatist's imagination, his understanding of social, emotional, and spiritual problems, his brutal and stark but also symbolic style, and the incandescence of some of his poetic sequences. To direct Büchner, Lassalle wrote, is to live sheer joy, sheer excitement, to divest oneself of traditional forms, to alternate actors and acting styles—"to explode performance" (*Pauses*, 236).[16]

Lassalle directed Nathalie Sarraute's *Elle est là* (*She Is There*) and *Silence* in 1993 to commemorate the momentous reopening of the Vieux-Colombier Theater, founded in 1913 by Jacques Copeau. In a salient article, he discussed the validity of calling Sarraute's stage pieces "anti-theater." Was it because she labeled her masculine characters H (1, 2) and her feminine ones F (1, 2)? Or because the author did not allude in her dialogue to their sex, age, and social or racial origins to establish their identity? What counted for her, as her audiences and readers well know, were those now-famous *tropisms* that she considered to be the foundation of human behavior. For Sarraute, and for Lassalle as well, speech—the "advent" of the word—was crucial. At such time the actor becomes the "bearer" of the word: "His respiration, his voice, his rhythm, his blood, his lymph glands, his nervous system, his gestures and mimicry, his course, the manner in which he occupies space, moves about in it, expands it until he dissolves into it," is basic to the creation of a character. The word, as Lassalle phrased it, "is born tenderly with forceps" (*Pauses*, 236).[17]

A director's function, in Lassalle's view, is not to mollify or comfort actors, set designers, costume designers, and other technicians. On the contrary, it is to make them feel the immensity of the dangers involved. Theater implies risks. How, for example, must actors handle stairs and platforms in performance? How can scenographs create heights, depths, and low points in order to destabilize performers and audiences? How can burlesque, clowning, mime, acrobatics, and comedy evolve in multiple dimensions?

A director learns from his actors by making their unhappiness his own. Their fears of joblessness, their overwrought imaginations, their yearnings, fantasies, certitudes, knowledge, talents, or faults sometimes serve to guide a director through labyrinthine situations or to make him aware of the pitfalls with which theater is replete. The actor is a most important "conductor" for directors—like a host and a guest.

The Argentinian-born Jorge Lavelli (b. 1931) reached Paris in 1960 and has remained in France ever since. As theatrical director, his roster of playwrights is large: Arrabal, Berkoff, Bernhard, Billetdoux, Copi, Grombrowicz, Ionesco, Lorca, Panizza, Pirandello, Seneca, Shakespeare, Tabori, Tardieu, Vauthier, and others. He has directed operas—*Idomeneo, Faust, La Traviata, Madame Butterfly, Norma,* and *The Magic Flute.*

As a man of the theater, Lavelli stresses ceremony, gesture, intonation, and a highly imaginative use of empty stage space. His frequently neo-baroque or surrealistic mises-en-scène are precise, rigorous, and sensitive. Each in its own way conveys his vision of *truth,* in the Artaudian sense. Thus, one may suggest that his is also a Theater of Cruelty.

Arrabal's *L'Architecte et l'Empereur d'Assyrie* (1967; *The Architect and the Emperor of Assyria*) focuses on two men who find themselves on a desert island. To pass the time, they indulge in ritualistically performed sado masochistic rounds, in role-changing and mirror-imaging, until the grotesque finale, when one of the men cannibalizes the other. Lavelli, who considers *L'Architecte* one of Arrabal's finest plays—a kind of summing up of everything the Spanish dramatist had done before—stressed the drama's thematics:

> the impossibility man experiences when trying to accept himself as he is. This theme is made obvious by means of the characters: their constant attempt at metamorphoses . . . their desire to escape, to become something other than what they are. Another theme is that of the Emperor, who symbolizes a decadent, rotting culture: a man who has never been able to commune with nature, even to come into contact with it on the most superficial level. Nor has he been able to experience God. His anguish lies in his various attempts to become God. Such an attempt on his part is in direct opposition with the Architect's domain: the one who is master of nature—a type of pocket God. The theme of solitude is also intrinsic to this play. No one can escape his own solitude: even master and slave cannot reach each other. . . . Each tries to leave the other in order to escape his anguish but cannot do so. The fear of being alone is so devastating, so insurmountable, that they prefer to accept a kind of sentence to be united, to continue together, rather than experience the intolerable pain of loneliness. (Quoted in Knapp 1975, 58.)

Lavelli chose García Lorca's *The Public*, a little-known surrealistic work by this "sulfurous, homosexual, ironic, and despairing poet," for the opening production in 1988 at the National Théâtre de la Colline, of which he was the newly appointed director. The play revolves around the anguish experienced by the disconsolate Lorca, a poet of the avant-garde, who kept his homosexuality secret because he feared he would shock and lose his "public." The theatrical director in *The Public* sounds out the question of how far a dramatist can take spectators into his dark, secret realm—his backstage to which audiences are never admitted—where truth and not illusion prevails. The magician in Lorca's play, unlike the director, has the power and the gift to transform unpalatable truths into acceptable ones. During the course of the drama, actors impersonating spectators are changed into brutish, repressive, and sanguinary creatures who invade the stage space and wreak havoc. An agonizing "red nude male" chained to an iron bed evokes the Passion of Christ; white horses, a clown disguised as a butcher, and marionettelike actors in various sorts of disarray people the stage. The play concludes with a confrontation between the director and the magician: the one willing to run the risk of telling all; the other, adhering to conventions.

Witold Gombrowicz's *Opérette*, also staged by Lavelli (1989), is situated in an imaginary country that resembles decadent Poland prior to World War I—a fertile field for the rise of fascism and Nazism. A bitter commentary on a variety of ideologies, *Opérette* underscores the purity and immaturity of youth and their dreams of liberty, as contrasted to the corrupt adult world. It may also be viewed as a biting satire on the superficiality and emptiness of stereotypic plots inherent to the operetta, and on the society—built on artifice, prejudice, and social codes—that fostered it.

Flor, the supreme arbiter of fashion the world over, having run out of ideas for his collection, organizes a costume ball. There is one proviso: the guests must dream up their own costumes, and keep them hidden until called upon to unveil what next year's styles will be. A parallel event revolves around Count Agenor, son of a Himalayan Prince, who is in love with Albertinette, "the mignonette." Instead of dreaming of a "pure" love, this naïve and unaffected girl longs for "nudity." Agenor does not yield to her wish by undressing her; rather, he keeps trying to dress her in the most exquisite and fantastic garments. In this closed, aristocratic society preoccupied with material things—clothes and style—appearance is essential.

The masked ball contains the allegorical side of *Opérette*. Artifice reigns supreme in the incredibly fanciful, gaudy, and bizarre costumes and ornaments that are paraded on the stage—a commentary on the vacuous nature of the protagonists' lives. When, finally, the guests unveil their creations and the uniform of a terrorrist (Marxist) becomes visible, revolution breaks loose in the real and figurative sense: the staircase explodes, walls and columns crumble, chairs are broken, and in a feat of technical and mechanical wonder, smoke and dust fill the stage to the accompaniment of deafening noises. Agenor's castle, now transformed into a charnel house, features protagonists wearing even more eccentric garb: the Prince is covered by an enormous lampshade; a Nazi uniform and masks are superimposed on previous creations. From within a coffin rises Albertinette, who everyone thought had been killed in the melee—nude, in all of her youthful and *unmasked* beauty.

The sets in a style that might be called baroque and kitsch, featuring the interior of a castle with old rose columns and an impressive staircase, were perfectly suited to this iconoclastic work. Lavelli brilliantly achieved corrosive ferocity in his choreographed displacements of the robotized humans onstage—their garish outfits, self-indulgent mannerisms, and hypocritically banal statements all spelling decadence and mental putrescence. The sumptuousness of the costumes at the outset of the play, and their transformation into rags after the eruption of chaos, underscored the end of a culture. Music, dancing, and singing, the sine qua non of operetta, were exploited to the fullest, with melodies from Viennese waltzes and other pre–World War I popular tunes contrasting with the sordidness of the stage reality.

Gombrowicz's theater, which Lavelli staged to perfection, was anti-naturalistic, anti-sentimental, and anti-psychological. Its unidimensional characters were mystified by their multiple disguises. Living in a macabre and discordant kingdom of their own, they functioned as a prelude to the demise of civilization.

The Argentinian-born Jérome Savary (b. 1942) founded an itinerant troupe, the Grand Panic Circus, in 1961. Seven years later, this troupe became known as the Grand Magic Circus and Its Sad Animals. The originator of a special brand of theater, Savary saw performance as a celebration designed to bring actors and spectators together in communion of purpose, feeling, and spirit. In order to give the impression of spontaneity and of jubilation, Savary had recourse to all kinds of props and special effects: real fire, colored smoke, fireworks, and animals.

Savary's "spectacles" have been described as "orgies," "authentic ceremonies," and a blend of "church and bordello. Although rapture and
fun are essential to his creativity, method and thought go into each of his
endeavors. Because theater in medieval France was a communal project,
Savary followed suit, performing his works outdoors and indoors, in a
garage, a stable, a church—even in a theater.

Savary's *Le Radeau de la Méduse* (1968; *The Raft of the Medusa*) was
based on the horrendous 1816 event that Géricault depicted in his celebrated painting of the same name: the sinking of the frigate *Medusa*,
with 400 people aboard. Although a raft able to hold 150 people had
quickly been constructed while the boat was still afloat, the supplies of
food and water on the raft soon ran out. Cannibalism seemed to be the
only means of survival.

Savary's cast of 45 men and 15 women, wearing algae on their heads,
imitated the sound of waves and wind throughout the performance.
Percussion instruments manipulated by Savary were used to heighten
the atmosphere of danger and fright. Like an orchestra conductor, Savary
directed the entire performance from one of the balconies.

Sea ambiance was enhanced by a fishnet extending from the top of
the balcony to the bottom of the stage. Audiences could therefore see the
happenings only through this meshed fabric. Since they were seated
below the fishnet, they had to look up to see the actors in their raft. This
spectacle created a strange and disorientating atmosphere. As the pas-
sengers began eating each other, bloodied corpses fell into the net, giving the horrified spectators the impression that these cadavers were
falling on them. Since no one was left alive in the raft at the play's conclusion, the net, now filled with dead bodies, blocked the spectators'
vision almost entirely, thus creating blackness throughout the theater—
and terror in the hearts of many (Knapp 1975, 64–69).

Savary's play *Aventures de Zartan, frère mal aimé de Tarzan (1971)*, a
farce, is a critique of neocolonialism, while his *Robinson Crusoé* (1972) dramatizes the problem of solitude in modern society, in which people are
conditioned to live, work, and create a family without ever feeling the
need for communication. People perform the same tasks day in and day
out, repeat the same motions like robots, think the same way, eat at the
same snack bars, watch the same television shows, in a world of silence.
Men barely talk to their wives or children, but human beings readily
turn to plants and animals to communicate. They are prisoners of their
culture, of the "reactionary" political and educational conditions to
which they are subject. Savary's Robinson Crusoé, symbol of that same

class-conscious, retrograde society, refuses to converse with his man Friday. Indeed, he teaches him only three words: "Thank you, master."

The 1980 production of Molière's *Le Bourgeois Gentilhomme* (*The Would-be Gentleman*) fulfilled one of Savary's long-cherished dreams. His anarchic blending of theater and circus, feast and music, with minutely integrated pranks and overt farcical sequences was an instantaneous success.

Savary had always looked upon Jourdain, whom he portrayed, as "a petit bourgeois, as are ninety percent of French people . . . a petit bourgeois, similar to those who made the Revolution, but who neither won honors or power for their efforts, since, once the Revolution was over, the spoils were taken over by the upper bourgeoisie, intellectuals, or government officials." Molière had a special feeling for Jourdain, and despised the musician, the dancer, and the philosopher in his play—fools who daily sell their intellectual merchandise. Vendors always ready to accept Jourdain's money, they have only disdain for him since he is not of their class. They utter their banalities in what Molière called "brilliantly formated" convoluted phrases, while Jourdain expresses himself simply and straightforwardly. Savary was moved by the fact that Jourdain chose the most difficult approach to win the affections of the beautiful Marquise: not merely through lavish gifts but by learning arts, letters, and even philosophy—albeit without attaining his goal.

The comic and satiric scenes in *Le Bourgeois Gentilhomme* were memorable: the peg-legged Master of Arms, wearing a black patch over one eye, moved about the stage in a wheelchair; the pedantic, potbellied Dance Master was ridiculously costumed; and the arrogant and blasé Master of Philosophy harped continuously on the same themes. The extreme character traits of each of the protagonists were caricaturized in typical Grand Magic Circus manner—imaginatively, rambunctiously, and lucidly. Seventeenth-century music was heard intermittently, played in a most sedate manner on percussion instruments, flute, saxophone, viola, violin, and harpsichord, while at other moments the musicians played in a delirious and rhythmic manner. Firecrackers, as well as other types of novel gags, brought Savary's fantastic ceremony to its concluding *turquerie*. In this humorous apotheosis, the Mufti, Dervishes, and Grand Mamamouchie, together with scantily dressed, veiled dancers who made the most of their alluring backsides and breasts, paraded about to rapturous applause.

As was to be expected, detractors voiced their disapproval of this blasphemous treatment of Molière. Others praised Savary for having transformed a classical work into a popular festivity to be enjoyed by all.

Although the Grand Magic Circus disbanded in 1982, Savary, partial to the music hall, keeps producing new works. Broadway-style shows, with ironic and savory underpinnings. His 1986 production of *Cabaret*, a financial triumph, as well as works by Offenbach and others, reveals perhaps a creative "abdication" on the part of Savary. Or it may indicate a new beginning.

Outstanding among a new generation of young *metteurs-en-scène* and playwrights are Jean-Claude Penchenat, José Valverde, Eric Pelsy-Johann, and Olivier Gosse.

Penchenat is the director of the government-subsidized Théâtre du Campagnol at Corbeil-Essonnes, on the southern outskirts of Paris. Not only have several *lectures-spectacles* been performed under his direction, but numerous plays have been as well—Jean-Claude Grumberg's *Les Vacances* (*Vacations*), Fernand Crommelynck's *Une Femme qu'a le coeur trop petit* (*A Woman Whose Heart Is Too Small*), Henri Monnier's *L'Univers d'Henri Monnier*, Henri-Pierre Cami's *Cabaret Cami*, Claudia Morin's *Fin d'été à la campagne* (*End of the Summer in the Country*), Giraudoux's *Ondine*, Luigi Pirandello's *L'Homme, la bête et la vertu* (*Man, Animal, and Virtue*), Bertolt Brecht's *Noce chez les petits bourgeois* (*Wedding*), Shakespeare's *A Winter's Tale*, and Rudyard Kipling's *Le Bestiaire tropical* (*The Tropical Bestiary*).

José Valverde worked with and acted in the productions of Jean-Marie Serreau at the Théâtre des Noctambules (1949), and was his assistant from 1956 to 1959 at the Théâtre de Lutèce. A year later he struck out on his own directing, and frequently acting in, innovative stagings of Gorky's *Mother*, Brecht's *The Good Soldier Schweik*, and other productions.

As director of the Théâtre Essaion since 1978 (in 1992 Alida Latessa was appointed director and Valverde artistic director), he fulfilled his dream of producing works by unpublished living French authors. His *théâtre à une voix,* a type of public reading, has showcased such plays as Anne-Marie Kraemer's *Une Mouche en novembre* (*A Fly in November*), Roland Shon's *Et si je?* (*And If I?*), Rose Delham's *La Quête de la femme-oiseau* (*The Quest of the Woman-Bird*), Jean Bois's *Titre provisoire* (*Provisional Title*), Varoujean's *Quand fera-t-il jour?* (*When Will Dawn Break?*), René David's *Macabête*, Alain Rais's *La Machiniste têtu* (*The Stubborn Machinist*), and Alain Bosquet's *Kafka/Auschwitz*.

Bosquet's *Kafka/Auschwitz* (1993), the first play by this well-published writer, was based on a dream he had had: Kafka had not died of tuberculosis in 1924 (as was the case) but had survived to find himself incarcerated at Auschwitz. As Bosquet wrote, "The Nazis drove out the little Jew, and locked him up in Auschwitz. But the second in command, an erudite intellectual, knows Kafka's works. He summons this unusual prisoner, feeds him, talks to him, plays checkers with him. Months pass. . . . What did they say to each other?" Bosquet warned his spectators that he, a close friend of Beckett and Ghelderode, should not be expected to dramatize meekness and tenderness. On the contrary, hard, cruel reality is his way. As for Valverde, he chose this work to direct because he found it "dangerous," both psychologically and theatrically. The "nightmare imagined by Alain Bosquet is situated in a historical period that one cannot evoke without passion." The play "disturbs, not because of its incredible references to the past . . . but because this strange parabola speaks of a certain kind of relationship, indeed an active complicity between artists and intellectuals and the dominant ideology."[18]

Eric Pelsy-Johann is a director, actor, and author of such plays as *L'Homme égaré* (*The Misguided Man*), adapted from Jean Cayrol's novel *Les Corps étrangers* (*Foreign Bodies*); *Les Survivants* (*The Survivors*); and *Le Doute—Cours de philosophie No. 1.*

Le Doute, a one-character play, is deeply moving in its poetry, profound in the thoughts enunciated, and searing in the mental and emotional pain experienced. The character, perhaps a professor of philosophy, seeks to discover the origin of things during the course of his increasingly painful probings. Such self-interrogation, relieved at times by ironies or humorous plays on words and ideas, sounds out the reasons for and the nature of his sometimes hesitant and fearful but continuous and relentless questioning. Perspectives broaden during his painful travail. Probings are centered on words, letters, syntax; religious and political certainties that are, in fact, uncertainties; impressions concerning one's own body—its height, weight, agility—that are as illusory as everything else. Family relationships, likewise, are as secure as quicksand. That doubt persists throughout the unearthing process of self-interrogation, which calls anxiety, fear, and love into play and serves to further *enlighten* the one—today's hero—who seeks to *know.*

Pelsy-Johann delineated his thoughts concerning the dramatic unfoldings in *Le Doute:*

> I retained Brecht's stylistic discontinuity in *Le Doute,* along with his famous syncopated effects as to the play's general rhythms. The "songs," however, no longer serve as "explanatory" syntheses, as in Brechtian tradition, but take on the function of true digressions: "blows" to humanity, emotional breaks, serving to enlighten the character in his reality as a sensitive being.

The play takes the form of a jazz composition [jam in the original sense, meaning excitation, music, dance, musicism], played by a living instrument, a man's life, a person who has doubts as to his identity—that fundamental doubt that haunts us all—and corresponds to the doubt of being.[19]

In *L'Homme égaré,* another single-character play, the character is like a polyhedron with its "infinite, thus indefinite" sides, always adapting to circumstances, endowed with a multifaceted personality. Thus could the play be performed in many ways, depending on its director and performer. The scenes could be reordered, thereby changing the rhythms and drama of relationships, chance, or hazardous factors. Thus would the character's linearity be abolished. Time and space would function as does memory, discontinuously and aleatorily. While the sum of the surfaces of the polyhedron would remain the same, its sides would alter in dimension and contour, thereby inviting multiple interpretations.

The thematics of *L'Homme égaré* are self-deception and the self's refusal to accept the truth. Such intentional or unintentional blindness becomes

> the very instrument which makes for a person's awareness as to what he or she is or could have been. The fluidity and malleability of an individual's identity, altering in keeping with the circumstances, seems to be responsible for a character's being. His manner at a certain moment—a means of paying his respects to the world of appearances—seems to engulf his or her entire person. To see a mirror image of oneself would allow the very essence of our being, at least during its duration, to become apparent. As if one's identity were soft—a constant structure to be sure, but whose form took on the contours of the "objects" encountered.[20]

Another important member of the new generation, Olivier Gosse, director and actor, is also the author of *Cargo, Nature morte* (*Still Life*), *Naro, ou La Vie à retardement* (*Naro, or Life as Delayed Action*), and other provocative plays.

Cargo (1992), like a Beckettian inner drama, may be viewed as a parable of an artist's struggle to bring forth what lies latent within. This two-character (or dual aspect of a single being) play takes place in the storeroom of a ship. Within this tightly sealed area—like the brain or the unconscious—each man in his own way uses the other to probe his own rich inner world. In so doing, he tries desperately, but also cerebrally, to find a means of recalling a past, of discussing his views on life, people, travel, relationships, feeling, in order to discover a way of finding a direction within a time/space continuum, a way of hanging on to life in what seems to be experienced as an eternal, sinister, even deadly vise. Where do human beings fit in this dimensionless inner/outer world? *Cargo* may be looked upon allegorically: as the excoriating pain experienced by an artist during the creative process. Words, gestures, and facial expressions intensify until they finally explode, physically and phonemically. One of the two men survives in this tightly structured work—in this hermetically sealed atmosphere in which language is sparse, pared down to essentials, preventing seepage of any kind.

Still younger are the newest wave of directors, actors, and dramatists, as passionate, innovative, and unspoiled as the preceding generation: Christian Schieretti, Stéphane Braunschweig, Jean-Luc Lagarce, François Rancillac, Robert Cantarella, Dominique Pitoiset, and Eric Vigner. This generation—which mocks styles imposed by Paris and works outside of institutions and media-dominated systems—was never helped or formed by older and well-tried people of the theater because, according to Robert Cantarella, *"They wanted no part of us!"* Children in 1948, these new-wave directors lived through the downfall of utopist ideals. Eric Lascaride explains their situation:

> We are a lost generation. We have no guiding voice, no History. We did not participate in any real struggle . . . the only thing I really recall when I was fourteen was the reign of a brutal and absurd terrorism. For us today, the only thing that's worthwhile is love—the imaginary.
>
> [N]or did we have a "father"! The others, Vitez, Bourdet, Vincent, Chéreau could at least situate themselves in terms of Vilar; question the goals of the famous "popular" theater as an "institution." The only problem was that they too dreamed of an institution! So, as soon as they were named, these attack dogs became guard dogs! And what they created was yogurt, soft stuff. One cannot even confront them, oppose them.[21]

Chapter Two

Theatrical Risks and Experiments: Lucien and Micheline Attoun's Théâtre Ouvert

Although founded by Lucien and Micheline Attoun in 1970, the Théâtre Ouvert (Open Theater) was born as a reality in 1971, when Jean Vilar invited the directors and members of the company to read or perform their works at the famed Avignon Festival. Itinerant and underfunded, the Open Theater's idealistic venture was a difficult one. The perseverance and vision of the Attouns was rewarded in 1976 with a government subsidy enabling them to establish a permanent Paris-based theater, also to be put at the disposal of subsidized regional art centers. The Open Theater moved in 1980 to the Cité Véron, near Pigalle and the Place de Clichy, known at the turn of the century for its famous Winter Garden and Moulin Rouge. Under the vigilance of the Attouns, and thanks to the financial aid received from both the national government and the city of Paris, architects in one year transformed the old-fashioned buildings into a modern and perfectly appointed theater seating 200. The Open Theater now housed a foyer, offices, and space for writers, directors, and actors, where practitioners of the theater could meet to lay out plans for future productions.

As a *théâtre d'essai* (try-out theater), the Open Theater became a center for play reading, staging, production, discussion, and publishing. The goal of its founders and of those who became associated with this remarkable enterprise was altruistic. The staging of plays, the Attouns maintained, must be made accessible to a new generation of talented theater people and the artist's freedom of expression must be protected against subversion by attractive government subsidies or offers from popular directors of professional theater companies presenting boulevard fare. The Attouns also demonstrated their principles by giving the same salary to everyone involved in a production, from the director on down.

Lucien Attoun, who had been involved in journalism, teaching, criticism, and radio (France-Culture and its dramatic repertoire), introduced the *tapuscrit* (typescript), an inexpensive mimeographed duplication of texts. The approximately dozen plays by untried dramatists chosen each year for duplication were printed in editions of 500 copies, which were sent to professionals and nonprofessionals in the hope that theaters, both national and international, would perform them. In 1993 the Attouns began printing bilingual typescripts—among them, Eugène Durif's French/German version of *L'Arbre de Jonas* (*Jonas's Tree*). Initiated by the Attouns as well was a new and inexpensive imprint (plays, documents, play texts, essays, program texts), brought out by the commercial publisher Stock, as a platform for creative artists to communicate with the outside world.

Some dramatists were so well served by the typescript imprints initiated by the Attouns that their reputations grew: Patrice Chéreau discovered Bernard-Marie Koltès's *Combat de Nègre et de chiens* (*Combat of Black and Dogs*); Pierre Léaud's *Fugue en mineur(e)* (*Minor Fugue*) was selected for performances at the Petit-Odéon; and Eduardo Manet's plays, first appearing in still another collection, *Théâtre/Ouvert/Enjeux,* were reprinted by Gallimard. Indeed, to date, several hundred theater pieces have appeared in the format of Open Theater imprints, which have diffused the works of such writers as Liliane Atlan, Enzo Cormann, Michel Deutsch, Eugène Durif, Paul Edmond, Colette Fayard, Jean-Claude Grumberg, Gérard Gelas, Victor Haïm, Bernard-Marie Koltès, Madeleine Laïk, Daniel Lemahieu, Armando Llamas, Eduardo Manet, Philippe Minyana, Claude Prin, Noëlle Renaude, Michel Vinaver, and Jean-Paul Wenzel. The Open Theater also established the reputations of directors such as Philippe Adrien, Armand Gatti, Jean Jourdheuil, Georges Lavaudant, Marcel Maréchal, Daniel Mesguich, Roland Monod, Roger Planchon, Jacques Rosner, Jean-Pierre Vincent, and Antoine Vitez.

Added to the already impressive list of publications was a news sheet, *Ecritures* (*Writings*), carrying articles with pertinent information by and on dramatists and directors, as well as works in progress and descriptions of the activities carried on at the Open Theater. A producer at France-Culture, Lucien Attoun organized radio performances of the plays he considered outstanding. Thus, he was able to popularize as well as explore the potential of new and untried dramatists.

Always reassessing their goals, forever searching for new dramatists, innovative texts, and different staging formulas, the Attouns and their group developed the following system for weeding out the poorer plays from the 350 to 600 received yearly:

(1) *Le gueuloir* (the talking shop) allows any playwright who wishes to have part of the program first to read his or her unpublished text before spectators, then to discuss it with them. Depending on the audience's favorable or unfavorable reactions, one of two actors chosen by the author may be called upon to participate in the recitation process.

(2) Should the text be well received, a director is then named—or names himself. The rudimentary working method allows the director—minus sets and costumes, and with only limited technical means—to plot out a mise-en-scène. The performers reading their texts onstage are thereby given some semblance of structure. As the newly born production begins to take shape, actors, dramatist, and director are forever exploring ways of enhancing the play's thrust. Performance takes place after a two-week rehearsal period.

(3) The *cellule* (cell), instituted in 1975, consists of three weeks of laboratory work, during which director and actors sound out the potential of the text they are working on. The public is now invited to afternoon rehearsals to explore and comment on the director's vision and the performers' interpretations of the work in progress.

(4) Informal Tuesday meetings at the Open Theater provide for get-togethers with people involved in the performing arts. Conferences are also organized to develop a national policy vis-à-vis theater. These serve not only to encourage playwrights to write, but to challenge them to question and to reroute their work—thus forever rejecting the status quo.

The Attouns see the Open Theater as a public workplace where they and those associated with their enterprise are determined to discover tomorrow's heritage today. Some of the works of the playwrights whose stage pieces I discuss in this chapter were either printed by the Open Theater or were performed on its stage. Many dramatists, such as Armand Gatti and Michel Vinaver, who began their careers at the Open Theater went on to stunning successes in France and throughout the world.

Creators of Disjointed, Contradictory, Inconsistent New Realities: "Workaday Theater"

The plays of Jean-Paul Wenzel, founder of the Théâtre du Quotidien (Workaday Theater) in 1975; Michel Deutsch; and René Kalisky introduced a new hyperrealism to the stage, which fractured, so to speak, space and time. The techniques used were a deconstruction of dialogue, verbal manipulation designed to heighten tonal and visual violence, and fragmentation and disjointedness of scenic sequences. Such devices allowed transcendence of the gulf between reality and illusion in a scenic tableau. The resulting discontinuity also permitted playwrights to circumvent rationality, thereby bringing into being an achronological stage world. By liberating space and time, spectators were no longer imprisoned in logico-temporal straitjackets. Freed from the constant incursion of dramatic continuity, a new truncated and scattered postmodernist world was born—one breeding malaise, ambiguity, and confusion.[1]

What Picasso, Braque, and other cubists had achieved in the domain of art, and Apollinaire, Cocteau, Vitrac, Artaud, Breton, Genet, Ionesco, and Beckett had accomplished in theater—the splintering of the human image—was pursued by Deutsch, Wenzel, and Kalisky. Their nonlinear, spasmodic, and fragmented proceedings disrupted all semblance of logic in a world that worshiped rationality as a mental concept. In so doing they heightened the irrational comportment of the creatures of their fantasy by setting them, paradoxically, in a realistic world and believable situations.

By effacing straightforward spatial concepts, Deutsch, Wenzel, and Kalisky fractionalized and chipped away at the heretofore sacred doctrine of unity of being. Having either lived through or heard their parents and relatives speak of the horrors of World War II, it was understandable that these dramatists would be preoccupied with problems revolving around human motivations, human cruelty, and the fragmentation of the human psyche. Each attempted to find an answer, a possible explanation to an impossible question. The first step in formulating the potential for a modus vivendi on an individual or on a collective basis was to project their inner climate onto concrete stage happenings.

Mention must also be made of the influences of such German filmmakers as Rainer Werner Fassbinder, and of Austrian dramatists such as Peter Handke on Deutsch, Wenzel, and Kalisky. Their works pointed up disjuncted and paroxysmal events in the lives of average or below-average people, as well as the repressed violence in the psyches of those unable to articulate their thoughts and feelings. The three French dramatists added their rage, shock, and disgust at a world that had allowed the Holocaust to happen. Deutsch, Kalisky, and Wenzel also heeded some of Artaud's suggestions. Aside from his techniques of fragmentation and virtually plotless drama, he emphasized new ways of conveying feeling and thought via the effect of sound: harsh, abrasive, clanging tones, yielding at times to mellifluous and velvety ones. Artaud's macabre humor underscored humanity's inhumanity through strident, excessive laughter and exaggerated volubility, thus forcing a huge cleansing process—a catharsis—upon some of the promptings. Such emptying out of pent-up rage through paroxysmal expulsions brings to mind in many ways Louis-Ferdinand Céline's unforgettable vomiting scene in *Mort à crédit* (*Death on the Installment Plan*), as well as Sartre's sequences focusing on nausea in his novel of the same name.

The forms used by Deutsch, Kalisky, and Wenzel are not, for the most part, new: they continue the tradition of disjointed plots that serve frequently to obliterate melodramatic elements, thus inviting, in Brechtian manner, a distancing or momentary break in audience/actor identification. Along with some of their predecessors, Deutsch, Wenzel, and Kalisky may be regarded as demythifiers of age-old images: loving mothers and fathers, seductive young women and men, gentle husbands, and utopist politicians. What is innovative in their theater, however, is the manner in which the three convey and attempt to deal with their emotional trauma in the light of the inexplicable and untenable sufferings during World War II. Without questioning or rationalizing, and explaining in depth—and, most important, without ever offering pat answers—the three playwrights were hard put to find redeeming qualities in the world around them. Brutal and bloody facts were served up to their audiences. A feelingless world had opened its doors.

The theater of Michel Deutsch (b. 1948) seeks to assess people through their sociocultural heritage. To this end he uses forceful and direct language. Self-referential images, frequently marked by a variety of time factors to heighten the drama's intensity, have a significant role in making the play's philosophical and aesthetic statement.

Deutsch's works replicate society as *he sees it*. He casts around for ways to create a condition of life onstage and seeks to view problems globally in order to effect change. Sets are used to divide stage space, thus fragmenting it visually but also, paradoxically, giving his text a deceptively solid structure.

More important than the theatrical text for Deutsch is "the dimension of theatre in the text." When writing or reading aloud, for example, he listens for the "echo of a voice," or for its resonance in his text. The written word's oral qualities take on stage reality for him: "Literature is constituted through its unlimited noisy depths." Maurice Blanchot's "literary space" becomes, for Deutsch, "musical space," comparable to the countings of *numbers* in the measureless rhythms of Gregorian chants. Just as Friedrich Hölderlin attempted to balance imbalance, rhythm, and tempo in his writings, so Deutsch aspires to transform song into language. Such an undertaking requires the discovery of a fundamental "punctuation," or "respiration," that succeeds in separating subject from narrative.[2]

Most of Deutsch's *centerless* characters, drawn from the lower classes, are divested of purpose. They exist in terms of the discontinuous sequences of events in which they participate, reacting to these in a programmed manner. Dominated by both people and circumstances, they are like robots being acted upon. What is not said in the text is of great import: silences, therefore, are used as an effective dramatic technique to create an aura of mystery. Small talk is used as a mask, and it underscores a sense of alienation. Violence is not limited to verbal outbursts; sometimes grand-guignolesque bloodcurdling murder takes place, as in *L'Entraînement du champion avant la course* (1975; *The Champion's Training before the Race*), and in Deutsch's 1978 direction of Hölderlin's *Antigone*.

Just as the nine scenes of *Dimanche* (1974; *Sunday*) are dispersed and fragmented, the fragile discourse, involving everyday people, is neither continuous nor progressive. To build up a character or a point of view is not Deutsch's aim. Each statement, whether revolving around values, judgments, or momentary desires in the lives of the protagonists, may be retracted, contradicted, or annulled by the next. Silences, ellipses, syllogisms, and other rhetorical devices serve either to attenuate or accentuate the violence buried within the word. By dignifying the needs and values of everyday people via linguistic and semantic rhythms, Deutsch succeeds in reconstructing both a period and a behavioral pattern.

Dimanche, which revolves around a young girl who lives to fulfill her ideal of becoming a perfect majorette, defies all semblance of chronological time schemes. Obsessed with training, she exercises continuously, attempting to imitate the stereotypic American high-kicker. Although she fulfills her dream, her body has been "consumed" in the process and she dies of fatigue. The simultaneity of the scenic moments onstage on that special Sunday of her final performance and death, and the continuously accelerating speed with which images multiply as groups of majorettes expend their sexual energy, leave the spectator breathless. The massive and rapid high-tech effects, accentuated by filmstrips projected on screens, at times frenetically and at times in cadenced sequences, serve to heighten the compulsiveness and the viscerality of the majorette's schizophrenic episodes.

The majorette's working-class parents suffer from vertigo as they observe the instantaneous, fragile, and fractured world onstage and the delicate lives—including that of their daughter—on the verge of falling apart. Deutsch creates a hyperrealistic world, ut lu "shadow play," through repetition, dispersion, and speed, but when by concealing reality. Events, therefore, are enacted offstage and viewers are invited to use their imaginations.[3]

Does the reigning atmosphere of hysteria in *Dimanche* allow us to label it tragedy? No, since the young girl's life inspires neither pity nor fear. Nor does it lead to catharsis. Aristotle would have labeled Deutsch's play comedy. The protagonist is vacuous; she lives in a world without meaning. Her clownish antics and her excesses liken her to a comic character—a buffoon.

Jean-Pierre Vincent's direction of Deutsch's *La Bonne Vie* (1976; *The Good Life*) stresses an attitude of nonlinearity, of discontinuity, and of dialogic hostility between a working-class couple. They disagree on everything, be it child rearing and bearing or aborting. They convey their feelings of emptiness in clichés, remnants of vocabulary: their words, divested of fire and energy, signify nothing. Only their tirades revolving around their desires for freedom from harassment remain unflawed, for these allow language to relive—although momentarily—a past, a time when word/feeling counted. In this play Deutsch's use of silences, vocalizations, and monologues serves to emphasize the atmosphere's disparities rather than to stabilize it. They underscore the alienation between husband and wife. Because aporia reigns, the gruesome outcome of *La Bonne Vie* is predictable: the husband had observed a gun hanging on the wall at the outset of the play, anticipating his ultimate crime and suicide.

Also directed by Jean-Pierre Vincent, *Convoi* (1980; *Convoy*) is one of Deutsch's most compelling and poetic plays. Its theme is exile and bonding. The action takes place in a small town in southwest France, in 1942, during the German Occupation. Marie, an 18-year-old Jewish girl, whose real name is Hannah Friedmann, lives in hiding in the home of Anne, a 60-year-old peasant. Anne loves Hannah like a daughter and has, at the risk of her own life, provided her with a false identity: that of Marie Lupiac. Although Hannah/Marie tries to return Anne's affection, her memory of her own suffering at the hands of the Nazis erodes any possibility of conveying her emotions on a conscious level.

The sense of mystery and urgency communicated by Deutsch, as he builds suspense via silences and tension by the nonsaid, reaches almost unbearable intensity. When Marie finally does speak, launching into her lyrical rendering in a quasi-trancelike state, she does not refer to herself as subject of her narration. Rather, she retraces someone else's—but really her own—harrowing exodus from the German concentration camp to France.

Oblivious to her surroundings, Marie stands for long periods of time at the door or at the window, her eyes glued to the pane, waiting for someone. Fear marks her countenance. A prey to amnesia, to mutism, or to its contrary, obsessive talking, she recalls bombings, burning flesh, starvation, escapees running through the fields, the dead—with their gaping mouths. Robotlike, she repeats the conversations and enumerates the names of those who died—starkly, as if life were being extinguished before her eyes, and by extension, those of the spectators. Despite Hannah's inability to respond openly to Anne, the thought that Anne might possibly leave her alone, even for one moment, overwhelms her with panic.

Waiting periods follow, each showing the inevitability of the power principle at work and the problematics of Marie's situation, thus paving the way for the play's shocking conclusion. Fear holds the villagers in grip after the Nazis have crossed into the so-called Free French Zone. Terror of reprisal may account for the fact that Anne's sister, her husband, and some neighbors denounce Marie/Hannah to the authorities. Both are arrested by the Vichy police. Anne, we are told, will not leave Marie—even in death.

Not only does the variety of Deutsch's pacing—from rapid to slackening tempo—intensify *Convoi's* dramatic elements, but the dichotomy between a present reality and the souvenir of past tortures, as enunciated by Marie, is a source of anguish. Marie's sufferings and her lyrical outbursts recalling segments of her past transform her into a figure of mythical dimension. As the archetype of the persecuted and the hounded, the figure lives her own twentieth-century Exodus.

For René Kalisky (b. 1936), essayist and dramatist, history is to be understood as a succession of cycles, of eternal beginnings. If progress exists at all, it is only superficial, like successive tides or recurrent nightmares, or like the ascents of Sisyphus, who climbs a mountain daily only to find himself at its foot in the morning. The same repetitions are true of theater: the same scenario is written over and over again, as if authors lacked imagination or mastery over their art and its mechanics. Despite Kalisky's nihilistic viewpoint, his dramatic unfoldings are rife with humanity's struggle to achieve some good, some serenity. Nevertheless, his anti-heroes are victims of history.

Sur les ruines de Carthage (1979; *On the Ruins of Carthage*) opens on the musical theme of Brahms's *German Requiem,* which is sung four times in the play, not only underscoring the pathetic plight of the protagonists but also organically linking them to their situation and to the progressive development of the play's tragic outcome.

Kalisky's play revolves around a rivalry between two literary professors: Koschitzke, a Jew, and Baron, a Nazi who has preempted the former's chair of Carthaginian history at the university. Although in his sixties, Koschitzke is living with the 16-year-old Elissa, a kind of dream figure he has named after two Carthaginian princesses who burned themselves alive rather than yield to the enemy. Jealous of Elissa's relationship with his rival, Baron seeks to harm her by revealing her name, Lisa Doch, and her Jewish—thus impure—origins to the Nazis. To destroy Koschitzke's reputation and thus enhance his own prestige as a historian is another of Baron's motivations. The earning of a promotion at the university requires that one make an astounding archaeological discovery. Baron, who knows that Koschitzke has hidden his "world-shaking" notes in his apartment, is determined to avail himself of them. Calling on Koschitze, Baron demands them, but Elissa refuses to hand them over.

In an extraordinarily macabre scene in which black humor reaches its apogee, audiences see Koschitzke slipping into one of his "dream stupors." Removed from the world of reality, he is unaware of Baron's attempt to harm Elissa physically. She, however, is cognizant of the fact that to survive Baron's onslaught, she must seduce him. As the two indulge in sexual manipulations on one side of the stage, Koschitzke, in a trancelike state, begins reciting a prayer to the Carthaginian lunar goddess, Tanit.

Breaking out of his trance, Koschitzke intones Brahms's *German Requiem* and then tells Elissa to let Baron read his notes. She obeys. After perusing them, however, Baron has learned nothing. His ire is fueled to the point of striking Koschitzke in the face, pushing him to the floor, kicking him, and demanding his diary. When Baron begins sniffing about like an animal in search of his prey, black comedy reaches its pinnacle.

Paroxysmal sequences follow as Koschitzke begins reading from his diary. Detached is his tone as he evokes the trial in which a judge condemned him for sexual instability, he also assails Baron. Meanwhile, Elissa, now identified with her Carthaginian namesake, begins her poignant incantation: "In a moonless and starless night, there resounds a cry that will never be forgotten by those who have heard it. A pitiful cry resounds over the Carthaginian plain." In sharp contrast is Baron's strident laughter as he states, "Carthage must burn," and Koschitzke reiterates, "Carthage must be destroyed."

While Baron, on one side of the stage, kisses Elissa on the neck and crushes her with his weight, Koschitzke, on the other side, takes his lighter and sets his manuscript aflame. The room glows as Koschitzke, paralleling his act with verbal terms, depicts the horrors experienced when Carthage burned. Koschitzke suddenly grabs Baron by the hair, beats him until his enemy's body rolls on its side. The fire spreads. Koschitzke takes Elissa in his arms, caresses her hair, and, in a kind of *Liebestod,* both prepare for death. His books—which have given meaning to his life—will also be destroyed.

Artaudian in many ways, Kalisky's characters are like raw nerves emerging from some abysmal depth, pointing to history's periodic return to blood-soaked totalitarianism. Recurrent images, such as piles of dirty laundry or rats, reminiscent of Fassbinder's degenerate Germany, clothe the stage world in ugliness, harshness, and brutality. Brahms's *German Requiem,* along with other sound effects—screams, howls, falling objects—in addition to Kalisky's own dry, jerking, halting, yet at times highly poetic and sensual language—exacerbate the central situation. Kalisky's *mise-en-abyme* reflects not only the contradictions but also the potential of a world in ruins; it also preludes future totalitarianism.

Jean-Paul Wenzel (b. 1947) was influenced in the 1970s by the works of such German playwrights as Franz Xavier Kroetz, whose writings invited audiences to view heinous crimes onstage as well as to listen to concrete and hostile verbal assaults. Fassbinder's raw and archaic beings similarly lured Wenzel into a sordid ultranaturalistic world where violence, if not overt, existed covertly.

Unlike the heroic and "pure in heart" working class dramatized by Brecht, Wenzel's characters are "real" people, whose problems, secrets, and anguishes he sought to reveal to his audiences. In *Loin d'Hagondange* (1975; *Far from Hagondange*), directed by Patrice Chéreau in 1977, Wenzel focuses on a working-class couple. After a life of patient saving and hard work, husband and wife are ready to retire. They have bought and moved into their "dream house," reminiscent of a Magritte painting, for, unlike others, it is situated in a desert. Viewed symbolically, it mirrors the protagonists' own arid inner condition. The Pinteresque silences punctuating the text reveal not inner riches but emotional emptiness and repressed feelings. Rather than devoting their early years to enjoying each other's love or expressing interest in community activities, the couple had focused their energies on acquisition: the purchase of an ideal home.

Outside of banalities, no communication takes place between the two. The patterns set during their early years together have never altered. The husband, who used to leave daily to go to the steel mill, returning tired in the evening, now makes his way to the shed in the garden. His homemaker wife keeps cleaning [...] linens, which never gets dirty, just as she has throughout her entire married life. Wenzel's acerbic ironies are cool and devastating. Stereotypes, the vacuous couple pursue their passive existence as they reduce life's complexities, but also its riches, to a bare minimum.

Wenzel's metalanguage, including sequences of prolonged silence and nonstop talking, discloses the dichotomies implicit in a whole unconscious realm: the problems facing those who love each other but are unable to convey their feelings.

After the production of *Les Incertains* (1979; *The Uncertain Ones*), directed by Alain Mergnat, concerning a conflicted domestic relationship, Wenzel reached an impasse in his writing. Volker Schlöndorff's 1971 film, *Der plötzliche Reichtum der armen Leute von Kombach* (*The Sudden Wealth of the Poor People of Kombach*), was instrumental in unblocking Wenzel, in helping him find a new way of conveying his anti-traditional theatrical views. Also effective in helping him break out of his own aridity was his work on collective projects and the realization that he had been locked into the form and formula of tragedy. His discovery of laughter allowed him to question his doubts and probe his inner desires, enabling him better to understand the public he was attempting to reach. Rather than keeping his fears and hesitations bottled up inside, where they had grown increasingly tenacious, he would share them with the world. His inner chaos had motivated him to cowrite *Vater Land* (1983; *Fatherland*) with Bernard Bloch.

What secrets had corroded Wenzel's world, terrorized his existence, inspired him after his 15-year friendship with Bloch to suddenly desire to cowrite a play with him? Wenzel discovered that his father, stationed in France during the German Occupation, had been a member of the Wehrmacht; that he had fallen in love with a French girl, deserted the German army to marry her, and had vanished from view at the age of 53, leaving his wife and two children to fend for themselves. Bernard Bloch's father, a German Jew who had feared Hitler as early as 1934, left his *fatherland*, went to France, married an Alsatian, enlisted in the Foreign Legion, and fought the Nazis. His parents are shopkeepers in Mulhouse.

Wenzel's and Bloch's common origins incited them to travel to Germany to gather documents and photos that would enable them not only to assess the country in the light of events of the 1980 but also to learn more about their fathers' land. Chance also played a role in the creation of the play: on one of their trips to Germany Wenzel found his missing father.

Vater Land is composed of two parts. The first is a series of *récits*—first-person accounts or narratives by the protagonists—that enunciate the play's theme: two men's search for their fathers. The second focuses on the the play itself: it is an attempt to create a new theatrical form by having the authors suggest during the play to a group of that they perform the story as told by the authors, refining it and inserting pertinent commentaries in the process.

The action takes place during Germany's so-called de-Nazification period. Beginning at Saint-Etienne in 1944, the story pursues its course in Baden-Baden in 1945, then Frankfurt in 1946, Wuppertal in 1947, and Hamburg in 1948. The sequences encapsulate a variety of landscapes and events: cities in ruin, people making merry, a man attempting to escape after having accidentally committed a crime, occupation by the French and Americans, the black market, fornications in cellars and elsewhere.

As Wenzel links the protagonists to their lives and times, he uses this technique: While a protagonist begins relating certain happenings to a friend or a bystander, he is, so to speak, superimposing his thoughts and impressions on the basically inattentive individual to whom he is speaking, who then mindlessly repeats these statements according to his own fragmented understanding to another, thus continuing the story—or round. So alienated are the protagonists from themselves and from each other that despite their conversations, they are never really heard by their interlocutor(s), nor do they really ever listen to what is being said. Uttered with gestures and tonal rhythmic changes, the words, revolving around insignificant reminiscences, are spoken mechanically. Thus are people saved from the excoriating hurt of extracting what has been buried so deeply within them; and audiences learn the real meaning of *deconditioning.* Such an innovative verbal technique, which Jean-Pierre Sarrazac calls *polylogue,* underscores the ambiguity of the talker, who is cut off from himself; in the protagonists, who never hear each other; and in the audience, who may or may not succeed in penetrating the objective and subjective universes of those on stage.

A Theater of Discourse

The interests of Philippe Adrien (b. 1939) as director, dramatist, and actor, at the Open Theater and elsewhere, focus mainly on collective creations: *La Baye,* first performed in Avignon, then staged in Paris at the Théâtre National Populaire by Antoine Bourseiller, and *Albert 1* (1969), first heard on France-Culture.

A psychodrama of sorts, *Albert 1* was conceived for a group of improvising actors. Its technical intensity is reminiscent of a jam session. It questions and probes but offers no answers, since characters have their individual understanding of reality.

The action takes place in a fourth-floor apartment. A knock at the door is heard. Claire, a heroine who seems to have stepped out of a prefabricated novel, has come to see Albert 1. How is it that he is at home? she asks. When she telephoned the day before, he told her he was staying with a friend. Why did she come if she knew he would not be home? Albert 1 keeps up the quid pro quo, going as far as to invite her to his home to meet the other Albert, the one she loves. After multiple ins and outs, we learn that there are not only two Alberts, but three.

The ambiguities, complexities, and mishaps lived out onstage increase in geometrical progression, particularly when two young girls, Anna and France, join in the happenings. Although the latter's name is strangely allegorical, the author interpolates, it has no relevance to the situation. As each protagonist attempts to pierce the barriers of the others, reality vanishes and stage madness dominates. Are the characters marionettes? Is their discourse an example of togetherness? rape? sadism? Is their verbal activity therapeutically sound? What is reality? truth?

Eugène Durif's (b. 1950) theater, like Artaud's, attempts to reveal a deeper reality: a world in which the unconscious takes on a strange vitality of its own. But whereas Artaud did not emphasize the word, Durif works within a poetic framework, thereby linking text to theater. He uses words at times as had Villiers de l'Isle Adam: like powerful tools to gain access to hidden and repressed inner spheres. He seeks—be it in *Croisements, Divagations* (1993; *Crossings, Ramblings*) or his other works—to discover what lurks within the personal and collective memory of the individual or group and what lies buried in the unarticulated. His monologues, interspersed with seemingly banal conversations give the impression of accessing everyday reality. Embedded within his imagistic phonemes is a fantasy domain in which a new gestural/visual and word/icon language activates perspectives, stirs elusive shadows cohabiting multivalent, conflicting worlds.[4]

Conversation sur la montagne (1986; *Conversation on the Mountain*) focuses on a woodcutter living in a remote village with its endless winters. The drama is built on the protagonist's past, which emerges slowly into a present reality through a type of soliloquy.

A condition of extreme alienation is experienced in *L'Arbre de Jonas* (1989; *Jonas's Tree*) as each of six voices, although monologuing along with others, is never heard by the rest. The speakers alone understand the harrowing nature of their losing battle: the pain and struggle involved in attempting to *reach* another human being. Although the plot is at first reminiscent of Camus's *Le Malentendu* (1944; *The Misunderstanding*), its focus is completely different. Ten years after World War II Jonas returns to his native town in France. Before making his presence known, and perhaps to divest himself of the nostalgia and hurt buried within him, he decides to hide out in the snow-covered woods. The white-toned, glacial images implanted everywhere in Durif's text not only lend the work a deeply poetic element but also serve to mask Jonas's physical whereabouts as well as his inner inextinguishable incandescence. Deftly placed allusions and subtly interspersed sensations yield fragments of an ever-deepening mystery, as Durif invites spectators to glimpse a secret world of memories—a domain they will never be able to understand.

Daniel, Jonas's brother who has been mutely staring through the window of his home for days, senses something, as he searches the snows for the slightest movement, the slightest indication of anything lurking somewhere in the gleaming white forest before him. Consumed with fear, "his mouth is closed, another having closed it for him, imposing silence upon him, to better speak within, in a voice unheard by us, murmuring, and at times from the deepest areas reaching us in fragments."

Daniel leaves the house in search of Jonas, telling the audience how he feels. He knows he will not be heard, yet he cries out his desperation. Exhausted, he lies down in the snow and sleeps. Meanwhile, Jonas has walked up to him, speaks to him as if from afar, lies down beside him in the snow—both warmed by the sparkling crystalline cover. Is it aphasia that keeps the secret of their torment? Is the recurring image of the snow, which covers and thus protects the brothers, also a means of subverting a return to a dead past—one that can never be forgotten or extracted, despite the mind's desire to cleanse it of its noxious effect?

The tension in many of Durif's plays emerges not only from his tremulous and sensation-laden style but also from his very real fear/need to become involved with words. The dichotomy between the said and the unsaid, soundings and silences, the recalled and the forgotten or repressed, is part of a buried continent of gnawing shame that adults seek to annihilate via speech.

In such plays as *L'Arbre de Jonas, Le Petit Bois* (1987; *The Small Woods*), and *Petites Heures* (1992; *The Wee Hours*) the monologues disclose a search for self within a past that keeps creating and re-creating itself. To talk, to relate, to get into another's inner world by way of strategies, detours, and circumlocutions in Durif's goal His sounds and dull or strident echoes, however, fail to produce an answer. They are an infinitesimal part of virtually imperceptible feeling.

Serge Ganzl (1925–92) wrote more than 40 plays, including *Le Coeur battant* (1989; *The Beating Heart*). Fragmentation, superimposition of one tableau on another, music, lighting, and interspersed dialogue serve to breathe new life into the stage happenings. Although *Le Coeur battant* contains 26 scenes, the playing time for each does not exceed four minutes. The action takes place in the village of Dieucourt in Picardy. The time: prior to the French Revolution of 1789. Known since medieval times for its textile industry and its strong communal spirit, Dieucourt has also been victim of exploitation by manufacturers, who, during depressed times, have abandoned the workers to poverty and wretchedness. (The feelings of destitution experienced in prerevolutionary France returned to Picardy in modern times, with the closing of textile factories in 1983.) Although *Le Coeur battant* is not a naturalist drama, it is thematically reminiscent of Gerhart Hauptmann's *The Weavers* (1892), a compelling drama revolving around the human suffering of Silesian weavers; and of Ernst Toller's *Man and the Masses* (1919), focusing on an attempt to stop smoldering hatreds and violence among revolutionary comrades.

Above all else, *Le Coeur battant* is a love story, revolving around Adrienne, the daughter of a count, and Niçaise, a young man who, as an infant, was found in a sack on the banks of the Somme. Adrienne is a daughter of the Enlightenment, the Encyclopedists, Diderot, and Rousseau. She believes in the spirit of the Revolution and in the New Man who will be born in its wake. After divulging her "occult" knowledge to Niçaise, however, in Artaudian manner, she grows weak, fallow, as if she has been emptied of blood—that is, of her worth to others. No longer useful or fascinating to Niçaise, she fades into oblivion. He, on the other hand, unaware of his spiritual "vampirism," has transcended not only his destitution but his environment as well. A kind of demiurge/alchemist, he has learned, thanks to Adrienne, how to speak and to struggle. He becomes deputy of Dieucourt. His rise has precipitated Adrienne's downfall.

To accentuate the economically depressed condition of the population, Ganzl had recourse to multiple and perpetually mobile scenes that transported viewers from one circumscribed stage space to another. Groups in village, castle, and church each told their tales. The rapidity of the scenic changes—superimposed one on another—was designed to give the audience the impression of but a *single* stage space within the multiple sets, accentuating thereby the universality of human bondage.

Comedy: The Ironic Rictus of Pain

Jean-Claude Grumberg (b. 1939), who was born to proletarian Jewish/immigrant parents, uses humor, irony, puns, and distortion rather than rage to cope with his world of sorrows. Despite his father's deportation from France by the army of the German Occupation and his mother's backbreaking work as a seamstress to support her children, laughter is his way to avert depression.

Influenced by classical, boulevard, and avant-garde theater, Grumberg's works deal with such fundamental issues as racism, intolerance, and violence. The author manipulates with expertise a whole range of moods, from cruelty to whimsy, and of vocabularies, from the most elegant to the crudest. As advocated by Artaud, Grumberg shocks his spectators, thus opening up a whole instinctual and repressed side of humankind. Like Alfred Jarry, he uses farcical and grotesque elements, captured from the workaday world, to expose and exaggerate life's foibles. Although his plays are mainly based on his own painful experiences, he also allows a world of whimsy to emerge—although he subverts it moments later by life's realities.

Produced by Jacques Rosner, Grumberg's *Dreyfus* (1974) is not a play about the Jewish army officer wrongly accused of treason by the French military. Its focus is on anti-Semitism in general. Its technique: the Pirandellian play-within-a-play. The scene opens in a small Polish ghetto in the 1930s. A Jewish amateur theatrical group is rehearsing a play written about Dreyfus by Maurice, one of its members. The performers decide to do away with traditional stock characters and musical interludes characteristic of Yiddish repertoire and become instead involved in worldly reality. They want something meaningful to emerge from their performance: they would seek an answer to humanity's continuous hounding and killing of Jews.

Although the participants try to understand the motivations for past anti-Semitism, they seem unable, despite their miming, gestures, pleadings, and frustrations, really to get into the play. They disagree over the causes of injustice; some are embarrassed to play the part of those who accused Dreyfus of treason; others cannot understand why Dreyfus did not consider himself a Jew but a French officer. An actor named Michel, playing Dreyfus, remains alienated from his role. The Marxist Maurice is convinced that there is no basic difference between Jews and Christians—except for the fact that the former are the victims. The professional tailor thinks costumes are most important aspect of the performance. Another member of the troupe feels more comfortable by returning to traditional Yiddish theater with its songs and dances.

Reality intrudes when several drunkards bang on the door and begin hurling anti-Semitic remarks at the actors. The oldest member of the troupe rises quietly, folds his Yiddish newspaper, and orders the others to hide. He opens the door. The drunkards enter, castigate, threaten, and beat him. Tensions increase between the victim and those in hiding. Only when one of the intruders grabs the old man by the neck and brandishes a knife does Maurice, along with others, run forward. That he first tries to reason with the irrational hatemongers is so absurd that it becomes humorous: "Why do you mistreat this old man, aren't we all brothers?" Only after the drunkards pursue their beatings and threaten to burn down the place does Michel, donned in Dreyfus's uniform, step forward. Introducing himself as "Captain Dreyfus from Vilna," he orders them out. Undaunted, they attack him. Michel brandishes his sword; the drunkards, terrified, run out, at which Michel states, "I have found the character."

Time elapses. Maurice, having joined the Communist party, writes a letter to those remaining in the troupe, who find solace in their religion. In the letter he expresses his Marxist view of history and his faith in the proletarian revolution—unable to predict the collective acts of extermination that were to occur only several years later.

En r'venant d'L'Expo (1979; *On R'turning from the World's Fair*), directed by Jean-Pierre Vincent, is grandiose in concept. The café-concerts of the belle époque, star-studded with such names as Paulin, Paulus, Artistide Bruant, and Eugénie Buffet, singing their catchy ditties, are set against more serious parts of society such as the union movement, warmongers, and reactionaries.

Jean-Claude Penchenat staged his 1979 production of Grumberg's play in a large arena where audiences were invited to sit in the center, thus participating directly in the charged happenings. The opening scene features highlights of the World's Fair of 1900: French military might, scientific discoveries such as electricity, "new art," "universal cookery." Attending the fair is the 10-year-old Louis, son of a waiter, through whom Grumberg questions the meaning of the new machine age.

Eight years later we meet the same protagonists in a small café. Louis has become an actor. Cleverly used stage space is cut up into groups of military men, workers, and students, who express many political views—leftist, rightist, centrist—some favoring the Action Française and castigating the Jews. Antipodal to these groups are the "Egalitarians," idealists meeting in the back room of the café, who, because they have diverted their focus from reality, lay the groundwork for such catastrophes as World War I.

The last act, which takes place between 1913 and 1914, opens onto a variety of café-concerts that serve as meeting grounds for union groups. Louis, the scenelinker, is ever present with his humor and satire. Fervor grows in a brilliant finale as soldiers march around the arena to the accompaniment of a band playing heroic battle music. The groups that were formerly opposed join in; their gestures and expressions grow increasingly frenetic and violent; finally hysteria sets in, forecasting the madness and cruelties of war.

The themes used by Victor Haïm (b. 1935), although drawn from life, are imbued with lyrical qualities. Because he possesses that marvelous ability to laugh at himself, he knows how to make others chortle. In *La Peau d'un fruit sur un arbre pourri* (1971; *Fruit on a Rotted Tree*) Haïm caricaturizes through lively dialogue a former French minister, Raoul Réal, who had fled to the desert to escape a government that refused to endorse his projects. He had proposed the use of preventative torture to gain one's ends. The vulgar, simplistic, truculent, absurd, and cruel logic of Réal crystallizes a fantastic world that could and has become reality. That the fruit is rotten is not the question for Haïm. Rather, who will avail themselves of it is the issue.

Theater for Jeanine Worms (b. 1923), whose taste is eclectic, is a means of attacking all that is stereotyped, hackneyed, narrow, and decadent in society. Very much of an individualist, her plays are original and personal. From Beckett, Genet, and Ionesco she learned what implements to use for satirizing superficial love, banal relationships, and perverse political situations. Her weapons for denouncing error and illusion are grammar and syntax. She juggles her words, indulging in puns and a medley of verbal acrobatics. She enjoys inventing words, like *intuitionyinner,* to spice up her humorous interludes and expose her characters' fads and tics, as well as simply to amuse herself. As an example of her epithets, a baby is referred to as "that little consumer" or "that little audio-visual." Her characters are frequently victimized by words (banalities, stock phrases); they are carried along by slogans, believing the prognostications of publicity mongers and dictators.

Un Chat est un chat (1968; *A Cat Is a Cat*), revolving around love and friendship, is set in a world of gossipers and prodigious slanderers. *La Boutique* (1971; *The Store*) dramatizes the economic and emotional aridity

in a couple's world after 15 years of marriage Capitalism and petit bourgeois turpitude constitute the theme of *Le Goûter* (1972; *Afternoon Snack*),
revealed most innocently by two women as they gorge themselves on
cakes during an afternoon snack—even while their respectful husbands
devote their efforts to making profits. Worms's plays are marked with a
common stamp: the conformity, narrow-mindedness, and mediocrity
implicit in a consumer society.

Play, Banter, and Badinage

Humor, wit, and an understanding of the corrosive nature of solitude
mark the dramas of Madeleine Laïk (b. 1944). Behind their façade of
quips and ironies lies deep pathos. In *Double Commande* (1982; *Double
Order*) the protagonist, Monsieur Paul, leads a double life. By day he is a
monitor in a driving school; by night, a hack writer. Why does he
despair? Because his publisher insists that female characters be included
in his novels. Try as he may, he simply cannot see into a woman's psyche
to understand her needs or desires. Lights out. Change of scene.
Grinding is heard. Monsieur Paul's student, Mlle Gloria, is taking her
driving lesson. Laïk's manner of interspersing multiple topics of conversation during the lesson—Mlle Gloria's dream the previous night,
Monsieur Paul's driving instructions, his difficulty in finding a suitable
woman about whom to write—shows her technique to best advantage
and adds hilarious confusion to the stage play.

Banter and jocosity are also implicit in Corinne Atlas's (b. 1952) *Le
Coin d'ombre* (1983; *The Corner Shadow*), which dramatizes events in the
lives of a family vacationing in a house facing the English Channel.
Because grandparents, parents, and children are all involved, each
behaving in keeping with his or her age, audiences are swept up in
swirling sequences of drollery verging at times on pathos. As the protagonists live out their imaginings, longings, torments, dreams, intermit-
tent disputes, outbursts, flirting, boredom, and love, stage time is
fleshed out and extended. Atlas effectively applies theatrical, technical,
and dialogic methods: lights reveal the hour of the day; sounds emanate
from a radio, even while a whole range of vocal modulations—lamenta-
tions, whispers, murmurs, bursts of laughter, hushed kisses, and sighs—
disclose a host of overt or covert flurries in this microcosmic family.

The plays of Colette Fayard (b. 1938) are unusual, thematically and
technically. *Effacement* (1987), for example, a play-within-a-play, focuses
on an actor, Maurice, obsessed with the idea of creating a play based on

Antonin Artaud's years of internment during World War II in the mental institution of Rodez. The members of Maurice's troupe, however, consider such an undertaking unthinkable. Who would be capable of writing such a play? As the members of the company attempt to dissuade Maurice from pursuing his project, the energy funneled into their dialogues triggers a counter-movement within them: the more they talk, the more possessed they become by Artaud's world and words. But do they really understand Artaud? and the depth of Maurice's commitment to his project? During the rehearsals Maurice becomes increasingly aware that the production he envisions cannot reveal Artaud's truth. Nevertheless, the more deeply he immerses himself in his role, the more his behavior is marked by irrationality: he eats as Artaud had, following certain maniacal rituals such as spitting out his food only to put it back into his mouth to chew again. He recites psalms during episodes of glossolalia: "I am collecting my urine, my excrements, my perspiration, I lose nothing, I do not blow my nose, I swallow my saliva in order to contain it." As Artaud had been forced to submit to electroshock at Rodez, so Maurice, unbeknown to the others, will not simply undergo a fake treatment but will actually experience it onstage on opening night. The company, aghast at seeing Maurice writhing in a state of semi-consciousness, rings down the curtain.

The scenic space features offices—those of the director, secretary, and others—and the protagonist's dressing room. As actors pass from one area to another, frequently simultaneously, they work their movements into their text, according to its rapid or slackening rhythms, thereby evoking feelings of frenetic or chaotic activity. Remarkable is Fayard's ability to interweave quotations from some of Artaud's works into the reality of her dialogue. *Effacement* elicits a rictus.

Fugue en mineur(e) (1978; *Minor Fugue*), *Passé composé* (1986; *Past Indefinite*), and *Les Murs n'ont pas d'oreilles* (1987; *Walls Have No Ears*) underscore the penchant of Pierre Léaud (b. 1909) for verbal devices intended to draw laughter, in light and clever banter à la Raymond Queneau. The plays also reveal a Giraudoux-like tenderness and whimsy. Although filled with wordplay, Léaud's dialogue—the very title *Fugue en mineur(e)* can be translated as *Minor Fugue* or *Flight of a Minor*—is frequently unsettling.

Fugue en mineur(e) opens on a road in some unidentified place. Fourteen-year-old Jacqueline, on her way home from school, meets 25-year-old Louis. They begin talking. Jacqueline loves to use slang. And Louis, forever correcting her, wonders why she resorts to such improprieties of speech.

Because she is unhappy; her mother does not love her, her stepfather beats her, and her siblings get on her nerves. We learn that Louis is also unhappy. He used to sing at small parties. When his voice broke, doctors treated him, but when he had no money left, they no longer helped him. Deciding to leave society for parts unknown, Louis asks Jacqueline to follow him, to leave her old life and join him on his great adventure. He warns her to tell no one of her whereabouts. Nor must she think. To reason is to interrupt action. Just say "good-bye" here and now. They leave on his tandem, riding over mountain and dale. Most poignant is Jacqueline's excitement at seeing the sea for the first time. "It's beautiful . . . it's large . . . it's infinite," Louis tells her, "it carries you away and transports you . . . it's the cradle of the world." One evening, while camping outdoors, Louis speaks to her of the stars and the planets. The rational world vanishes, as does linear time, while the two are transformed into two universal beings existing in infinite space.

During the course of the play Jacqueline awakens to life with rapture, sensitivity, tenderness, and a share of bitterness. Like some of Giraudoux's young girls, she, too, discovers that life is not always candy-colored and that growing into womanhood is serious business.

Dialogic Situation and Environmental Theater

Combat de Nègre et de chiens (1979; *Combat of Black and Dogs*), *Dans la solitude des champs de coton* (1987; *Solitude in the Cotton Fields*), and *Roberto Zucco* (1990), all by Bernard-Marie Koltès (1948–89), are stark, intense works revolving around environmental and racial multiplicity and intolerance. Dialogues are trenchant, at times fierce. Each character attempts to subvert the other in order to save his skin—or an ideal.

Combat, directed by Patrice Chéreau, takes place on a construction site some place in West Africa. The decor, designed by Richard Peduzzi, consists of a huge concrete bridge under construction, set against an empty sky, which thus emphasizes an atmosphere of extreme alienation. The presence of a real truck onstage and grating, grinding, metallic sounds—whistles blowing and shots emanating from the dark in keeping with Artaudian dicta—are jarring and disturbing.

Koltès maintained that his play does not deal with blacks, whites, or neocolonialists, nor does it focus on racial issues. Like Genet, Koltès claims neither to take sides nor make value judgments. Nevertheless, he fleshes out the inequities existing in European colonial policy: settlers were usually not civilizing agents but exploiters. As Joseph Conrad did in *The Heart*

in *The Heart of Darkness,* Koltès sought to deal with those hidden but
raging demons in the darkest, most archaic levels of the human psyche—
that "primeval mud" or slime.

Combat features two engineers employed by a French company. The
60-year-old Horn is fatherly in his outlook and intent on maintaining
peace and equilibrium in the compound. On his last trip to Paris he met
Leone, a woman who had never left her native city, and brought her
back with him to Africa. The 30-year-old Cal works for the company
strictly for money. He considers himself superior to the natives and is
attached to his dog alone.

The play's relatively conventional plot revolves around a black man,
Alboury, who has come to the building site to claim the body of his dead
brother, a worker who was killed that very day. Horn, whose motto is
cooperation no matter the cost, tries to handle Alboury diplomatically:
he offers him whiskey and invites him to sit at the table with him.
Alboury, aware that Horn is using smooth talk, remains adamant.
Tension builds when audiences learn that Cal, given to violence, had shot
Alboury's brother, driven the truck over his body to create the impression of accidental death, and then hidden the corpse.

Horn is also plagued by Leone, a strangely negative woman who finds
it impossible to relate to her new land or to Horn. The only one she can
begin to understand is Alboury, and she is even attracted to him. After
Cal is shot dead offstage by, one surmises, some mysterious African
guard, Leone leaves for Paris, while Horn remains alone with Cal's dog.

Although Koltès frequently waxes trite and his stage action is predictable, as are his stereotypic arguments, his animistic language and his
macabre humor serve to emphasize his characters' deep sense of solitude.
Excitement and fright are also implicit in the play, when, for example,
Alboury is awaiting his brother's hidden body. Spectators have the feeling that multiple hidden presences are lurking offstage, lending this
highly realistic drama a metaphysical dimension.

Koltès is far from trite in his approach to dying and death in *Roberto
Zucco,* directed by Peter Stein in German and Bruno Boeglin in French.
In fact, the play treated the theme so radically that it elicited scandal
and polemics. Patrice Chéreau wrote, "The play was born out of a violent
revolt against the world and its fascination for murderers, [and] it is
true, it is scandalous."[5]

Koltès divides humanity into two categories: those who are condemned and those who are not. Roberto Zucco is among the former.
Recounting this solitary serial killer's story in a detached manner, Koltès

offers audiences no explanations or justifications for his animal acts. The mysterious, utterly closed Roberto Zucco became for the author a mythical hero. Because Koltès is dealing with real feelings and not cerebrally constructed thematics, *Roberto Zucco* may be considered one of his most troubling dramas. As he himself said, "I must speak out because I am going to die. It must be said that no one is really interested in anyone else. No one. Men need women and women need men. As for love, there isn't any" (Quoted in Le Roux, 28–29). Nor are there answers for gratuitous crimes; nor for the gratuitous nature of life itself. Nor is there any reason for living. Koltès himself was murdered by AIDS.

Thinking/Language in Action Theater

Theater for Daniel Lemahieu (b. 1946) is a crisscrossing between language and history, the one deriding the other. *Usinage* (1983; *Machining*), the third play in a trilogy that includes *D'siré* (1983) and *Entre chien et loup* (1981; *Between Dog and Wolf*), takes place in a factory town somewhere in the north of France; *Nazebrock* (1993), a comedy, is, like the trilogy, studded with regionalisms and idiomatic phrases that frequently violate both syntax and grammar, it is universal in spirit. Lemahieu knows how to inject the flavor of the times and of a people's mentality— a vitality—into his dialogue and action.

Lemahieu describes *L'Idéal* (1990) as a "confrontation," an "inner combat" in the minds of his characters living in a space/time continuum. "Thought alone is action," he maintains. Because dramatists, directors, and actors all "juggle with notions, concepts, ideas, emotions," nothing is certain in theater any more than it is in life. The nine sequences in *L'Idéal,* each viewed as a response to life's quandaries, can be approached as a vocal quartet or opera made up of two male voices (Ernst and Wolf), one female (Lodli, Wolf's wife and Ernst's friend), and a piano score.

Time in *L'Idéal,* as in myth, is reversible. Seasons and hours are announced as each scene unfolds on a passionate or hate-filled note. Events unfold in an "apocalytic climate," in a kind of surreal Vienna— once the home of such great figures as Gustav Klimt, Egon Schiele, Oskar Kokoschka, Arnold Schönberg, Sigmund Freud, and Lou Andreas-Salomé. Indeed, Lemahieu's creative protagonists are inspired by famous artists: Ernst, a budding author, resembles Nietzsche, Rilke, or Adamov; Wolf, a composer and pianist, old and at the end of his career, calls to mind Wagner, Verdi, or Alban Berg; and Lodli suggests Cosima Liszt, Lou Andreas-Salomé, or Alma Mahler.

Ernst enters the stage space on a fine spring day. Chords struck on a piano offstage convey a mood of dissatisfaction and suffering. Ernst is in love with Lodli, Wolf's wife. His appearance is disorienting: he is wearing an outmoded traveling outfit and black glasses, and although he is not blind he uses a cane. His seemingly irrational soliloquy reflects his passion for work and his admiration for Wolf, who is his friend but also his rival and thus his enemy. Ernst's obsessive affair with Lodli and his fear that his liaison may be discovered produce emotional havoc within him. Feelings of guilt punctuate his monologues and are paralleled by the tones hammered out on the piano.

Throughout the play Ernst's, Lodli's, and Wolf's moods reach extremes of anger, jealousy, pleasure, fulfillment, alienation, solitude, creative fury, or aridity, measured in staccato beats. Lemahieu's linguistic sounds as well as his thematics do not depict one life, but many; not one era, but an infinite number of them, in a single theatrical universe.

Some of the plays of Philippe Minyana (b. 1946)—*Laura dans l'Olivette* (1980; *Laura in the Olive Grove*), *Le Dîner de Lina* (1983; *Lina's Dinner*), *Fin d'été à Baccarat* (1985; *Summer's End at Baccarat*)—are powerful for their poetry. *Laura dans l'Olivette* in some ways in comparable to García Lorca's dialogic use of nature. Sun, moon, and olive grove imbue the stage space with a panoply of sensations, as if plants, trees, and grasses were all participating in a pantheistic revel.

Set against a Mediterranean backdrop, *Laura dans l'Olivette* concerns a girl named Laura who rejects her tradition-obsessed father. Only in the "vibrant silence of the olive grove" into which she retires does she enjoy a sense of peace and protection. Laura refuses to accept the prevailing male-dominated, restrictive, and demoralizing establishment. Her world is experienced in opposition to that of "the others"—those leading staid and well-regulated lives. Shunning the heat of the summer day, she yearns "for ice and mountains. The odor of ether and silence."

Her mother, siding with her father, castigates Laura for her disobedience: "Your jaw is steel, your eyes are black." But Laura is not one to yield. Violent and piercing images reveal her inner rage: "When I hear father, I'd like to drive my fork into the table." Because he is a conventional man, he has always behaved with "traditional dishonesty." As the richest man in the district, his successful candidacy in an election is predictable. Even the dead vote for him. Just as cutting to Laura are his insensitivity and egoism. His loves are hunting, acquisition, and dominating others. Understandably, he has neither time nor love for his family; he enjoys being surrounded by men, indulging in male talk and games.

Like Antigone, Laura has the makings of a heroine, she is strong, vital, unafraid of martyrdom. Although she loves and is loved by Adrien, she refuses to marry him on her father's terms: to follow in her mother's footsteps. Launching into a passionate poetic discourse, she tells her fiancé that she is attracted to his body's heat and contours. Adrien, interested in money and the luxurious future his marriage to Laura would assure, tries both to please her father and placate his nonconformist fiancée. Laura, feeling free only when away from her father, tries to convince Adrien to leave with her. "No one gives me orders," she says aggressively, whereupon Adrien slaps her. Laura spits in his face and leaves, but only momentarily.

The confrontation between daughter and father is the high point of the drama. When her father informs Laura that for reasons of economy he intends to cut down the olive grove and sell the land—the only place where she finds solace and beauty—she threatens to kill herself. An angry exchange ensues. Aware that such antics will neither see him through his electoral campaign nor ensure the wedding he has planned for his daughter, the father yields somewhat by promising to delay the sale of the olive grove.

Adrien and Laura's wedding day has arrived. A friend rushes in moments before the ceremony is to take place. Speaking with immense sorrow, he informs the family that the father's little truck has "plunged into the void"—in the olive grove. Both Laura and the truck have burned to cinders. Despite the still flaming embers, the friend got out of his own car to look around for signs of life. Only Laura's wedding bouquet was intact.

Not only is *Laura dans l'Olivette* effective theater; it is also stylistically and ideologically striking. The viscerality of its poetry, punctuated with musical interludes replicating high-powered mood swings, is memorable. So, too, is the manner in which Minyana contrasts the daughter's idealism with the mediocrity of her family life. Impressive as well are the stances of the robotlike mother, who thinks of nothing but fulfilling her wifely obligations. Having accepted herself as *object,* she has become *abject* in her daughter's eyes. Words spoken by such "defunct" individuals as the mother become *pretexts* for life itself.

France's "internal organs are revealed" in the theater of Noëlle Renaude (b. 1949), wrote Minyana, and "their stench is expelled." Brutal, trenchant, raw, yet non-naturalist, Renaude's protagonists are caricatures spiced with touches of black humor.

Petits Rôles (1992; *Small Roles*) deals with the pain of being. It probes and digs relentlessly, crushing the barriers behind which hides a disquieting, even menacing, world. Sam, the play's psycho-pomp, is implacable in his interrogation of the widower Livio. Because his focus is on death, he demands to know the purpose of Livio's life. Does this widower, who has spent his days tending to his grocery store and whose only solace in old age is his dog, have anything to look forward to? Despite the fact that the skeletal Livio looks like a "mummy," that his store is dirty, dark, and run-down, and that he reeks of old age, Livio is not yet ready to die. Try as he may to parry his interlocutor's incessant talk of his imminent demise, he is entrapped by his artful interrogator. When asked how he would feel were his dog to die, Livio refuses to face such a probability.

A third voice, endowed with its own speech patterns, enters the macabre round. Madame Verdure, a widow for nearly 50 years, has been contemplating suicide but has never taken the action because she fears death. The verbal cantatas of a fourth voice, that of gold-digging Johnny, evince his killer tactics and anticipate Madame Verdure's death. That he is a real devourer, *eating* everything in sight, including the deceased's pocketbook and its contents, implements Sam's merriment at a job well done, which he conveys in his dance at the play's conclusion.

Blanche Aurore Céleste (1992; *White Dawn Celestial*) opens with a caricature of marriage-bed antics: "Papa struck mama. Mama fell on the bed. Papa, filled with remorse, jumped on mama," and the narrator was conceived. Relating her tale in a detached and flippant manner, the protagonist informs her audiences that she had been given the name White because she was born at the cock's crow, while Dawn and Celestial were added on later. Her days flow by as do her nights. Her dreams, more like nightmares, feature worlds in collision, hideous forms constantly popping into view, such as a maimed horse or a "horrible mouth" crushing her screams. Nor are viewers spared the details of her empirical reality: the shock of her first menstrual period, her initiation into sex, her leaving home, her loneliness, her innumerable sexual encounters accompanied so frequently by the death of one or more of her partners. When she questions one of her men friends, Sélim, whose presence is a momentary consolation, about the incandescent sands of his North African homeland, he refuses to reply. They separate because the cultural chasm between them is too deep. Never do White's fleeing encounters bring her fulfillment; the men with whom she beds are unpleasant, sexually

Insufficient, or dull. Her numerous and repetitive *motions* cramp her life negatively—until she is utterly incorored by a love experience.

Renaude's direct, powerful, and stark style is expertly interspersed with slang, which adds mightily to its flavor. As she hammers out her verbal truths, her nails penetrate deeply into her protagonists' flesh, sometimes drawing emotional blood and surprises, but never answers.

Political, Social, Aesthetic, Confrontational Theater

Enzo Cormann (b. 1954) is deeply committed, both socially and philosophically, to the plight of the laboring class. His dramas, dealing with empirical problems, are with but a few exceptions thesis plays directed against capitalism.

Takiya! Tokaya! (1992) deals with death, sickness, drugs, alcohol, murder, and illusion versus reality. Life is a valley of sorrows, disease, and mutilation. All is worthless. Why continue to live when we are fated to be plowed under? Hatred and violence reign in a Bosch-like atmosphere of human degradation. To say that *Takiya! Tokaya!* is nihilistic would be an understatement. The play opens as a 60-year-old hemiplegic, Mademoiselle, pushes her old-fashioned wheelchair about the stage space and talks with her young interlocutor, Lila, about her writing. The characters emanating from her fantasy world come to life. In a second scene, aptly entitled "Bandy-legged, But," a 45-year-old saxophone player, Frank McBollan, is in the process of disclosing his explosive feelings and thoughts to his doctor, Pepin.

The clever mood of irrationality Cormann seeks to portray in his staccato sentences and phrases—in the manner of James Joyce's *Finnegans Wake* (1939), is hardly successful. The Irish writer created an elaborate language made up of puns, neologisms, slang, and foreign words, in which he incorporated literary, historical, and philosophical allusions. He always related his linguistic skills to every facet of the human experience, thus lending his work a mythical dimension. The same cannot be said of Cormann. His proliferating flow of words, including such overworked nouns as *bullshit* and *cunt*, is simply a hodgepodge of meaningless banalities. Predictably does Cormann's saxophone player say to his doctor: "Cut my head off."

Images de Mussolini en hiver (1984; *Images of Mussolini in Wintertime*) by Armando Llamas (b. 1950) is innovative in its attempt to subvert destructive rule through the characters' insalubrious and irrational comportment. Although references are made to Mussolini's Italy, the action takes place in a timeless era. A quartet of amoral, anguished beings are attempting to live out their lives in a war zone. Joseph and Eric are friends, bound together for some mysterious reason. Marthe and Isabelle are hoping to find husbands. Joseph marries Marthe; Eric, Isabelle.

In a world where human emotions are repressed, killing seems par for the course. No one mourns the death under bombing of Isabelle, or of Joseph's mother, who never liked Eric. Eric moves into the home of Joseph and Marthe, who soon dies of some strange ailment. Joseph buries her in a nearby forest, then returns to Eric. They finally sleep together, only to separate the following day. The sound of a soccer match on the radio drowns out Joseph's voice as he enunciates his hope for a better humanity in the future.

The Marxist play *Les Nonnes* (1969; *The Nuns*) by Eduardo Manet (b. 1932) was directed by Roger Blin. This ingenious stage piece, which takes place in Haiti, features three nuns—really three men—who have invited a wealthy woman into their cellar, promising to help her escape from the clutches of revolutionary slaves. Instead they murder her and take her jewels. But their frantic attempts to leave their cellar are to no avail; a sense of anguish sets in. That there is no hint of transvestism, homosexuality, or sex changes among these "women" members of a religious order heightens the drama's import. That they use their positions to further their own interests, and indulge in carnage on the way, is for Manet the most extreme kind of demystification of Catholic doctrine.

Manet's *Les Chiennes* (1987; *The Dogs*) takes place in a devastated war zone. The last living man is seen pulling two enchained women. Because they obey and fawn over him, they have debased themselves to such an extent that they merit the title of his dogs. A strange character wearing hunting boots, elegant pants, a poncho, a sombrero, and a revolver enters the stage space. The surprise element occurs when audiences discover that *he* is a woman who has singlehandedly transformed part of the devatastated war zone into a kind of paradise. Relationships alter. The once autocratic man has now become an object to be manipulated and crushed.

Serge Rezvani (b. 1928) is ferociously opposed to any kind of specialization in the arts. A playwright, he asserts, must know how to wield hatchet and pen; how to cultivate land, cook, and play one or more musical instruments. To remain imprisoned within the narrow confines of one's concepts or milieu is to become *un homme de métier*—a pedestrian author.

Were it not for Rezvani's acidulous humor and provocative language, which stress the farcical elements in life, *Le Palais d'hiver* (1976; *The*

Winter Palace) would verge on the nihilistic. Based on an ancient Russian tale set in the court of Peter the Great, the play relates the story of two of the czar's dwarfs who fall in love. They ask their sovereign's permission to marry, and their request is granted. To enhance the wedding festivities, the czar has a special ice palace built to their dimensions, containing everything they would need in their household. The wedding ceremony completed, Peter the Great orders the couple to lie down on their nuptial bed, which is also made of ice. He then has the massive block of ice used as a door sealed with water. So cold is it in St. Petersburg that night that the following morning the dwarfs' bodies are found congealed in death.

Theater for Rezvani is a political and social weapon. As such, the play becomes a substitute for action and must remain so until the day when action becomes a substitute for the play. Whether a dramatist takes an active part in politics or not, Rezvani reasons, his work engages him in political action. If he rejects such involvement, he becomes a criminal—since he *lets* things happen.

Chapter Three

Feast, Frolic, and Ferment: Ariane Mnouchkine's Théâtre du Soleil

The credo of the Théâtre du Soleil is celebration—feast, frolic, and ferment. Its repertoire includes documentary theater with a politico-socio-Marxist twist; Shakespeare with a touch of No; clowning with lazzi license; Aeschylus and Euripides with Hindu highlights. The Théâtre du Soleil's productions have led to some of the most startling and innovative spectacles in contemporary French theater: *1789, 1793, Mephisto, The Clowns, Richard II, Twelfth Night, Henri IV* (Part 1), *L'Histoire terrible mais inachevée de Nodorom Sihanouk roi du Cambodge* (*The Terrible but Incomplete History of the Cambodian King, Norodom Sihanouk*), *L'Indiade, ou L'Inde de leurs rêves* (*The Indiade or India of Their Dreams*), and *Les Atrides* (*The House of Atreus*).

The Théâtre du Soleil was founded as a cooperative in 1964 by Ariane Mnouchkine and a group of nine actors and technicians from the Theatrical Association of Parisian University Students. Unlike most directors, who sought to name their companies after themselves, Mnouchkine called hers the Théâtre du Soleil because it answered a need: that of life, light, heat, beauty, strength, and fertility. Nor did she seek to dictate to the actors, technicians, and set designers who joined her company. Rather, she worked with them in creative collaborations. Like Jacques Copeau, Mnouchkine had the members of her company spend a month with her in the Ardèche, learning to work together as a group and within the parameters of arduous communal disciplines.

Like other theatrical enterprises of the 1960s, Mnouchkine's was socially oriented and left wing in theory and practice; it produced such plays as Gorky's *Petits Bourgeois* as adapted by Arthur Adamov (1964). Equality reigned on all levels in her company: each member was paid the same salary; roles were rotated, a small part going to an actor who then played a large one at another time; and all were expected to perform menial tasks when the need arose. Thus the notion of hierarchy was done away with. Because the Théâtre ... the ... il ... good ... to entertain even while also activating social conscience, members would make a concerted effort to produce works of interest to all—the intelligentsia, the worker, or simply the pleasure seeker.

The group's production of *The Kitchen* (1967) by Arnold Wesker opened at the Cirque Médrano in Paris with intriguing sets designed by Roberto Moscoso. Because Mnouchkine transformed the circus ring into an arena stage, spectators sat in a semicircle on benches. To create the right ambiance for Wesker's theater piece, which dramatized the lives of restaurant workers, the troupe visited some restaurant kitchens where its members learned about the preparation and serving of "assembly line" food. In turn, various chefs, waiters, and kitchen workers were invited to attend rehearsals of the play and comment on the accuracy of the company's presentation, the player's movements and gestures, and the spatial layouts of certain scenes.

The sets for the large kitchen of a restaurant where the action takes place consisted of a group of counters placed center stage. The audience was made privy, during the course of the action, to the jealousies, animosities, and love-hate relationships manifested during the course of a working day. A microcosm of a macrocosm, *The Kitchen* is a metaphor for the repressed world of instincts—a sphere where unregenerate feelings take root, burgeon, and are released.

Wesker's play centers on the culinary sphere: food is cooked, served, eaten, and digested in the kitchen, or inner sanctum, which is, paradoxically, in full view of the audience. The Théâtre du Soleil's idea of weaving the various stages of the transformatory processes into ritualistic designs was genial since it underscored both the drama's rhythmic and visual elements. Even more significant was the mythic quality and the sense of continuity injected into the proceedings: since food is the source of life, what remains unconsumed is recycled.

The excitement and mystery generated by the Théâtre du Soleil's presentation also stemmed from the actors' pacing in their rapid or slow entrances and departures from the kitchen. The audience was riveted by the variety of movements, gestures, and mimed sequences—particularly the manner in which dishes and trays were carried or twirled—enacted rapidly, even frenetically, or slowly and sometimes in a barely perceptible way. Enriching the production as well was the orchestrated quality of the dialogue, the soft asides alternating with strident vocal tones accentuating growing perturbation or satisfaction. The interacting visual centers created a whole network of polarized spheres of action, which not only energized the play but also mesmerized the audience into following the performers' antics in their patterned circular or linear formation. *The Kitchen*'s success enabled the members of the Théâtre du Soleil to leave their jobs and devote themselves full time to their art.

Mnouchkine's innovative 1968 production of Shakespeare's *A Midsummer Night's Dream*, also performed at the Cirque Médrano, stimulated viscerally the spectators' unconscious by placing stress on the play's lustful, lusty, and Dionysian side. To this end Moscoso built a set consisting of a sloping stage covered with hundreds of variously tinted goatskins, which were smooth and soft when stroked during performance. A magical climate was born when moons, sculpted of wood, copper, and metal and placed above the stage, cast their remote and matte luminosities on the vast expanse of carpeted earth.

As fairies, wearing goatskin pants and resembling frightening satyrs more than ethereal beings, danced and leaped about the stage, a fantastic subliminal universe was dredged up before the viewer. That Titania fell in love with an ass injected a singularly illicit, yet shockingly realistic, note into the stage play. Two members of Maurice Béjart's dance company, invited to portray Oberon and Titania, pranced about on the fur's opulent softness, lending truly comic grandeur and flame to one of the most beloved Shakespeare works.

Not until May 1968, when political ferment reached its height in France, did the Théâtre du Soleil discover its real aim: to create a new theatrical language, a fresh aesthetic, and, perhaps most important, to become politically militant. No longer would the group merely work together as a cooperative or collective experimental theater. The Théâtre du Soleil's goal was twofold: to trigger a revolutionary spirit in those associated with the troupe and to have a lasting influence on the spectators. No longer only interpreters of drama, the players were henceforth to be participants, activists, and future revolutionaries, inciting people to act on behalf of their fellow beings. While continuing to entertain and amuse their audiences, they would function as educators, forcing direct contact with social issues. To encourage change in cultural outlooks, history was to be recounted as a living reality serving as an instrument of change.

Les Clowns (1969; *The Clowns*) focused on the role and function of the artist in society. The Théâtre du Soleil's approach to this collective textless play liberated the performers as much as possible from their preconceived notions and their psychological constraints by transforming them into clowns. Descendants of the mythical fool or jester, victims and companions of rulers, clowns, with their chalk-white faces, black-ringed eyes, reddened mouths, and baggy costumes, have for centuries brought laughter and merriment to audiences. Nevertheless, they are complex and ambiguous in disposition, often harboring a melancholy or even tragic nature beneath their comic disguises. Associated by some scholars with the devil of the medieval mystery and miracle plays, they serve to relieve protracted anguish with moments of comic relief.

To prepare for the production, Mnouchkine, unlike many other directors, refused to impose plot, form, or a written text on her performers. Actors were given full rein to search out their own clown and story, their costume, and their mask. Acrobatic, gestural antics, rhythms, dialogues and monologues were based, to a large extent, on sequentially paced puns, jokes, and associations of ideas composed by each individual. A meaningful scenario, replete with fitting gestures and a personal body language, emerged in each case.

In true commedia dell'arte style, the performers improvised, moving about at their own pace, sounding out their wants, needs, and functions. They also attempted to understand better the reasons for taking on their roles and creating their particular scenario around the clown icon. Most frequently, the actors interwove autobiographical elements into their scenarios, projecting their personal and collective experiences onto the stage happenings. Mnouchkine, endowed with a keen and shrewd theatrical sense, sought to bestow a sense of unity on the individual creations. To this end, she went over the individual sketches daily, reworking them into meaningful units. In so doing she rounded out the dramatic elements in the scenarios, while also sharpening their political and philosophical innuendoes. A dazzling theatrical performance resulted: activity set against moments of repose; comedy blended with tragedy. Paramount, however, was the sense of rambunctiousness and absurdity of farce brought to life within the perspective of both the individual and his or her society. The thrust of the performance underscored the company's belief that the voice of the artist must be heard in society.

The press, although laudatory on the whole, nevertheless had some reservations about *The Clowns*. Many felt its thematics to be banal: struggle for power, fear for the future, the woman's role in the home.

The year 1970 was a momentous one for the Théâtre du Soleil. Mnouchkine and her group rented and then moved into the Cartoucherie, a huge warehouse that had once served as a cartridge factory in Vincennes, just east of Paris.[1] The immense lobby, the large transitional area, and the huge wall-less theatrical playing space now available to the group encouraged a free-flowing interchange and inter-stimulation between actors and audiences. Such vast acting spaces, unparalleled in European theatrical history except in the circus or village squares, or in medieval productions, emboldened performers to sweep and leap about and increase their range of portrayals as they allowed their imaginations to roam free. The new acting space was to become the ideal locale for the festive, collective, and politically oriented ventures Mnouchkine and her troupe had in mind.

Everything about the Cartoucherie was different. Numbered seats were abolished; for some productions there were no seats at all. Because of the immense acting space available, Mnouchkine did away with the restrictions imposed by a proscenium stage and arch, instituting instead a *scène éclatée* (open stage). Actors, then, could wander about during a performance. Whenever they considered their presences effective, they might even intermingle with the audience. Thus the sense of separation usually associated with theater was exchanged for feelings of intimacy and camaraderie. In some future productions audiences would be invited to wander about from one acting area to another. This enabled them to enter into an emotional as well as an intellectual dialogue with the players, thus increasing their involvement in the events.

Unwilling to make a tabula rasa of their national theatrical heritage, Mnouchkine and her troupe retained whatever conventions from medieval and classical French theater they believed could help them in their creative enterprises. The use of mansion sets, for example, allowed the Théâtre du Soleil to set up a variety of platforms or rectangular stages, galleries, and interchangeable backdrops. Groupings of tables and benches—a theater within a theater—were also constructed when the need arose, allowing alternation in focus and interest.

Having discovered the forms most suitable to their needs in their new home, the members of the Théâtre du Soleil gave birth to extraordinary collective creations: *1789* (1970; subtitled "Revolution Must Stop When Happiness Has Been Perfected") and *1793* (1972; subtitled "The Revolutionary City Is This World").

Extensive study was required for the preparation of the two historico-political plays dealing with the French Revolution—*1789* and *1793*. The Théâtre du Soleil wanted not merely to resurrect a lost past in these two plays but to show how modern capitalistic society evolved out of the French Revolution: the destruction of the nobility paved the way for the insurgence of the wealthy and powerful bourgeois. Chronologically structured, *1789* dramatized the attempts of both monarchy and clergy to destroy the people; *1793*, the people's attempts to fight the maneuverings of oppressive bourgeois and military interests.

To lend authenticity to the productions, professors of the Sorbonne were invited to lecture to the members of the troupe on the political, literary, and economic situations existing prior to and during the momentous historical events. Impressive reading lists were also distributed to the cast and instructive discussions were held among the participants. Films on the French Revolution and its aftermath were shown: Renoir's *La Marseillaise,* Gance's *Napoleon,* Griffith's *The Two Orphans.*

A Marxist view was adumbrated, using the past as a type of sounding board to point up society's deficiencies and excesses as well as its sufferings and hopes. The French Revolution was looked upon, however, not as an intellectual concept only, nor as a panoply of dead issues, but as a living reality into which Mnouchkine and the cast poured the fire of their ideals. To prod their audiences into reaching a common goal—the creation of an egalitarian society—the performers tried to propell them into a state of rage or fervor. Only then could begin their struggle against what the company banally labeled the bourgeois oppressor. At the start of *1789,* for example, audiences saw a peasant woman followed by a priest and an aristocrat demanding tithes and taxes. Because she did not acknowledge their presence, they hit her with a cooking pot. When spectators heard her screams of pain and desperation, their angry reactions to the heartlessness of the perpetrators was immediate and visceral.

Nothing was fixed in the elaboration of *1789* or *1793*. Dressing rooms were eliminated: costumes were donned and makeup applied along the side of the first of the three wings of the Cartoucherie. As the spectators entered the theater, they were able not only to familiarize themselves with the techniques of applying makeup and costumes, but, perhaps more important, they could talk with the actors. The sense of participation and involvement between spectator and performer began even prior to the spectacle.

The period costumes, both thoughtfully accurate and wilfully inaccurate, accented both the historical and the contemporary, unifying past and present from the outset. Some characters, costumed in grotesquely elegant clothes, represented the overindulgent lifestyle of the nobility; the poor elicited pity by wearing tattered bits of clothing that were skillfully draped around their bodies; the nouveaux riches bourgeois, in the process of taking over royal and church properties, were identified by their garish togs. For months prior to the opening, rehearsals were held in costume, giving the clothing a well-worn look and thereby adding to realism.

Instead of conventional sets, Moscoso and Guy-Claude François opted for environmental stage techniques. The original architecture of the Cartoucherie injected a tone of historical accuracy into the atmosphere. "A rectangular stage consisting of five elevated platforms . . . with four wooden walkways connecting them" could be transformed, if the action so required, into gangways, tribunes, foot bridges, galleries, tables, or other forms, thereby centering the energetic clusters activated by the Revolution.[2]

The creative and exciting work method adopted by Mnouchkine's 35-member company injected as never before a sense of unity of purpose and of intense joy in collective creation. Months of training were required to achieve the company's goal. Groups of four or five performers were asked to improvise skits enacting certain key events of the revolutionary period. At the end of the day the scenes brought to life by the individual groups were performed before the company as a whole. With an eye to unity of structure, the troupe retained some skits and discarded others.

Frantic and frenzied activity alternated with more passive, calm, and deeply moving moments in *1789*. One word or a single gesture served at times to bring to life the Bastille, the Tuileries, and other historical areas in Paris. Scenes rippled along, including the calling of the Estates-General, the betrayal of Louis XVI, the storming of the Bastille, and the festivities following the victory. One of the most terrifying scenes featured performers standing at various points in the acting area and describing the harrowing events occurring during the taking of the prison. As spectators gathered around, they listened in rapt silence. The verbalization of happy as well as sanguinary deeds triggered feelings of excitement as well as sharply farcical moods in the audience, who felt they were actually participating in the events.

During other interludes, past and present interlocked when an actor, standing on a chair, began haranguing the populace, generating a popular *kermesse* atmosphere. Was he speaking his mind about revolutionary matters, or about contemporary political and moral conditions? High points were reached with Lafayette's nomination as Commander of the Bourgeois National Guard. Jean-Paul Marat, remaining sacrosanct in his perfection, warned the people at the close of *1789* that only through civil war would power be directed away from the aristocracy and channeled toward the people. Gracchus Mabeuf's words advocated the overthrow of government along with its institutions. Such grandiose statements were intended, of course, to trigger emotional upheavals in the citizenry of the time as well as in contemporary spectators.

Audiences were fascinated by the way individual actors or groups of actors addressed the populace, attempting to convince the listeners to become active proponents of the fight for Liberty, Equality, and Fraternity. As staged riots broke out, performers moved about the acting areas in mad arrays of dazzling burlesque sequences, ridiculing mimetically those in power: king, noble, clergy, bourgeoisie.

Several different actors were given the task of portraying political figures, such as Louis XVI, in order to underscore the reactions to them of the sansculottes. Some saw their monarch in a relatively positive light; others as a bitter foe. When in *1789* Louis XVI entered the stage area leaning on a crutch, walking slowly up the gallery to the accompaniment of music by J.-B. Lully, the Narrator intoned, "This poor king, sensing death to be near, called his subjects together." To show the people's contempt for their monarch after he had tried to disperse the "courageous" Estates-General, who were "working for the people," Louis XVI was represented onstage as a small hand puppet. When the angry women of Paris decided to take their king from Versailles to Paris, he came to life in the guise of a huge marionette, reminiscent of one of the Bread and Puppet figures.

Louis XVI, Marie-Antoinette, the clergy, the banker Necker, and all those who sided with royalty were derided ironically in a variety of burlesque scenes. Painfully grotesque satiric effects were achieved in the scene of "The King's Betrayal," in which Marie-Antoinette and two of her ladies-in-waiting, hypnotized by the charlatan magician Cagliostro, performed a wild serpentine dance routine onstage. Mingling with members of the audience, performers pursued their dialogues, monologues, and concatenations, frequently gamboling, hopping, leaping, jumping into the air, spreading fun, frolic, and terror throughout the vast performing areas. History for the Théâtre du Soleil was celebration.

Whether Lully, Berlioz, Mahler, Bizet, *La Marseillaise,* folk songs, or nineteenth-century romances were sounded in *1789* and *1793,* affectivity, parody, humor, and irony were felicitously elicited. Mahler's melodies were used at times to point up narcissism in effeminate nobles during, for example, the ritual held on 4 August 1789, divesting them of their clothing.

Despite the clownish antics, the mood of *1793* was purposefully meditative, indicating an increase in the sansculottes' political awareness of the events taking place at the time. In *1789* the people were not conscious of the impact of the happenings.

To the strains of Berlioz's *Symphonie funèbre et triomphale*—a willed anachronism, to be sure—the Announcer, armed with a microphone, reported what took place between *1789* and *1793*. To familiarize the audience with the revolutionary figures, he introduced Louis XVI, Marie-Antoinette, Catherine of Russia, Francis II of Austria, Pope Pius VI, generals, emigrants, and others. As those who had used their power and treachery to defy the people passed in review on a platform stage, the sansculottes cried out, "Long live liberty!" Once the ceremony was completed, the characters on parade removed their costumes and pointed to a backdrop that was then lifted. Spectators and actors were invited to enter another area of the Cartoucherie, built to look like the gigantic Mauconseil Assembly Hall in Les Halles.

Lighting for *1793* underscored both the divisiveness and the unity of the chaotic period. Fluorescent tubes, hidden in a meetinghouse roof or outside a window, pointed up the harsh or more subdued realities of the day. Incandescent reds, yellows, and whites or nuanced tones showered the acting space with variety as well as vitality: brilliantly cold winter daylight or more delicate evening hues, ushering in exciting (albeit traumatic) events.

Unwilling to repeat what had been so successfully accomplished in *1789*, the Théâtre du Soleil's *1793* focused more specifically on the lives of the sansculottes. To this end the Cartoucherie was divided into various sections (*quartiers*) for public happenings and on-the-spot political encounters. Unlike *1789*, for which audiences stood or walked from one hall to another in order to keep up with the events, spectators of *1793* sat in galleries or on chairs at ground level. The latter, designed to pivot, enabled the viewers to observe the action of the actors, standing or seated, eating or drinking around the three huge tables set out on elevated wooden platforms on the sides of the immense hall. Such proximity involved the audiences in the pros and cons of the arguments being proffered by the actors. Whether a scene took place in a wash-house, a disused church, a barracks, or a meeting hall, it was as if tension-provoking history were unfolding before the viewers' eyes.

The storytelling technique that had worked so effectively in *1789* was used with even greater felicity in *1793*. Plot lines revolved around a variety of themes, particularly the problems touching on volunteers leaving for the army and the economic difficulties—even starvation—faced by the women who remained behind. As performers discussed and reasoned about their political situation and their ideological differences, some demanded the King's death (July 1792); others, the abolition of the very notion of sansculottisme (September 1793). Moved by the participants' emotions and confused by the multiple opinions they expressed in their discourses, the spectators, through projection, felt uncertainty, jubilation, malaise, and even distress. Indeed, when opinions favoring or opposing the philosophies of Marat, Jacques Roux, and Robespierre were expressed, audiences were stirred into taking sides. The more the performers identified with their roles, the greater were their passions and their feelings of solidarity with other *sectionaires*—even those holding contrary views. When talk revolved around the King and Queen's escape to Varennes (June 1791), compassion was sparked in some and satisfaction in others. As moods altered, voices sounded to condemn the wealthy of the period, when in reality the targets were modern-day capitalists. In other sequences actors, quoting from the Declaration of the Rights of Man, alluded to the inhuman manner in which criminals were treated in the eighteenth century. In reality, however, they were referring to the manner in which modern French riot police trapped their prey.

A sense of urgency invaded the stage space when the political events of 1792 were explained to a friend by an actor impersonating a servant employed in a Girondin home, or by a postal employee who had been present at the Battle of Valmy. Miming of Prussian and French soldiers accompanied these eyewitness accounts of people's behavior during the struggle. Music celebrating the Valmy victory added to the illusion of historical accuracy. The scenes in the wash-houses, in winter and in summer, were endowed with vitality, as women talked about their problems while washing their imaginary clothes. One of the most important and inspiring events was the Civic Banquet of 23 August 1793, held just before the volunteer army's departure. When the "Hymn to Reason" was sung, the sense of actuality was so great that faith in the future glory of France invaded everyone's mind and heart.

Despite these sequences, a prevailing logical and thinking tone encouraged audiences to evaluate situations objectively to better understand the events. Gone were the familiar stereotypic sequences such as the "Terror" that always comes to mind when one recalls the French Revolution. A more Brechtian approach, rather than hyperemotionalism, encouraged an increasingly detached view of the period as a whole. The ideas discussed by the actors enhanced the spectators' political education undidactically. The questions posed in the dialogue were the same ones the spectators asked: What was in store for the masses? for humankind?

L'Age d'or (*The Golden Age*), performed in 1975 and composed of eight scenes, purports to deride contemporary culture based on gold and directed by business magnates. Issues such as drug addiction, feminism, unwanted children, immigration, exploitation, corruption, and the lowering of standards in the building industry, among other problems plaguing society, were dramatized to the hilt. *L'Age d'or* centers on a Moroccan, Abdallah, who arrives in Marseilles, works under difficult conditions, and suffers injustice until his death resulting from a fall from a building under construction. The play concludes with the thought that a new Golden Age may be forthcoming with the birth of an egalitarian society.

Techniques for *L'Age d'or* included the use of commedia dell'arte stock characters, such as Capitano, Pantalone, and Arlecchino with their masks, songs, and dance routines. Because the masks for females characters were not considered adequate to define character, new elements from Chinese theater were introduced.

In keeping with Chinese theater, certain performers in *L'Age d'or* covered their faces with chalk-white makeup, drawing thick black lines around their eyes, brows, cheeks or chin areas to signify either violent or tame responses. The raising of an eyelid or the contracting of a mouth were stark manifestations of shock, astonishment, joy, or sadness. Performers were their own decorators and creators of environment, each adding individual luster, style, and ceremonial details to the performance as a whole. Actors also brought in their own accessories, such as pieces of string, which they felt were needed properly to mime the tale they had in mind. Unlike Chinese theater, there were no sets or stage props, allowing the delighted troupe the freedom of physical and emotional abandon.

The spectators, instead of using galleries, wooden walkways, bridges, and similar structures, now had to climb and frequently slide down four large hills and hollows—or craters—in order to follow the action. These rounded elevations made of earth, over which a thin layer of concrete had been poured in preparation for the laying of carpeting, gave the impression of endless expanses. Likewise, the ceiling was different from that of previous productions: it was made of copper sheets to which hundreds of little bulbs had been attached. Their illumination gave the entire area a warm glow, in sharp contrast to the harsh realities of life. When the spectators entered the hall, they were greeted with both a global vision of the entire space.

Unlike *1789* and *1793*, the written text for *L'Age d'or* was virtually nonexistent. The results were not brilliant. The spoken dialogues for the most part were dull and overblown, as were some overly obvious stage antics. The simplistic political answers and social commentaries concerning injustices that were proffered throughout the performance were uninteresting.

Even the carnival atmosphere, one of the Théâtre du Soleil's fortes, with its ongoing capers and acrobatics, farcical humor, and irony, were so repetitive as to lose their verve and power. Nonetheless, specific characters radiated humor, charm, and grace as they defined their roles mimetically. Protagonists such as the forever optimistic Abdallah, Mimi la Minette, Marcel Pantalon, and the gluttonous capitalist took on vitality.

Mephisto (1979), adapted by Mnouchkine from Klaus Mann's novel, is a roman à clef. Covering the years from 1923 to 1933, it tells the tale of Hendrik Hofgen, modeled on the famous German actor Gustav Grundgens, and of Otto Ulrich, in real-life Hans Otto, the actor and Communist. The play highlights Hofgen's increasing dependence on the Nazis for his career and well-being, and his final apotheosis as manager of the German National Theater. Ulrich's fate is not so pleasant. Once aware of the political situation, he struggles against the Nazi propaganda machine. He is fired from the theater in which he performs and is assassinated by the Gestapo on 24 November 1933.

A *Götterdämmerung* atmosphere prevailed in *Mephisto*. In one wing of the Cartoucherie, spectators sat on aligned wooden seats in front of a stage adorned with frescoes of Germanic mythical heroes adulated by the Nazis. As the curtain rose, audiences attended a play-within-a-play: the concluding moments of a performance on the proscenium of the Hamburg State Theater, viewed from backstage. Hofgen, seen from the back, stops the applause of an imaginary audience, informing it of the good news that Hitler's Munich putsch has been unsuccessful. When the play's action shifted and scenes were enacted at "The Stormbird," an anti-Nazi political cabaret, spectators pivoted around in their same seats to follow the events taking place on the opposite side of the hall. There they could admire a fresco evoking a naïve, romantic Germany with its beautiful and peaceful countryside. Most disturbing and terrifying were the sets—or nonsets—in the second wing of the Cartoucherie: a huge, empty room surrounded with wire mesh. Its barenness lent a concentration camp effect to the atmosphere, like those of Nazi Germany or of Stalin's gulags. The continuous presence of this large, empty, imprisoned space during the course of the play served as a constant reminder that history repeats itself and that no culture, in any century, is impervious to persecution.

Everything in Mnouchkine's *Mephisto* was based on duality: two destinies, two theaters, two attitudes toward politics, art, and production. The play itself was divided into two parts: the first, spanning the years from 1923 to 1924; the second, from 1930 to 1933. The single connecting link was the protagonists' involvement with theater. In good existentialist tradition, Mnouchkine believed that individuals not only have the right to carve out their destinies but must do so. If they do not, they are guilty of not-acting—and therefore of joining the enemy.

There were those in *Mephisto* who followed the Nazi line, like Hofgen, prostituting themselves along the way for fame or other reasons. Otto chose a different course, deciding to live as independently as possible. Striking allusions were made to the choices given to French dramatists, directors, and actors during the German Occupation. Most of them had their works produced and performed to packed houses.

When persecution began in Germany, the members of the acting troupe who followed the Jewish religion also had choices to make. They either emigrated or were slaughtered. Carola, Otto's beloved, unwillingly left for Moscow. A painful scene was played out between a non-Jewish theater director and his Jewish wife, who preferred dual suicide to separation from her husband.

The verve, satire, lazzi antics, and improvisations tinged with black humor, particularly in the cabaret scenes, were unforgettable. Even the masks, false noses, bombastic clownings, overstated gestures, and exaggerated stentorian voices elicited peals of laughter within the most macabre of frameworks.

Deeply disturbing was the atmosphere resulting from the intertwining of fact and fiction. Jean-Jacques Lemêtre, for example, composed the music for the spectacle; he also performed as a member of the orchestra in "The Stormbird" cabaret scenes. Reality took over when Martine Rouvière sang a poem composed by Archangelski—verses that Resistance fighters interned at Buchenwald had sung in homage to their assassinated comrades.

Mnouchkine considered Shakespeare's *Richard II,* which the Théâtre du Soleil produced in 1981, one of the greatest plays of all time. It revolves around a fatally flawed hero, Richard II, the son of Edward the Black Prince, who arbitrarily settles a quarrel between Henry Bolingbroke and Thomas Mowbray by banishing the two men. After the death of "the time-honored" John of Gaunt, Bolingbroke's father,

Richard comes his property to pay for the Irish wars in which he partici
pates. When Bolingbroke returns to claim his inheritance, he succeeds in
taking back part of his heritage—namely, Berkeley Castle. When
Richard comes back to Wales, he discovers that his supporters have
deserted him and that Bolingbroke has executed his favorites. Richard
loses all hope and surrenders to Bolingbroke. He follows him to London
and abdicates in his favor. His wife, Queen Isabel, is sent to France.
Richard is imprisoned and assassinated. After Bolingbroke proclaims
himself King Henry IV, he curses the plotters who attempt to kill him
and weeps on Richard's tomb.

Mnouchkine's mélange of the styles of fourteenth-century Japanese
No theater, seventeenth-century Kabuki, and Shakespeare's sixteenth-
century dramatization of fourteenth-century British history was appro-
priate. Serious parallels between East and West can be made. No, a
composite art that includes song, dance, and poetic recitation, was created in feudal Japan in the same time frame portrayed in *Richard II*—an
epoch of great violence and factional strife. The ritual nature of No, with
its ceremonious and formalistic protocol, was eminently suited to underscore the visual splendor of the English army parading in full battle
regalia: standards flying, trumpets sounding, plumed horses prancing,
helmeted men in their coats of mail, carrying spears and shields was a
feast for the eyes and ears, a celebration of life and death. To impose the
restraint, discipline, and artifice of traditional Japanese theater onto the
extroverted Western European knightly and courtly ways was a feat in
itself. Even the text, as translated by Mnouchkine, imposed its own tones
and dissonances, as well as its distinct modulations and rhythmic patternings, as in Japanese music.

The square acting platform, covered with light-colored, black-striped
carpeting, was divided into two parallel spaces by brown strips of cloth.
Lateral passageways were separated by two swinging doors, allowing
performers to enter or exit. In a corner two musicians sounded their
drums and gongs at proper intervals, punctuating the brutal—yet on
some levels deeply compassionate—proceedings. The music, composed
by Jean-Jacques Lemêtre, called for percussion or traditional Japanese
instruments and audiovisual elements of recitation and chanting. Such
mixing of sound and visual elements had been suggested by Artaud in
The Theater and Its Double because of its increased ability to evoke and
invoke sensate and sensuous worlds.

The emphasis placed on ritual, pageantry, and the festivities surrounding an aborted reign and an overt divestiture of authority was

heightened by multihued lights. The lights pointed up the banners furling and unfurling in the wind, as King and soldiers charged their enemies. The sheer fluidity of the lights, when focused on the large gray, red, gold, black, and white silk curtains hung about the immense acting area, altered shapes and contours, injecting increasing awe, but also malaise, into the events. The painted masks, created by Erhard Stiefel, and the hairstyles shaped to resemble those of No and Kabuki players, were also impressive. The wide, somber-colored skirts worn by the men were made of metallic fabrics that reflected the various hues projected on them from above. The belts, kimonos, and felt boots were all instrumental in creating powerful mood swings, thus adding to the compelling nature of the drama. Incredibly, Mnouchkine suceeded in transforming Frenchmen into ancient hordes of sword-brandishing samurai riding imaginary steeds. As they moved about, light fell on them in sheets and waves or in rapid and prolonged flashes. The acting spaces left in darkness evoked a shadowy and spectral atmosphere of terrifying strangeness.[3]

Spectacular effects were achieved as Richard II (played by Georges Bigot), a fabulous but frivolous young king with piercing eyes, greeted his "turbulent court." His appearance alone was arresting: garbed in black and wearing a high white collar à la Rembrandt, his face bearing stark white makeup and his eyes circled in thick black lines. White-faced as well were the groups of young men surrounding him and older, sumptuously bedecked samurai. They stood immobile in hieratic postures, anticipating an interlude of precisely choreographed, irregular dancelike movements. Then they wheeled their imaginary steeds around and made ready for battle. The colors of the curtains partitioning the acting space, ranging from blood-red splattered with gold to grayish lunar tones, signaled variations in mood.

In certain scenes, as when John of Gaunt was about to die and admonished the young king to administer his domain wisely, the unexpressed, so vital a part of Japanese theater, became more important than what was being said. The impression given by the juxtaposition of speech and silence was one of mystery and terror, but also of hope. It was as if some outer-worldly power had wanted to single out the ritualistic death scene for symbolic reasons: to convey the end of the old world and the birth from blood and fore of a new one.

No's extreme reserve, its disciplined gestures and stances, underscored the extent of Richard's non-noble acts. Rather than follow the sage advice offered him by John of Gaunt, he pursued a politics of unrightful annexation of properties and wrongful administration of state revenues, resulting in his abdication and subsequent murder. The scene featuring the feudal lords united against their monarch was stark: they deprived him first of his kingship, then of his clothes, leaving him a prey to an assassin's strike. The concluding image, reminiscent of Michelangelo's *Pietà*, featured the dead body of the nude monarch, bound by immense ropes, lying draped over the knees of the new ruler, who bends over him and kisses his lips.[4]

Body language, voice, and eye movements were integral parts of the scenic composition and added to the excitement required in Shakespeare's play. As crowds passed from one expressly limited scenic space to another, energy seemed to be contained, compressed to the point of explosion. At certain junctures a sense of panic was instilled into the action: when, for example, Richard II, seen frontally—tall, immobile, a replica of the life-size marionettes of Japanese Bunraku—and flanked by his white-faced foot soldiers and horsemen, suddenly rushed forward as if he and his retainers were about to seize their prey. A mood of apprehension, remoteness, and mystery was cast at the sight of such unnatural countenances—as if death's pallor had become a reality. In other parts of the play the detail and precision of the performers' stylized gestures, ritualized stances, and rapid or slow gesticulations enhanced duels, joustings, and battle episodes.

The scene in the garden of the Duke of York (3.4) is noteworthy for the slapstick quality and parodic features it injects into a murderous climate. While a gardener and two assistants bounce and clown about, as in Western folk and peasant tradition, a composite figure, the *kyogen,* a stock comic character of No, also intrudes. His presence is particularly apt since his function is to dance, dialogue, and mime in rhythmical yet restrained, patterned, and nuanced ways, even while peppering his performance with hosts of "mad" words—which speak truths as only he, an earthly creature, knows how, through mimicry, informality, and jocosity.[5]

Some Shakespeare traditionalists reacted unfavorably to the No-influenced mise-en-scène, considering the hieratized stylization of the acting and the abrupt, hatchetlike, artificial diction of the performers irritating, outlandish, even outrageous. Nevertheless, most critics, including Gilles Sandier, considered the spectacle "fabulously beautiful"; Pierre Macabru compared it to a feat of "magic," declaring its "rigor" and "sumptuousness" to be extraordinary.

Mnouchkine introduced a decidedly Indian and feminine flavor to her 1982 production of Shakespeare's *Twelfth Night.* The action—in the distant land of Illyria—was bathed in soft lights, evoking a world of subliminal desires that at times exploded with carnival frenzy. The dream-soaked land of Illyria, on which Sebastian and Viola, twin brother and sister, are separated after their shipwreck, became onstage a blend of natural sensuality and spiritual yearning. Upon reaching land, Viola disguises herself as a young man (Cesario) and takes service as a page with Duke Orsino, who is in love with Olivia. Later, when Sebastian makes his presence known, he is taken for his sister. Many quid pro quos and mélanges of ambiguous passions filled the lyrical, gently melancholy, but also festive and happy atmosphere. Much of the humor deriving from the play's subplots added bounce to the events. One of these hilarious scenes, featuring Sir Andrew Aguecheek, recalled Louis Jouvet's unforgettable portrayal of this character in Jacques Copeau's earlier production of the play.

Mnouchkine's approach to *Twelfth Night* was neither stereotypic nor did it sound out psychological questions revolving around the theme of travesty. Because Viola's disguise is a metaphor for her adventurous soul, representing her need to experience life to the fullest, its sexual symbolism did not have to be overplayed. Shakespeare's ingenuity, his ability to open up a person to passion—to an unregenerate, instinctual childhood world with all of its desires, fears, repressed intuitions, and narcissism—carries his play into the twentieth century.

A selection of hybrid costumes artfully put together with multiple bits of colorful cloth or even rags disclosed the individual actor's search into his or her depths.

As spectators entered the vast stage space, a smaller area covered with a rug, around which four lamps had been placed, became visible. Lights, casting their subdued nuances and golden glows on this limited area, focused on a single dancer performing the Hindu *bharata-natyam*. Danced by the women of southern India, this religious piece evokes a realm of magic and mystery and avatars of divinities, who, during their earthly trajectories, were incarnated in mortals carving out their own fate. While musician/singers relate the epic of Ganesha and Krishna, emotions ranging from detachment to passion, spirituality to viscerality—even murderous intent—are woven into the ceremonial rituals of love.

Cloths used as partitions or rugged hills in later interludes of Mnouchkine's production cut the vast, nude, horizontal expanse into geometric or circular designs. A throne room, gardens, or battlefields crystallized. Moods were accentuated by melodies created by speech tones and rhythms; breath, as Artaud had suggested, was instrumental

in enriching the resonance of the words. The blending of Indian instru
ments, such as the sitar, and ancient French ones, including a spinet, also
had great effect. Intoned or aspirated, music punctuated the drama.

Novelist, poet, playwright, and essayist Hélène Cixous also wrote
L'Histoire terrible mais inachevée de Norodom Sihanouk roi du Cambodge
(1985) and *L'Indiade* (1987), both produced by the Théâtre du Soleil. In
her other plays, such as *On ne part pas, on ne revient pas* (*One Does Not
Leave, One Does Not Return*), word is strikingly and successfully used as a
catalyst. Cixous sometimes uses homonyms, plays on words, repetitions,
metonymies, alliterations, metaphors, and images to carry the reader or
spectator along. Her talent, unfortunately, does not shine in either
L'Histoire terrible or *L'Indiade*.

The former historical play is divided into two periods: the first,
1953–70, a time when Marxist students, such as Saloth Sar, the future
Pol Pot, left Paris, where they had studied, to return to Cambodia. In
1954 Sihanouk, then in Geneva, was given sovereignty over what had
been the French protectorate of Cambodia. A year later he abdicated in
favor of his father, King Suramarit, who called for and won the elections,
thus becoming head of a socialist, monarchist, and Buddhist state.
Sihanouk became the head of state in 1960 but was driven from power
10 years later by American forces under General Lon Nol. Some of the
events under scrutiny in the play are the American bombardment of
Cambodia and the involvement of the Communist Khmer Rouge and
Vietnamese, who "liberated" a land only to occupy it.

Critics not only were surprised by Cixous's political stand but found
her play wanting in drama. Once siding with the poor, the destitute, and
the reviled, Cixous now chose, some critics maintained, to support a king
who ruled according to medieval tradition, virtually by divine right,
under the guise of benevolent paternalism. Because of the lack of character probing and evaluation of economic, religious, or political conditions, Cixous's play was considered by many to be naïve, banal, and
didactic.

L'Indiade, also didactic, is an account of the Ghandhi-led independence movement. Although Cixous neglected to transcend the single
personalities involved and sound out the reasons for their politics, she did
mention some of the politically and perhaps religiously conflicting elements separating this vast land, and perhaps this accounts in part for a
more interesting theatrical production.

Mnouchkine's direction and translation of *Les Atrides—Iphigénie à
Aulide* (Euripides), *Agamemnon* (Aeschylus), *Les Choéphores* (Aeschylus),

and *Les Euménides* (Aeschylus)—in 1990 reaches one of the high points, if not *the* high point, of her career. These four epic pieces, which probed the fundaments of myth, magic, and the magnificence of theater, invited her to use, as she had in her Shakespeare productions, words as verbal icons. Through words and staging, she succeeded in re-creating archetypal creatures, universal in scope and organic in their aesthetics. In so doing she evoked Nietzsche's "strange and barbaric" approach to theater, Artaud's visceral Theater of Cruelty, and secrets imparted by Copeau, Meyerhold, Vilar, and Peter Brook in their productions of these plays.

The Greek tetralogy spans approximately two decades of tragic conflict and violence within the House of Atreus: infanticide, regicide, matricide, patricide, cannibalism. In *Iphigénie* Agamemnon sacrifices his daughter to placate the Gods, who then allow the winds to blow, thus consenting to his embarkment for the Trojan War. *Agamemnon* focuses on his wife, Clytemnestra, who avenges her daughter's killing: she and her lover, Aegisthus, murder her husband and the prophetess Cassandra, his Trojan captive/mistress. In *Les Choéphores* Orestes, Agamemnon's son, together with his sister Electra, murder their mother and Aegisthus.

Les Euménides (the "kindly ones," also known as the Erinyes, or Furies) focuses in part on these chthonian powers but mainly on Orestes' trial, argued by Apollo and Athena, and ending in Orestes' acquittal.

Because Mnouchkine understood the importance of the woman's role in *Les Atrides,* she opened her cycle with *Iphigénie.* Rather than emphasizing a traditional historical order (Aeschylus, 525–456 B.C.E., preceded Euripides, 480?–405? B.C.E.) she sought to stress the battle raging in Greece between matriarchal and patriarchal cosmic powers. *Les Atrides* was played out by Mnouchkine's troupe as a religious mystery. Audiences were no longer exposed to a male-dominated Olympian ethos that relegated womankind to a hideous underworld. The blood bath initiated by Agamemnon and Achilles pitted male treachery and violence against primal female power.

The performers' faces, daubed with layers of chalk-white makeup as in No and Kabuki, bore heavy black trapezoid designs around their eyes—one of Mnouchkine's hallmarks. The violent opposition between black and white colorations not only increased feelings of terror but freed the characters from the trappings of traditional stereotypic icons.

Abolished as well was the individuality of these archaic collective forces donned in intriguing masks, headpieces, and eye-catching costumes. It was as if spectral powers, silhouetted against empty space, were moving about the stage in ritualistic sequences. Although disparity was visible in the hybrid nature of the costumes—a composite of southern Indian, Babylonian, and Egyptian styles—a condition of unity was also imposed by the strange harmonies created by the brilliantly conceived garb. Skirts were full; vests shone brightly; colorful and ingeniously designed ornaments glittered under the projection lights. Although the dance steps varied—the *bharata natyam,* combined with Kathakali, Balinese, folkloric, and Western elements, including turns, twirls, leaps, and shoulder shakings onstage—a sense of unity imposed itself. When, at certain critical intervals, the dance reached a peak of frenzy, the emotions of the characters flowed into the hearts of the audience.

Continuous music, composed and performed by Jean-Jacques Lemêtre, was provided by instruments placed on the side of the acting area and thus in full view of the audience. As Lemêtre played one instrument and then another, sound, speech, rhythm, and tone were indelibly fused. Chantings, moans, grunts—whatever the modalities to be replicated—were accompanied by bells, chimes, drums, or other instruments.

The tetralogy begins as a double door at the rear of the hall swings open. Dawn is about to break. A striking chorus of 15 women (some are actually men) clad in red, black, and gold with embroidered, mirror-encrusted panels surges forth, stomping, swaying, kicking, and whirling about in a primitive joyous frenzy. Their mood alters as events change: they are high-spirited and buoyant in *Iphigénie,* shocked and grief-stricken in *Agamemnon,* scolding in *Les Choéphores.* In *Les Euménides* they are transformed into creatures of the underworld—terrifying, fantastic beasts that growl and snarl, ready like harpies to tear their prey apart.

When Agamemnon enters the stage space wearing multilayered clothing, his movements are stately and ceremonial, underscoring his sense of authority and hubris. Achilles, donned in white and black, speaks to him in favor of the army's demand for Iphigenia's sacrifice. Prior to her solo dance, Iphigenia is unaware of her fate. Only after completing her patterned rhythmical body movements does she come to understand the necessity of her sacrifice and its religious dimensions. She realizes that her death will not only give her the status of a heroine but will empower her to save her country and people. Her mother Clytemnestra's rigid chalk-white mask and black and yellow garb suggest the depths of her sorrow: learning that Iphigenia must die, she falls to the ground in shock.

Apollo's presence in *Les Euménides* takes on the power of an epiphany. Tall, slender, and clothed in white, his body gives the impression of gliding along in space. Adding to his outerworldliness are his long locks, which flow in the wind as he moves/dances about or bounds onto a parapet only to return most elegantly to Mother Earth. Athena, rational and poised, argues for Orestes' acquittal, basing her judgments on her understanding of justice. But expediency is also a factor in her decision. While the Furies dig deep into the heart of divine and/or human motivations, they blame both Apollo and Athena for Orestes' heinous crime. Athena, in her wisdom, convinces the Furies to yield to new ways of thinking, thus establishing a climate of harmony rather than one of hatred.

That the three chief Furies are dressed as bag ladies, each clothed in a medley of rags and wearing dirty, worn sneakers, creates a startling and unforgettable stage image, as does the chorus of dogs emanating from some hideous underworld, growling and cavorting about the stage, ready for blood. Once Orestes is acquitted, the formerly vicious dogs rise on their hind legs, symbolizing the birth of a higher level of understanding.

That one actress portrays both Clytemnestra and Athena adds to the complexity of the scenic fare. That a queen should be judged for her murderous act by a goddess, that her responsibility should be scrutinized from different standpoints, introduces greater objectivity into the question of punishment and retribution. When, however, a goddess is judged by a queen, traditional hierarchies have altered. Because the divine and the mortal are viewed on the same level, each protagonist is forced to look into herself with greater clarity.

Does Athena's judgment suggest an abdication on the part of the gods to rule the destinies of humankind? If so, the responsibility for personal acts falls on the individual. Although the cycle of murders ceases— at least for the time being—the birth of what Athena considers a new democratic and just civic order indicates a return to a patrilineal society. The Furies are forced to abandon what has been theirs for centuries: their power to punish wrongs committed against kindred blood, regardless of the motive. They are, in the Orestes myth, Clytemnestra's agents of revenge. Once Orestes has been absolved of the guilt of matricide and the Furies have accepted Athena's decision, they function as the Eumenides, "the kindly ones."

In keeping with Athena's dicta, the court—the Areopagus, representing the ancient council of elders—is henceforth to hear and judge cases not in terms of revenge or retribution but within a new and just legal framework. All seems perfect except for the fact that the Areopagus bars women.[6] Because absolution and simplism remaining are included from Mnouchkine's nonlinear approach to timeless problems answers are inconclusive, as they are in real life.

That the cast in *Les Atrides* not only played multiple roles but hailed from different lands—Armenia, Lebanon, North and South America, Spain, India, and elsewhere—gave the production an international flavor. Unfortunately, in certain instances the diversity of the accents, coupled with some actors' poor articulation, rendered certain segments of the plays incomprehensible, thereby detracting from the text's enormous power and the greatness of the performance as a whole.

Although the *Oresteia* has been produced at least three times in the past 40 years—by Renaud-Barrault, Ronconi, and Peter Stein—Mnouchkine's vision of this mythic stage piece was unique. Under her aegis *Les Atrides* was a feat of precision, concentration, imagination, and sensitivity. The silhouettes inhabiting her stage, wrestling as they did with universal questions revolving around moral dilemmas, evoked cultural icons and invested myth with renewed and ever-expanding meditative power.

Are they gods or humans, those estranged figures from beyond time and space?

Chapter Four

"An Aesthetic of the Disjointed": Antoine Vitez

Whether inspired by a novel, poem, article, anecdote, event, or the Gospels, innovation and tension are inborn in the stagings of Antoine Vitez (1930–90). Solitary, distant, ascetic, and discreet, Vitez shunned staid concepts, never wallowed in traditionalism or academism. He endlessly branched out in untried directions, searching for new elements and fresh insights. For Vitez, "theatre is that which passes, which dies . . . we live in the ephemeral."[1]

Certainly different from what the mainstream and even the avant-garde offered, Vitez's sometimes shocking productions inaugurated what has been called "an esthetic of the *disjointed.*"[2] Every word, character, and aspect of a drama was approached as a separate and living organism, each disquietingly antithetical to the other. Unlike Paul Claudel, who considered both metaphor and reasoning processes to be unifying devices, Vitez saw them as divisive and segmenting. Directing Claudel's *Partage de midi* (*Break of Noon*), Vitez atomized its salient qualities; he dismembered more than he assembled. Whether producing plays by classical or contemporary authors—Sophocles, Racine, Molière, Hugo, Lenz, Chekhov, Mayakovsky, Claudel, Aragon, Vinaver, Kalisky, Guyotat—Vitez's outlook was *hors-style.* He adhered to no one style. Every play, like every person, was endowed with its own personality, climate, variations, tones, colors, rhythms, and tapestried effects. Change, evolution, a continuous search for new forms, a relentless probing of the text on which Vitez was at work—all these became part of a growing and deepening process from which he drew inspiration and that endowed him with a sense of renewal. In addition to his open and malleable approach to performance, his remarkable visual memory of stage movement prevented him, both as director and actor, from becoming rigid.

That Vitez's work has been labeled "anarchical" is evident from one of his early productions, *Le Procès d'Emile Henry* (1967; *The Trial of Emile Henry*), based on the 1894 trial of the well-known anarchist Emile Henry, accused of having thrown a bomb into a Paris café, Terminus. He conceived of this "theater-document" in commemoration of his father, who was also an anarchist and participated in the protests leading to the bloody massacres perpetrated during the 1870 Commune. Vitez's production of *Catherine*, a *théâtre-récit* based on Louis Aragon's *Les Cloches de Bâle* (*The Bells of Basel*), also typifies his nonconformism.

The Paris-born Vitez began his career at the age of 19, as an actor. From his teacher, the celebrated Tania Balachova, he learned early on that "the actor is a creator."[3] Like some of his well-known predecessors—Jouvet, Dullin, Stanislavsky—Vitez combined acting, directing, and teaching, holding posts at such prestigious theater schools as the one bearing Jacques Lecoq's name, the Amandiers at Nanterre, the Atelier at Ivry, the Conservatoire National Supérieur d'Art Dramatique, and the Théâtre National de Chaillot in Paris. Vitez's approach to teaching was maieutical (related to the Socratic method); students thought out their characters for themselves in order to discover the right way of portraying them. This approach earned accusations that diction was not sufficiently emphasized and that a state of anarchy prevailed in his classes. Nonetheless, his classes were always filled to capacity, whereas those of more traditional teachers floundered.

Like Konstantin Stanislavsky (1863–1938), Vitez emphasized the natural use of the actor's body, voice, and breathing technique in the belief that if a performer sought to find his way into a role he had first to develop his "instrument." Since outer sensations catalyze emotional equivalents, the understanding of a character begins at the sensation level; the mysterious subliminal sphere is penetrated from the outside inward. Because Vitez did not consider a human being to be *one* but rather an entity of infinite elements, he espoused a *disjointed* approach that disclosed a complex of emotional truths about a character, and hence produced a climate of insecurity.

Directors and actors, Vitez suggested, should divest themselves of preconceived notions, working on a tabula rasa in the manner of Jacques Copeau. When first reading a text they should listen to their instinctive reactions and not ponder its historical or psychological motifs. Relationships between protagonists take root on stage, Vitez insisted, on that same visceral level that leads to deep understanding of the character to be portrayed. Only later do the refining processes and detailed work on performance and direction intervene. Vitez went beyond the concept of "biomechanics" of Vsevolod Meyerhold (1874–1940), which sought to minimize the actor's individual contributions in favor of the grand scheme of things. Vitez focused on both: the spectacle as a whole as well as the individual's creative abilities.

Vitez's intent to free both director and performer from established norms was accomplished by adherence to a very personal notion of the "arbitrary" and of the "incongruous or extravagant." Members of his troupe felt at ease discussing items involved in production or even disagreeing with the director's interpretations of a particular role. Such interaction worked both ways. The storehouse of views to which Vitez was made privy during the troupe's conversations did much to enrich his understanding of the play(s) under discussion. Because Vitez was always open to suggestion, his troupe was described as one in which the actor was king (Dizier, 23).

When preparing a mise-en-scène, Vitez listened for what he termed the "arbitrary" component, identified with "intuition." He did warn directors, however, not to follow their inner voice before setting their guidelines clearly and explicitly. If the play's central idea is not first explained to a troupe, results might be remarkable but at the same time disastrous. Since gestures, body movements, pantomime, and facial expressions are inextricably linked to the text, they should not be choreographed haphazardly. Each element must be studied and patterned to suit the continuously changing, discordant, irregular, and clashing nature of the character portrayed. For example, in his production of Racine's *Britannicus*, Vitez, seeking to reveal the ambiguities in Nero's relationship with his mother, Agrippina, had the emperor in certain scenes play his part virtually riveted to the ground, fixed like a statue. Thus did he accentuate Nero's efforts to restrain and constrain his inherent volatility. In so doing he heightened not only the mysterious and latent elements within the emperor's personality but also created a climate of anxiety that was to reach its apogee in the bloodbaths to come. In another scene, to illustrate Agrippina's terror as she waited for a storm to die down, Vitez had the weeping actress actually crawl at the bottom of a jetty (Dizier, 13, 52).

Rehearsals were hard and taxing under Vitez. Each scene of the play under production was studied separately until meanings were clarified and inner substances revealed. Once each segment was worked on "disjointedly," it was set into the whole. The integration process, however, frequently presented unexpected problems arising from new dichotomies between text and performance. Rather than dissimulate these antitheses, Vitez sought to accentuate them gesturally, thereby increasing disquietude. To this end he might have an actor enunciate his text in an even and smooth manner, while his actions would be played contrastingly in an unassuming, mobile, fitful, jerky, and jarring manner. Thus did Vitez break up what could have become the play's *unity* and *harmony*. He desegmented what he regarded as antithetical to the real-life experience, since he wished to demonstrate that human beings do not perceive real life as a cohesive, meaningful series of events.

Language, as essential to Vitez as it had been to Louis Jouvet and others, acted as a catalyst. Once his senses reacted to the verbal abstractions on the printed page, to the sight and sound of the performers ambulating or standing rooted in place on the acting space, the distillation process began. Gestures were now studied in their individuality as well as in their relationship to those of other protagonists; displacements were evaluated with equal discernment, whether the actor performed a major or minor part. So closely together did the troupe work with one another that roles were frequently exchanged. One actress, for example, played both Andromache and Hermione; Orestes' tirade was recited by several actors, depending on the effect desired. In this regard Vitez, like Brecht, broke the identification between actor and role.

Critics did not always react kindly to Vitez's creations. Some referred to his productions as "dehumanized," comparing his performer to a "puppet" or describing him or her as an "actor-object" manipulated by the director; others denigrated his eclecticism, his use of cinematography in theater, his audacious interpretations, and his "strangified" characters, whose unexpected gestures and anti-imitative or unnaturalistic stances disoriented spectators.[4] Prior to Valentin's murder in *Faust,* for example, actors danced, beating out the rhythms of the music on the palms of their hands. To convey Faust's fear of the hissing Earth Spirit, Vitez had the aged doctor hide behind a tree trunk on all fours. Rather than resort to artifice, he preferred to "strangify" the performer's stance, thereby relating his problems to reality. Mephistopheles was poised onstage not only photographing the insalubrious activities of the *Walpurgisnacht* night scene but also singing jazz. Such comportment not only stamped the scene with a temporal cast but served to portray the Devil in a manner that emphasized the transpersonal side of this august and feared figure while also pointing to the humor of it all. The stifled voices of the performers howled out their dismay at Faust's words referring to the New Testament: "The love of God enraptures me." Minutely orchestrated polyphonic sequences of imitative sounds (such as buzzing of insects) surprisingly prevented Faust from pulling the trigger to murder

Valentin. Thus did Vitez modernize what could have been a dead classical work (Dizier, 52, 53).

Rather than imitate nature, Vitez was attracted to the unusual and the unexpected in the visible world, thus eliciting drastically positive or negative reactions from his audiences.

To appreciate Vitez's nonconforming mise-en-scène of Racine's *Andromache* (1971) requires a close reading of the classical text. Seeking to acquaint audiences with the barest outline of the play, he had directed an actress to announce from the stage on three different occasions: "Orestes loves Hermione who loves Pyrrhus who loves Andromaque who loves Hector who is dead." Such a simplistic presentation of the profound notions implicit in this French classical tragedy was disarming because of its absurdly humorous cast.

The stage environment created by Vitez was equally astonishing. Not only did the properties yield an impression of randomness, but the objects themselves suggested that the action took place in a gym rather than in the conventional palace. The table, ladder, two white wooden chairs, a saddle horse, uneven parallel bars, ropes, and other body-building equipment on the acting space made a strong impression on the audience. The two benches placed front stage on either side allowed performers to sit and rest after their physically taxing efforts. Although the stage climate and properties lent a fragmented quality to the play, its pictogrammatic effect as a whole, which brought into play Vitez's concepts of the "disjointed" and the "arbitrary," created a fresh and intriguing vision of a classic.

There were even more innovations. Believing the roles should be alternated, Vitez had three young men and three young women wearing loose-fitting pants and shirts play the four protagonists. Different actors played different aspects of a particular character. Thus Andromache, Pyrrhus, Hermione, and Orestes became complexes of opposites or of disconnected and frequently conflicting traits. On entering the stage space, the actors took hold of the gymnastic appliances chosen to distinguish the individual from the collective. Each said, "I am playing Andromaque. . . . I am playing Pyrrhus . . ." But Pyrrhus, like the others, was played by more than one actor, according to the fragments of his personality that were to be incarnated. A slim, angular, and very supple actor portrayed Pyrrhus' youthful and athletic side: he was featured at the outset either seated or standing on a chair ("throne") placed on the table, then sliding down from it and landing on the floor at the feet of the recumbent Orestes. A second performer portrayed him in a more traditional manner: jealous and excessively intense A third incarnated him as a stately, even rigid, monarch, particularly in his encounters with Andromache and Hermione. In the last two acts he was seen in a state reminiscent of animated suspension: a flesh-and-blood being slowly disappearing—degrading physically—as he passed into death.

Despite the metamorphoses, each aspect of a personality was clearly identified as the actor spoke the verse that belonged to the particular protagonist he or she was conveying. A surreal atmosphere was achieved, however, when one actress unexpectedly took over the role of Hermione (3.3) from another, thereby breaking the continuity of Racine's "sacred verse," which so many French audiences knew by heart. Vitez had defied and rejected tradition. Such a disruption shook spectators out of the mood of Greek tragedy and propelled them into the equally harrowing reality of the contemporary world.

Seduction attempts and rejection were replete in scenes that crackled with repressed anger and threats. Hermione, for example, sought to win Orestes' love, but physical obstacles barred her way: his friend Pylades, lying on his back at her feet, acted as the impediment. Andromache, a most complex figure, was a mélange of three distinct and contradictory portrayals. Reserved, distant, and dignified vis-à-vis Pyrrhus and others to whom she felt no emotional link, she changed her character completely when she was possessed by fear for her son's life. Moments of panic were accompanied by a howl emanating spasmodically from the very depths of her being, shattering the previous image of her self-control. Unexpectedly and brutally, action was interrupted by an actor's intonation of a chant (3.6) composed by Louis Aragon that recalled Andromache's deportation, while an actress, miming events in the presence of Pyrrhus, was joined by two other actresses standing front stage, and the three took on the shapes of wounded birds.

Vitez's staged placements and displacements were choreographed with such expertise that they looked "like overlays of great surfaces of color moving over Racine's original sketches, without being subjugated by the capriciousness of the lines" (Sarrazac, 87).

Catherine (1975–76), a *théâtre-récit*, was based on Louis Aragon's *Les Cloches de Bâle* (1934),[5] a dramatization of events in the life of a woman that revolved around her strength and feelings of independence. She freely chose both her lovers and her lifestyle—an existence composed of "love and anarchy."

A dining table surrounded by chairs was placed in the center of a large, rectangular acting space. There were no backdrops or other accessories. The light shed from the lamp hanging above the stage illuminated both the performing area and the audience seated in two rows of tiered benches on opposite sides of the stage. Thus did Vitez incorporate three elements into a single framework. The absence of sets, as well as the visibility and close proximity of spectators and performers, aroused in them variegated sensations, images, thoughts, and dreams. A climate of warmth and free-flowing communication was born between the individual and the collective.

Catherine is a montage and not a text; it is a *reading* composed by Vitez. Although made up of narratives, fragments, and descriptions, and spoken in the third person by 11 actors, it cannot be labeled a dramatization. Dialogue was interspersed as the actors, seated around the table, ate an entire *real* meal, divided into three parts: the hors-d'oeuvre, standing for anarchy; the main course, representing Catherine's illness; and finally the dessert, coffee, and champagne. The explosive noise of the uncorking of the champagne bottles occurred when the text called for "a burst of shelling." The food served as an agape, or communal repast, emphasizing the life force inherent in each of the individuals present; the wine symbolized the blood sacrificed by those who had fallen during World War I; and the table itself, transformed into a kind of casket, was identified with the dead body of one of Catherine's lovers. While the meal was really the excuse—the backdrop or anchor—for the action, the portrayals crystallizing around the table served to sustain the imaginary world of fiction.[6]

Vitez walked onstage at the outset of *Catherine* to put a copy of Aragon's novel on the table. Moments later he opened it and began reading aloud. Catherine seized the book and handed it to another reader, who in turn handed it to other participants: Father, Mother, Son, Uncle, Sister, Young Girl. The play came to life after the use of multiple readings, signs, innuendoes, and objects (such as a broom) to mime actions that brought reality into a world of fantasy. Although multiple time schemes coexisted onstage—the reality of the events depicted in the book as well as the actions mimed before the audience—they never fused. The characters did not use the book to recall past events but were stimulated by them to play the parts of those whose lives and reminiscences they had read. The medley of different vocal timbres, accents, rhythms, and tonal dimensions conveyed the emotions and accompanied the gestures of bourgeois women of the 1900s, army men, and different groups of militants and libertarians.

Questions were also posed. Did the performers rightly probe their imaginations as they narrated the anecdotes, passions, and brutal or sentimental relationships of the people living within the pages of the book? Did the performers authentically "evoke" the inner happenings of these arrangers whose vitality they sensed?

As the actors handed the book from one to the other during the course of the performance, roles, even genders, were alternated. Only Nada Strancar played Catherine throughout. Because of its excessive handling, the book became splattered with food and wine, was eventually torn, and finally burned in a sacrificial ritual.

Although not an exact enactment of Aragon's work, what did emerge in Vitez's production of *Catherine* was a constant and consistent change of faces, expressions, and moods of those guests invited to incarnate an all-but-forgotten past and to share in an agape.

Vitez's use of "contraction," "arbitrariness," and antithesis in *Catherine* created a world of paradoxes for audiences to probe. Thus did he transform the stage space into a meeting ground between the transpersonal, timeless, infinite sphere and the "disjointed" finite dimension. On many occasions stage space was endowed with an unforgettable mythic dimension.

Chapter Five
A Titan of the Theater: Armand Gatti

A fighter, anarchist, and lyrical, flamboyant, and perhaps even mystical poet, Armand Gatti (b. 1924) is a Titan of the theater. A stage piece for him is not merely a form of amusement or a pleasant distraction, nor is it designed only to give audiences an aesthetic high. It is a stimulant to action, a way of expanding consciousness, a force designed to liberate audiences from staid and established notions.

Gatti is a searcher, a seeker of artistic freedom and authenticity. He wants to stimulate the imagination and energize creative elements in those who participate in his experimental events. Once an active participant in the French Resistance during World War II, he still resists oppression and suppression, artistic or other. After he was arrested and condemned to death by the Nazis, his sentence was commuted, and he was deported to the Neuengamme camp near Hamburg; then he was assigned to forced labor. It was in the concentration camp that he learned the true meaning of theater. Everything he has accomplished in the performing arts, he maintains, was the direct result of a specific event that occurred in the camp. Although camp regulations forbade the performance of plays, some Lithuanian Jews decided that since they were scheduled to die anyway, it was worth risking their lives to create theater: to maintain their humanity by telling their stories. Gatti subsequently escaped from the camp. His courageous deeds as a parachutist in Free France and his work as a journalist in 1945 were largely motivated by the life/death theater he had helped create during his imprisonment. An independent, Gatti is anti-establishment. His intent in theater is to set everyone and everything aflame. The stage has become his battlefield—not to destroy, but to trigger Chaos, from which Cosmos will emerge.

One of the most memorable of Gatti's early plays—for its technical innovations and autobiographical elements—is *La Vie imaginaire de l'éboueur Auguste Geai* (1962; *The Imaginary Life of the Street Cleaner Auguste Geai*). Gatti's father had been a street cleaner, and Gatti himself had

been brought up in the slums of Monaco. The play, produced by Roger
Planchon and directed by Jacques Rosner, revolves around the protagonist (Gatti's father, Auguste), who is lying on his deathbed center stage,
as he recalls and recounts events he had either actually lived through or
had imagined at various periods in his life. He visualizes himself at ages
9, 21, 30, and 46 and fantasizes about his future retirement and his son's
career as a great film director—neither of which the real person ever
knew, since he died at 46. Onstage, past, present, and future time
schemes are lived virtually simultaneously. Since the play is based on
memories and dreams, sequences are not chronological; instead they
adhere to a logic and a pattern born from the protagonist's inner world.
Because each progression or regression evoked by the protagonist is
played by a different actor, segments of Auguste's life appear, reappear,
and disappear onstage, fleetingly, half-formed, like tropisms.

Because the divisions in time, abstracted from the protagonist's memories and fantasies, are spatially established onstage, audiences are invited to share in a "spectacular" arrangement of events: the child Auguste
reminiscing about a fire that destroyed the tenement building in which
his family lived and killed his parents; his army experiences during
World War I; his great love and marriage; his job as a street cleaner; his
participation in a strike that resulted in his bludgeoning by a French riot
policeman, accounting for his hospitalization stay and his death.

Not only did Gatti use the techniques of multiplicity and fragmentation of stage images—implicit in what he calls *théâtre éclaté,* but, like
Brecht, he also used filmstrips to underscore the vitality of certain of
Auguste's reminiscences. While the focus was on Auguste, the rhythmic
visualizations were diversified, ranging from frenzied overt action to
moments of extreme internalized stillness.

Gatti pursued his experimentations in stage techniques in an ongoing
effort to meld the "real" world with a new theatrical "reality." To this end
Gatti and Guy Rétoré, the director of the Théâtre de l'Est Parisien, asked
regular members of the TEP to participate in the creation of *Les Treize
Soleils de la rue Saint-Blaise* (1968; *The Thirteen Suns on Saint-Blaise Street*).

The scene: an adult evening course held on Saint-Blaise Street. The
teacher asks 13 students to write an essay on their reactions to the following situation: Saint-Blaise Street is to be destroyed to make room for
modern high-rise buildings. One caveat is added: the students must
detach themselves from their subjective worlds and ponder their answers
as though they were suns passing over the street. Here, then, Gatti uses
the doubling technique onstage to create both disparity and drama: the

actual students are viewed front stage, busily writing their answers at their desks; rear stage each of the sun characters, each with his or her own personality and name/epithet, comes to life in an imaginary world that keeps appearing throughout the play. As suns, the students must assess the validity of the architectural transformations about to take place by using historical events to throw things into perspective: for example, the Commune of 1871, which led to the burning of the Tuileries Palace, the City Hall, the Cour des Comptes, and other structures, not to mention the bloody massacres of people.

Gatti's intent in this play is to stimulate thought processes by inviting participants to go beyond their limited frames of reference and their repressed or stereotyped judgments and aspirations. By obliging them to distance themselves from an event that will certainly affect their lives— that is, to examine it from the sun's perspective rather than from their own—Gatti is really asking them to probe their world in a detached manner. To use the sun as a vantage point—as object and metaphor— would enable them not only to shed their facile and subjective approaches to life but also to transcend their job, group, and class mentality. Thus would they be encouraged to revaluate their long-held beliefs, their feelings, and their acts.

For Gatti, "the world's a stage" not to be circumscribed or falsified with stock and unrealistic creatures. He makes short shrift of theatrical systems that not only subvert living and dynamic elements implicit in continuously changing and evolving language but ossify it. He seeks to portray humankind in a theater of action based on multiplicity or fragmentation, by calling into being oral, sonant, tactile, visual, and gustatory dimensions, using all types of technological equipment to achieve his goal.

Although Gatti's plays differ structurally from one another, they usually follow a certain pattern. Each has an opening theme or topic (frequently social or political) dramatized over and over again throughout the work via a variety of frames of reference. The thematic fluctuations themselves become instrumental in opening up new optics for both characters and audiences. Because of the play's divergent vantage points, each possible explanation and analysis of situations or their repercussions emerges as something new and vital. Excitement frequently reaches such a pitch as to alter sharply the original impressions of both participants and viewers.

Gatti's prismatic approach also serves, as previously mentioned, to abolish Occidental time schemes. Past, present, and future, as witnessed in *La Vie Imaginaire* and *Les Treize Soleils*, can no longer be considered secure and concrete pillars on which one can build a strong and safe, albeit static, world. Because time is *one* for Gatti, despite its fragmentation onstage, each segment affects the other and activates and reactivates multiple experiences. As horizons alter and falter, depending on the angle from which they are enacted and observed, they may broaden perspectives or erode the vision of one or more characters, thus impinging, by extension, on the drama as a whole.

Gatti's fusion of time and space onstage in what he calls "flash time" does not imply the enactment of a series of flashbacks or flash-forwards. Rather, it enables the character or characters to face themselves as individuals or as aspects of the collective. Although hundreds of memories, feelings, and moods exist within each person, and although he or she may be conscious of only one at a time, they all interact with each other on an unconscious level. To shatter the restrictive and repressive nature of the conscious mind enables Gatti's protagonists to live on many different levels, each one enriching or depleting the other. It is not uncommon, therefore, to see a performer in a Gatti play assuming several possible attitudes and postures virtually simultaneously: he or she may stand before an audience in one way at a particular time, while reacting to the same set of events in a completely different manner shortly afterward. Nor is there any character development in the traditional sense. Nothing is predictable in Gatti's dimensionless and fluid drama. What the protagonists see, what other characters may or may not discover during the course of the performance, and what audiences project onto the happenings are volatile. Relationships vary; they grow, slacken, fade in and out, lending complexity but also at times excoriating tension. In no way are Gatti's characters replications of the rigid heroes of a Claudel; nor do they resemble the intellectual self-interrogating creatures of Beckett's world; nor even the hedonists of a Genet drama. They are elusive and forever fluctuating.

The year 1968 taught Gatti a bitter but crucial and enriching lesson. His play *La Passion du Général Franco* (1968; *General Franco's Passion*), later titled *La Passion en violet, jaune et rouge* (*Passion in Violet, Yellow, and Red*), was banned at the request of the French government after complaints had been lodged by the Spanish dictator. Although rooted in a historical event, like Gatti's other plays, it went beyond the mere dramatization of Franco's ironbound regime. By focusing on the theme of exile, even while using the technique of fragmentation, Gatti universalized the vicissitudes of four groups of Spaniards forced to emigrate to France,

Germany, Russia, and South America. Meeting at various intervals during their travels, and evoking the pain they suffered after their expulsion from Spain, the exiles frequently aroused both suspense and pathos. To further flesh out the already complex prismatic stage activities, Gatti included flashbacks and sequences recalling the country's political climate prior to Franco's dictatorship. He created an atmosphere of terror by grouping onstage some physically hideous prehistoric monsters—a metaphor indicating the anticipated Fascist takeover. He elicited these same terrifying forms to project a resurgence of the totalitarian credo at some future time—long after the dictator's demise.

When, after Franco's death, the play's ban was lifted, Gatti rewrote *La Passion* for its 1972 production, altering its focus. Once mere talkers, the Spanish émigrés had now become criticizers, "deconstructing" and finding fault with each other's arguments and stories in what was now a kind of philosophical, political, and existential debate. But the protagonists agreed to disagree, and while the play itself became "polycentered," the characters retained autonomy over their destinies, thus allowing for divergence and fragmentation (Sarrazac, 48ff).

Another innovation used with even greater facility by Gatti in *La Passion,* as well as in his future works, was its so-called choral structure. The variety of inflections, tones, and rhythms emanating from the various debaters or conversers, who articulated their views singly or collectively, increased in geometric progression during the course of the play. The effect achieved was mental and emotional dislocation, intensified by the fact that the narrators could no longer offer clear-cut answers to life's problems. At this time Gatti was particularly interested in encouraging actors and audiences to find their "own language"—street talk, dialects, regionalisms, localisms, neologisms, slang, or any other speech devices. The language would serve to discover a personal way of understanding or conveying contemporary society's deep-seated feelings of exile, alienation, or exclusion.

After the banning of *La Passion* Gatti realized that it was time for him to leave France and to broaden his life experience. He moved to West Germany in 1969, where he made films and produced such plays as *Rosa Collective* (1971), based on the life of the socialist revolutionary and cofounder of the German Communist party, Rosa Luxembourg.

In Belgium, Gatti directed his first "collective creation": *La Colonne Durruti* (1972; *The Durruti Column*), focusing not so much on the life of Durruti, a Spanish anarchist in the Spanish Civil War, but on the impact of his work years later in other lands. The production, open to all

interested, took place outside of Schaelbeek, Belgium, in a disused facto
ry. The inspiration for Gatti's second collective work, *L'Arche d'Adelin*
(1973, *Adelin's Ark*), was a Bousval farmer, Omer Labarre, whose land
had been requisitioned by the government to make space for a highway.
Like Noah, Omer Labarre left his village with his family and flock, setting down roots for his future tribe in Dordogne, France.

Gatti's production revolved around a fictional character, Adelin (a
farmer in the Brabant Walloon region), who, like Omer Labarre, was
tired of seeing his land cut away by huge factories, high-rise buildings,
and superhighways. He invited student-actors as well as the inhabitants
of Bousval and neighboring villages to be not mere observers but to
express their reactions to the progressive erosion of land by monolithic
industrial complexes.

The actual production of *L'Arche d'Adelin* not only took on gargan-
tuan proportions but created a carnivalesque atmosphere as well. The
acting space extended for 45 kilometers over the countryside, and the
accessories included a motorcade made up of 135 vehicles of different
sizes: tractors, trailers, trucks, and cars, each used as a stage for the performance of the play. Three thousand people were involved in this "spec-
tatorless" drama lasting 28 hours. The trajectory of Gatti's motorcade
not only served to link villages and farms but also became the nucleus of
dramatic playlets created and enacted by the participants along the way.
Thus did text and people relate. That all types of homemade foods were
offered to the participants along the way injected a festive mood
throughout the performing areas.

Gatti's goal was not to replace indoor theater with street theater but
to fuse actor and spectator with both the elements and the world of
objects in one single dramatic expression. Like the medieval mystery
plays, which frequently lasted for seven days and involved hundreds of
individuals from all walks of life, Gatti's entreprise brought together
diverse nationalities, races, and classes—entire villages—in his single
collective creation.

Associated with Gatti's company at this time were Hélène Châtelain,
a video artist; Stéphane Gatti, a set designer; and Jean-Jacques Hoc-
quard, a producer and administrator. Their goals were one: to unite writing, theater, painting, video, and film in a dramatization that would be
universal in scope. With this in mind, Gatti adopted a logo in 1976—
that of the wild duck. Just as this bird must fly 300 kilometers an hour
against the wind in order to migrate to warmer climates, so people must
likewise struggle against odds. To yield means freezing to death.

Although to fly against the wind had always been Gatti's credo, it now took on greater import, becoming the byword for another of his collective endeavors. This time it revolved around Vladimir Bukovsky, a Russian dissident who had been imprisoned in a psychiatric hospital in the Soviet Union. Despite the fact that the French Communist party tried to discredit Gatti's projected production, the event not only took place but bore fruit. The power of the audience's intellectual and emotional response transformed *acting* into *action:* a plethora of journals, posters, playlets, videos, and exhibits of all types suddenly appeared. The result was that Bukovsky was not only released from the mental institution but he traveled to Saint-Nazaire, where Gatti's event had taken place, to address the participants.

Gatti, the revolutionary playwright/poet, while still seeking new visual, oral, and conceptual ways to liberate the spirit, was also devoting more and more of his time developing and refining a fresh linguistic approach to the performing arts. To this end he required each performer to generate a word or phrase designed to cut through the defenses erected by individuals and societies as protective devices over the centuries. Every expression had to live in and of its own power, as an independent poem improvised by the person who created it.

Gatti adopted a Mayan term to describe his semi-improvisational theatrical technique. The term *porteurs de parole* (bearers of the word) was applied by the Mayans to those who fulfilled or enacted sacred ceremonial functions. Thus did their task—and Gatti's as well—take on greater status. The concept of the "bearers of the word" enhanced the production's ethos, adding to it a spiritual dimension. Moreover, the sense of sacrality such a function injected into the proceedings pointed up language's exorcistic function: its power through performance to raise the consciousness of those involved in the collective happening.

Language, then, must actively trigger thought, feeling, and mood. Expressions, vocabularies, vernaculars, syntax, and figures of speech must change, take on substance and depth, and resist aridity. To water down the spoken or written word of popular culture or folklore is to divest it of its succulence and its substance. The acuity of the thought process itself diminishes, thereby enslaving the mind, allowing it to be patronized by others. If language is allowed to lie fallow, it dies. Gatti actively resists such passivity onstage. To sharpen words, to keep them well oiled and polished, is to better equip a person or group to fight. Words for him are weapons, capable of activating or slackening thought and, by extension, reinforcing or weakening individual identities.

Gatti's God is grammar. To justify his faith, he quotes from John: "In the beginning was the Word, and the Word was with God, and the Word was God" (1: 1). The word, as an absolute, allows him to converse directly with his century and its people; it also invites him to feel into the *earth,* its rhythms, tones, and melodies. He waits for no future time—no *heaven* to come. He lives in the now, as an independent. Yet as a devotee of the Clementine Homilies, the Talmud, and other tracts of this nature, Gatti calls himself a mystic. Theater has become a spiritual exploration, as attested to in *Le Chant d'amour des alphabets d'Auschwitz* (1988; *The Love Chant of the Auschwitz Alphabets*).

Le Chant d'amour des alphabets d'Auschwitz is a play characterized by both abstract and concrete concepts. The protagonists are letters of the alphabet as well as flesh-and-blood humans. As "bearers of speech," their words, expressions, and tones become both sacred and earthly. Gatti suggested that the actors speak as "one articulates a piece of music," with its various amplitudes and rhythms. Each speech, if properly experienced, not only functions as the harbinger of meaning but also sets off rounds of energy. Such "musical play" helps create the word/sentence spoken onstage while also galvanizing answers.[1]

Le Chant d'amour features 22 trains leaving Auschwitz after the concentration camp has been liberated by the Soviets. Before the war's end the camp had been abandoned by the Germans, who took with them the healthier individuals, leaving the ill and the dying to fend for themselves. When the Soviets arrived the survivors were put into trains in the expectation that some war-torn European country would offer them asylum. Rejected everywhere, they remained incarcerated in the trains for nine months.

Gatti explained that the trains numbered 22 because of the 22 letters of the Hebrew alphabet. As for the concentration camp victims, they represented society's exiles. The train filled with outcasts continued its physical as well as its linguistic wanderings, "dragging languages about," as Gatti said, in search of "the Book whose pages had been reduced to ashes" and whose words might have shed light on the meaning of life in general, and theirs in particular.

The first production of *Le Chant d'amour* was performed in France by society's pariahs: rehabilitated drug addicts, former prostitutes, ex-convicts. The second was at the University of Rochester in New York State, where David Richman, who was involved in the American production, taught dramatic arts. Because Richman had been born blind, and because he was a Jew whose grandmother had come from a shtetl in

Central Europe and whose family—including himself—had been incarcerated in a concentration camp, he could easily identify with the notion of "exclusion."

When Richman told Gatti that the camp orphans—those without proper names or identities, without childhoods—called the rat that lived in their precinct "Besht," the latter used it to illustrate his concept of the word both as electric charge and as a linguistic meeting ground for humans and animals. For certain orthodox Jews, however, the word "Besht" took on sacrality: it was the name given the Baal Shem Tov, the founder of the Hasidic sect, by his followers. Understandably, then, did the camp children give the name of Besht to the only living creature with whom they shared a common language.

When work on *Le Chant d'amour* began, it was decided that because Richman's blindness was evident and accepted by him and the others in the group, it could not be looked upon as a handicap and a reason for his exclusion. Instead, Gatti made his blindness the play's theme: everyone in the cast wore dark glasses—they were all blind. The word *Besht* would serve as an icon for "linguistic exclusion," thus becoming a metaphor for the train people, their stories, and the distance separating them from the student/performers at the University of Rochester. When a group of deaf-mute people happened to attend one of the rehearsals, they asked why they had been "excluded" from the project, whereas the blind had not. To remedy a wrong, those trained in sign language—"bearers of the word"—were asked to commit the entire text to memory and to translate it into the "common language" of the deaf-mutes.

As the train people grouped and regrouped, singing their litanies, speaking their dreams, conveying their pain, fear, and anger, they also circulated among the spectators. At one performance the audience, grouped as usual in clusters (or islands, as Gatti referred to them), consisted only of deaf-mutes. They observed the physical action but heard nothing. Each island had been awarded a translator who faced his audience, his back to the performers. The "bearers of the word," like orchestra conductors, enacted the text gesturally, not only enriching the entire production but endowing audience and participants with feelings of warmth that come with a sense of *inclusion.*

In Gatti's 1993 production of *Le Chant d'amour* he altered and expanded the play's focus. The theme grew out of an inquiry begun by Francis Gendron and the city of Montreuil into an event that has been all but forgotten: the police roundup and deportation of French Jews, although other religious denominations were also taken to Auschwitz and other Nazi concentration camps. Gatti felt that the memory of this crime should be renewed for every generation. And he did not believe it really concerned Jews as much as those who were directly responsible for leading them to slaughter. *Le Chant d'amour* ran 10 hours, an infinitesimal time allotment for the commemoration of an event of such magnitude.

Gatti's nonpsychological, noninstitutional, nontraditional, nonhistorical collective form again tested its worth in *Ces Empereurs aux ombrelles trouées* (1991; *These Emperors with Leaky Umbrellas*). Like the first production of *Le Chant d'amour*, it was performed (this time at Avignon) by society's pariahs, and it, too, deals with the problems of exclusion. Gatti's understanding of the notion of being an outcast does not necessarily imply public rejection of someone who has, for example, stolen or who has a physical handicap. Language, accent, intonation, vocabulary, and speech patterns may in one way or another lead to ostracism. Once imprisoned in a niche, the categorized individual will remain there, the butt of society's need for the creation of stereotypes.

Inviting volunteers for his production of *Ces Empereurs,* Gatti shocked those who responded not only by quoting from the Gospel of John, as he had many times before—"In the beginning was the Word, and the Word was with God, and the Word was God" (1: 1)—but by asking them outright, "Do you want to be God with me for six months?" And by adding, "To be God and to speak and write His Words requires a great deal of work."

Gatti's goal in *Ces Empereurs* was to find, on both an individual and group level, a way of creating peace out of confrontation. He decided that an interdisciplinary approach to theater might achieve his end. Each volunteer was asked to search for a connection between word, image, music, art, and dance. In so doing he or she would be deconstructing or dislocating stereotypic words or phonemes, removing them from their traditional/limited definitions and, paradoxically, broadening and also personalizing meanings. The participants were required to undergo a kind of self-imposed exile. The resulting aloneness would compel them to burrow within soma and psyche—to reach down into their own solitude. Only then could a person *know* the vitality of the inner time/space continuum.

A journey inward, however, requires commitment and courage, for along the way fear, doubt, and questions of self-worth may intrude, discouraging further soundings. Such a pursuit, however, yields a sense of dignity and accomplishment. Similarly, the word(s) that grow out of the experiment become endowed with their own strength and durability—their own divinity. During the six-month training period for the staging of *Ces Empereurs,* the participants not only learned how to discover their individual word or speech pattern but conversed with each other as well. In time, sentences organized themselves, as does a musical score or a poem, one word taking on a strong beat or tone, another a weaker or intermediate quality. Silence, which taught variety in breathing, also became an active force in performance.

While trying to inculcate a feeling for words into his actors, Gatti also invited them to look for the riches that lay hidden within each phoneme. To this end he asked that each volunteer answer in writing, as well as verbally to the group, these questions: "Who am I?" and "To whom am I talking?" Although such questions may at first sound simplistic, they are quite complex. Self-discipline is required to work out a truth for oneself; the collection and organization of one's thoughts implies a consciousness of their ramifications. Although self-interrogation may trigger new insights in individuals and thereby enable them to exploit their unrealized or dormant potential, such probing may also help reaffirm a person's faltering ego. If one of Gatti's actor/students found himself or herself unable or unwilling to divulge his or her truth in the presence of others, he or she had to withdraw from the group. As a man of the theater, Gatti allowed no one to sidestep real issues. Only by facing them, he felt, could his volunteers live comfortably with themselves.

During rehearsals, if Gatti felt that a trainee lacked sufficient fire or drive, he entered the stage space to explain or converse with the performer in question. Rather than telling him or her how the lines should be spoken, he encouraged each to think out a personal point of view and not merely mimic his.

He might also explain the grammar factor, not referring to syntax but to the body's grammar. Just as the word *grammar* is associated with classes of words—their inflections, functions, and relationships in the sentence—the body must similarly discover those elements that frame, reframe, and structure physical form. Only then may the individual performer develop his or her own system.

Reading was (and is) another of Gatti's requirements. To better understand the concepts involved in a play, his volunteers were instructed to acquaint themselves with disciplines related to it. In the case of *Ces Empereurs,* some aspects of philosophy, religion, history, and art were involved, so Gatti required the volunteers to know something about the Council of Nicéa, the Battle of Poitiers, and the Auschwitz death camp. Without some sense of history, albeit slim, they would have difficulty understanding the meaning of the staged hypothetical battles called for in the text.

Only after the volunteers had passed their tests did Gatti outline the theme of the play:

> We are going to write an autobiography of God, according to the visions of different religions, each of which seek to invent peace: Jews, Muslims, Christians. Judges will be present. Everything will be authentic, except for the names, so as to avoid slander suits. Characters will be called: Curator (guardian) of the retired Gods, Synthetic Messiah, "Tuesday's Heaven" for the audience. The main performer—the Devil—will most certainly not be omitted. The Devil, incarnated in God's earthly form, represents all the Imams, all the priests and prelates—"Those Emperors with their leaky umbrellas."[2]

Although Gatti usually writes his texts after lengthy discussions with each of his trainees, his approach to *Ces Empereurs* was different. The initial text, although rudimentary, had been written prior to his work with the trainees. He adapted it to suit the evolving thoughts and needs. During the course of the text's transformations, each trainee was given a stage name: for example, Malika, who had walked the streets of the outskirts of so many large cities, was named Outskirts of Aleph; Farid's unusual interpretation of lyrical passages from Schoenberg's *Moses and Aaron*—he sang them with a strong Arab accent—was called Vowel in Abeyance.

After formulating the theme of the first improvisation—a Koranic view of the Devil—Gatti defined his view of this divine figure: he represented priests and clerics. When the text called for staged ritual battles, the performers replicated those fought throughout history by, according to Gatti, manipulative, power-hungry, and hypocritical men of the cloth in their attempt to prolong their power over people's thoughts. The Devil, Gatti asserts, is present whenever there is war. It is he who creates chaos, Gatti adds, enlarging his original definition of this divine figure, but it is he, as well, who is instrumental in fostering the thinking process. Thus does one associated with evil increase consciousness and pave the way for harmony.

The disused church in which *Ces Empereurs* was performed had been transformed into a museum housing stone sculptures, which Gatti rebaptized "The House of the Retired Gods." To enhance the area's inherent *mysterium tremendum,* Gatti had the walls draped with large, light-colored silk panels; a sandy-toned net hung above the stage served to hide the church's high vaults; and a vast platform occupied the center of the nave. He also camouflaged the blond-colored stone statues surrounding the acting platform by wrapping them in sandy-toned material. Lit from behind, the statues cast matted luminosities, lending an eerie quality to the entire space. The cloth covering each of the statues was marked with a cross, a crescent, or a Star of David. So striking was the symbiosis between decors and lighting that these ghostly powers took on reality for both performers and audience. The statues seemed to watch over and react to the stage happenings; their moods gave the impression of altering during the course of the performance, echoing reflective, strident, angry, or loving notes.

An outerworldly climate was ushered into the theatrical experience when actors began speaking to the covered statues, reciting lines from the works of Hölderlin and St. John Perse or describing the visualizations of Raphael, Michelangelo, Mondrian, and Malevitch. As they articulated their thoughts about these artists' canvases, they daubed their faces and bodies with green, red, and blue pigments, which were placed in canisters around the acting area. Soon, as if by sleight of hand, the actors had transformed themselves into fragments of the very paintings they evoked.

Musical sequences were also part of the performance. Ten students had been taught to sing extracts from Arnold Schoenberg's 12-tone opera *Moses and Aaron.* The biblical tale of Moses and his older brother, Aaron, contains, among other religious, philosophical, and psychological notions, a message of great brotherly love. It was Aaron who helped Moses call down the Ten Plagues, enabling the "Children of Israel" to leave Egypt. Not only had the volunteers learned the German text by heart; they had made the composition their own, musically, intellectually, and emotionally. Despite the technical and compositional difficulties of the operatic extracts, they sang with ease, brio, and *justesse.*

Because the thematic heart of *Ces Empereurs* is peace, Gatti placed onstage two groups in opposition: Jews, who believed in the righteousness of their claim to the Holy Land; and Palestinians, equally certain of their convictions. At the conclusion of the staged stylized battles, the performers embraced each other, united under one banner—that of Abraham. The understanding, emotion, and sense of friendship that emerged, although perhaps only temporary, was deeply moving.

His television screens replicated the stage activities throughout the theatrical space. Whether the locus was Baghdad or Jerusalem, or whether the scene entailed a Crucifixion, an Exodus, or a concentration camp experience, the Word resounded with an intensity rare in theater. Having taken hold of their text, the actors spoke it viscerally, or musically, or objectively. Indeed, they had become Masters of the Verb.

Gatti, seated at a small wooden table in front of the first row of spectators, mediated the stage proceedings. It was he who twice interrupted the performance to call for intermissions. He, too, decided when the play was to end. Since the recitation takes 12 hours, it will probably never be performed at one stretch. Spectators will see only those sequences that Gatti and his "friends," as he calls his trainees, choose to reveal on any particular evening.

Gatti's theater is poetry, scenic design, and drama. It is also resistance to staid concepts. He brings to the stage living language, which tears down the barriers of exclusion, allows chaos to explode, and invites peace to be "invented." So deeply had Gatti's cast in *Ces Empereurs* appropriated language unto themselves as individuals and as members of a group that the so-called pariahs who were the performers had become masters of their bodies and their words. Each had reached into his or her solitude and befriended it, transforming what had once been shattered into a solid and impregnable force. They understood now that every creative act is born of *solitude* and that it brings *independence*.

Just as the rod of Aaron, which he had placed before the Ark, had miraculously blossomed and bore almonds, Gatti's theater had transformed society's outcasts. "And it came to pass, that on the morrow Moses went into the tabernacles of witness; and, behold, the rod of Aaron for the house of Levi was budded, and brought forth buds, and bloomed blossoms, and yielded almonds" (Numbers 18: 8).

Gatti continues to search for ways of spreading harmony among people through his powerfully innovative art of the theater. In his remarkable 1993 play, *Marseille: Adam quoi?* (*Marseilles: Adam What?*)—the title being the last words spoken by a friend of Gatti's before his extermination in a Nazi death camp—the 150 nonprofessional performers enact the fatal journey by repeating the unforgettable chantings of the 800 deportees taken from Marseilles on 23 February 1943 to Sobibor, where they were murdered. The text consists of the performers' invented language—a new alphabet, unheard-of words, constructed from the names of those who had been put to death and based on nothing. Yet from nothing there did arise a breathtaking spectacle that is Gatti's theater.

Chapter Six
"Discourse of the Image":
Patrice Chéreau

The theater-spectacles of Patrice Chéreau (b. 1944) are orchestrations of visual poems. An actor-director acutely sensitive to color, form, and depth perception, he wills to set his imaginings into images, to give substance to his architectonic stagings. Working in conjunction with make-up artists, set and costume designers, and lighting and sound technicians, he succeeds in integrating unforgettable iconic patternings into his mise-en-scènes. Because these multiple elements give the impression of being isolated but at the same time viscerally connected to the dramatic unfoldings, Chéreau's productions take on a personality and patina of their own. He adds to his sets and to the machines used to heighten their impact—cranes, pulleys, and wheels—musical effects that underscore a feeling of outerworldliness and choreographed luminosities. He frequently divides the stage into two armed camps: brash sunlit realms and ominous shadowy spheres, thereby creating a condition of metaphysical anxiety.

Actors perform realistically on Chéreau's stage. They may be seen scrounging around for something or executing crablike motions, suggesting both emotional and physical awkwardness. At other instances their beautiful bodies, like mobile sculptures, are silhouetted against an empty sky. In Chéreau's dramatic world—the fruit of his constant in-depth search—variegated types spawn, ranging from the aggressive to the withdrawn, the macabre to the joyful, the monstrously repulsive (because of the sordidness of their intent) to the exquisitely beautiful. By triggering tension from within his being, he succeeds in injecting many of the historical fables he has directed, such as *Lear, Peer Gynt,* and *The Dispute,* with contemporary meaning. Chéreau fears neither violence and cruelty nor shedding light on darkened regions of a character's psyche. In the manner of Artaud's "master of ceremonies," he knows how to control the obscure and dangerous presences emerging in relief or in contours onstage.

Chéreau belongs to a generation of directors who have rejected the very idea of compromising personal vision in order to curry favor with audiences. Like Vilar, he is a firm believer in culture suited to the needs and means of the majority. Experience has taught him, however, that a popular approach to theater is unworkable in a capitalist society. Still, he has done his best to communicate with people of all classes, not waxing esoteric in his productions but always retaining his own deeply original and universal perceptions. He strives to clarify ambiguities in a play's fabulation and characterizations, exploring these, together with his group, better to understand their place in history and in the society and culture that gave birth to them. For example, for his production of Ibsen's *Peer Gynt* he studied in detail the importance of Norse mythology and the facts surrounding the playwright's life in his native Norway. When undertaking Genet's *The Screens,* Chéreau read the dramatist's many textual variations of his play to better investigate, even highlight, the text's many willed dualities.[1]

Chéreau's work habits have always been disciplined. After early readings of the play in question, intuition and instinct seem to trigger an inborn image-making process. Once visualizations are fixed, he and his associates gather around a table to study. Although he speaks at length in an attempt to extract the play's central idea, he is in no way authoritarian. Once the sedentary work is completed the play is brought to the stage, where Chéreau's phantasms are given credence or are drastically modified as his living characters emerge full-blown.

Chéreau still questions his instinctive reactions and perceptions, both as actor and director, and expects the same of his associates. Self-interrogation of the character portrayed and the actor's understanding of his role require sensitivity and strength. His approach to acting disorients some performers: to see lucidly into oneself, to face one's own void, and then to return to stage life takes diligence, discipline, and power over oneself.

Chéreau's critical and confrontational approach to theater provokes a battle at each phase of production. What is of import to him are, to be sure, text and ideas, but also their *intrusive effects* on both the protagonists and audiences. In what way, he questions, does their thrust distort—as does television—the psyches of the performers and onlookers?

The time/space dialectic, also significant in Chéreau's production technique, is aimed at impinging on the performer and the spectator. For example, the interaction between *signs* as spatial elements (sets, costumes, lighting, sound, performers, positions and movements on the stage) and their repercussions on abstract time, as experienced by the actor and the spectator, are designed, generally speaking, to shatter the coherent, to cacophonize the harmonious, and thus to create a complex of warring icons.

Either autonomous or balanced with or against each other in complementary or shockingly jarring visualizations, Chéreau's sets are endowed with their own space/time syntax. Rarely static, his sets become living and active powers in the continuously evolving process that is production. Thanks to the use of machinery, walls, houses, pools, mountains, greenery, and skylines expand or decrease the size of landscapes, thereby destabilizing or stabilizing the stage image.

The system of costumes created for a particular play also exists in a space/time continuum. Their materiality makes them *signs* of temporality, manifested either as strangely antagonistic to the historical undercurrents within the play or in concordance with them. A performer's dress reflects a play's personality, pace, and plot and a director's vision as well. What is worn, therefore, must not only be coordinated with the decor to achieve the desired plastic unity but, to use Roland Barthes's expression, must not undergo "hypertrophy."[2] Some of Chéreau's productions, such as Molière's *Dom Juan*, have spotlighted the anti-hero bedecked in leather togs, reminiscent of the the French *blousons noirs*, or America's "Hell's Angels," thus running counter to, or even violating, traditional concepts. In Marivaux's *L'Héritier du village* (1965; *The Inheritor of the Village*) young people appeared onstage with shaved heads, khaki costumes, and Chinese mannerisms, and they created a scandal.

Chéreau's mise-en-scènes are intuitively, imaginatively, and intellectually constructed and reflect his basic political, moral, and aesthetic views. He took a strong social stand in his production of Jakob Lenz's *The Soldier* (1967), choosing to emphasize the dichotomies between a decadent nobility and the so-called lower classes. He accomplished his goal via sets (houses with peeling walls) and lights (Strehler-like interplays of chiaroscuro effects). The psychological impact of these melodramatic devices increased the morbid misogyny inherent in the play.

Two Chinese plays by the thirteenth-century dramatist Kuan Han-Ching, *La Neige au milieu de l'été* (*Snow in the Middle of Summer*) and *Le Voleur de femmes* (*The Purloiner of Women*), in a different tradition, allowed Chéreau to introduce what was to become his hallmark: the *machine à jouer*. Sets created with his scenographer, the painter Richard Peduzzi, brought to the stage an entire mechanical frame of reference: gears, pulleys, winches, trapdoors, gangways, and footbridges. Equally intriguing lighting effects were achieved by André Diot. Masks with a slight

Brechtian twist and costumes by Jacques Schmidt set off a vigorous
conflicted climate.

The protagonist of Chereau's 1969 production of *Dom Juan* was no
longer the archetypal seducer of Molière's time. Chéreau shed formerly
sacrosanct interpretations but considered that he had remained faithful
to the religious, social, and political spirit of seventeenth-century France.
Yes, he made Dom Juan a more profound and far-reaching iconoclast
than he had been before, but had Molière himself not been anti-
establishment? Had he not lived out a marginal and ambiguous existence vis-à-vis the ruling classes of his day?

Jouvet had played Dom Juan as a great lord, "a solitary and frozen
hidalgo"; Vilar, "as a Cartesian and atheist musketeer." Chéreau's Dom
Juan (Gérard Guillaumat) became a leftist intellectual, a freethinker,
interested in politics and in clan relationships. He was a man stripped of
glory and wealth, as well as of power over his servant, Sganarelle (Marcel
Maréchal) (Sandier, 168–70).

Dom Juan's "rigorously constructed gestures" were *signs* charged with
meaning and reflected feelings of impotency and doubt. The scanning of
his phrases opens up a complex inner world: inchoate, repressed violence,
frustration, and anger against aristocrats who seek to keep their power
while oppressing people of his ilk who struggle for spiritual and emotional freedom. The new libertine type, aware that both God and the Devil
are dead, believes in the power of "reason" to assuage the wretchedness of
the human condition—a revolutionary concept for the time. Unlike the
decadent nobles against whom he fights, Dom Juan is viewed by friends
and foe as a redoubtable force "sufficiently audacious" to reject taboos
and consider morality a "masquerade." His monologues become dialogues as conversation is transformed into controversy (Sandier, 170).
Nevertheless, this depraved and outcast nobleman, this traitor to his
class, this sometime leader of a band of outlaws, imprisoned in his own
world of contradictions, is unable or unwilling to help anyone for fear of
betraying his own needs and failures. He lives in splendid isolation until,
victim of "those he had betrayed," he experiences his "sublime" punishment. In earlier versions the renegade had been put to death by the
commander's ghost, but in Chéreau's ultrarealistic production he is
crushed by something concrete: an "infernal machine."

The dynamic, inventive, jubilant, lyric Sganarelle is an explosive force
within "Chéreau's aggressively intellectual mise-en-scène" (Aslan, 41).
Clowning à la Chaplin, in a costume inspired by Callot's tramps, he was
unforgettable as he forever followed his master, sometimes mimicking

his role model's gestures and vocal prowess (Temkine, 2: 128). On one occasion, while listening to a love duet between Dom Juan and Charlotte, he lived out an erotic dream alone, upstage. Rather than portraying the valet as a stuttering or incompetent farce character, as tradition dictated, Chéreau played up Sganarelle's sense of alienation through inept speech, which elicited laughter. During a *real* meal onstage, when Sganarelle's mouth is filled with food and Dom Juan orders him to speak, his body becomes a center of conflict from which authentic gestures are extracted. At the play's conclusion Sganarelle does not weep over his lost wages, nor over his master's death. On the contrary, he realizes for the first time the joy that comes with freedom.

Richard Peduzzi's sets were, as usual, provocative. Whereas an elegant quarter with models of aristocratic houses were featured upstage, Dom Juan's farmhouse was seen in ruins. Also featured onstage, as in the two Chinese plays directed by Chéreau, were cogs, winches, wheels, reels, pulleys, cords, and wires, reminiscent of one of Leonardo da Vinci's intricate drawings of machines. These were activated in full view of the audience by six peasants dressed in rags and serving as stage mechanics. When not occupied, these flunkeys sleeping on straw brought to mind certain canvases of Le Nain, one of the great seventeenth-century artists who depicted the world of hungry, wretched peasants. As the apparatus functioned, spectators had the impression of following the distances covered by the hunted Dom Juan and Sganarelle: the pulling of Dom Juan's cart filled with his possessions, up hill and down dale, was reminiscent of Brecht's Mother Courage dragging her wagon. When the cart grows too heavy to move Sganarelle throws out a trunk and other assorted objects, which he sometimes puts back in when the spirit moves him, provoking sequences of gesturally choreographed comedy (Aslan, 46).

Charlotte and Mathurine, charming peasant lasses in Molière's day, were transformed by Chéreau into awkwardly shaped and overly and unbecomingly dressed women. At the discovery that they are rivals for Dom Juan, they lunge at each other with arched legs and outstretched arms in bouts of incredible violence. Paralleling the brutality of the peasants was the hysteria of the 16-year-old Elvire. This sick, immature girl, forever accompanied by her nurse—Chéreau's invention—suffers the pain of her unrequited passion for Dom Juan. Her brothers, remnants of a feudal age, dressed in long fur coats and looking like bears emerging from a cave, talk grotesquely of "honor" and "glory." Dom Juan battles them as though he were a boxer and, at the propitious moment, flees from the danger.

Although some critics felt that Chéreau's interpretation degraded a great mythical figure, Gilles Sandier wrote that what was unique in his staging was the manner in which the "encounter between two antagonistic temperaments" (Dom Juan and Sganarelle) had been handled. Unlike former Sganarelles, admiring of their masters, even a bit "in love" with them, certainly "fascinated" as well as terrorized by them, Chéreau's valet was new. Although blind to *reality,* he was, nevertheless,

indestructible and conscious of being blind: he is a man possessed, thrashed, driven to distraction: a conscience that escapes tragedy through derision. No longer knowing what he is, where he is, what the world is and if there is a heaven or just a bogey-man, he *knows* only that he has been divested of everything, of his being and his language: his drunken clown-like pirouettes no longer succeed in masking his pain . . . he will become aware of what is really his, his hate, only on the day he pushes with his foot the body of this progressive Puntila and crook, who died without paying him: only then will he realize the implications of liberty, a world without slaves. (Sandier, 170)

On an even more controversial staging was Chéreau's derisive and violent mise-en-scène of *Richard II,* triggered paroxysmal reactions on opening night. A new "Bataille d'Hernani" was in the offing as half the audience left the theater long before the end of the play.

Richard Peduzzi's stage sets were distinctive. An enclosed trench into which tons of sand had been poured became many things: a battleground, a deserted house, the inside of a castle-prison. When feuding lords occupied the space, the mounds of sand took on the grandeur of a broad plane. The brutality of the battling men gave rise to special effects, as the sand was kicked up by rival bands. What could be more realistic, yet at the same time illusory and fantastic? Some critics compared the antagonistic sequences peppering the drama to tournaments of Roman gladiators; others, to a circus ring (Godard, 18).

The cyclorama in the background gave the impression of expanding distances, of hills and valleys, as models of farmhouses and mausoleums passed in and out of view. The heavy stone pillars of the castle-prison surrounding the misty arena and the lugubrious "pale" and "blind" walls created an atmosphere of decadence and death. The castle-prison's long vestibules, abandoned rooms, war machines (modeled on Leonardo da Vinci's drawings), and coffins became a microcosm of court life. The stage's asymmetricality took on a psychological dimension: that of an unbalanced, destabilized subliminal sphere. Audiences were viewing not merely a dispossessed king but one who suffered irremediable pain (Temkine, 2: 109). Scenes of passion and tenderness relieved the macabre atmosphere, however, when, for example, Richard II bade farewell to his queen in the Tower of London. As they advanced toward each other for their last kiss, their arms held in back of them by their jailer/torturers, each bent over toward each other on the open space, symbolizing the emptiness that was their lives. Screaming and fighting, each one's hair became enmeshed in the other's as they were led away to face their separate destinies.

Chéreau played a morbid and languid Richard II. His face painted white gave him a clammy, waxlike, sickly, and vulnerable look. Sequins around his eyes suggested a grotesque and perverse disposition. Entering the stage space, carried on a four-armed portable seat by his darlings, he resembled an "enthroned Nero." The motility of the portable seat—a fetish of sorts—evoked the fleeting nature of time, a sign of all departures and arrivals. To impress audiences with the ambivalent mental state of a man on the verge of a breakdown, Chéreau frequently introduced bizarre and unexpected pauses at the wrong places in the poetry of his lines. Did his rejection of traditional syntax suggest a repudiation of life? (Aslan, 79).

Chéreau's Richard II has been described as "a corrupt adolescent, a kind of flabby, farinated Nero" surrounded by his "darlings whose luxurious tatters bring the hippies to mind." Irresponsible, weak, capricious, corrupt, and perverse, he seems unaware of anything and everything. His self-centeredness encourages him to despair over a feudal world that rejects his rapacious tyranny. Humor at its blackest was evoked when this once hot-spirited youth, now at the end of life, flees his enemies carrying his crown in a picnic basket.

When first performed in 1744, Marivaux's *La Dispute* was hissed, but Chéreau's 1973 production was received enthusiastically. It was considered not only a social satire and "a great opera" but "an allegory endowed with the power and violence of the novels of Sade and the tales of Hoffmann." Some critics, however, labeled his production "a nightmarish psychodrama." Nevertheless, as Pierre Macabru noted, "Something has taken place in theater, and this quasi-magical something is the source of enchantment in the strongest meaning of the term" (Aslan, 113).

Chéreau divided the stage for *La Dispute* into acting spaces. The first, hidden behind the closed stage curtain, represented Nature; the second, the lodgings of the Prince, Princess, and the Court. Prior to the start of

the play, the protagonists gathered on a square platform erected in the
first few rows of the orchestra. There they are, involved, and rolled
Linked to this "small island" was an "enlightened" astronomer's workplace featuring a spherical copper balance wheel, an opaque oval mirror,
and other optical instruments. A small, brightly lit ramp led from this
platform to a hall and crossed over the orchestra pit, or "mystical abyss."
A Prologue, in apposition to the text and lasting about 40 minutes,
fleshed out the play's philosophy. Marivaux's texts collected by François
Regnault for this purpose included *The Education of a Prince:* a discussion
on human nature, revealing the unfortunate lot of women, who were
kept, dependent and subservient, in a state of virtual captivity by men.

Once the theater lights were extinguished, the obscurity was relieved
by a red light beamed onto the cloth-covered orchestra pit from which
white sulfurous vapors escaped. Mozart's *Masonic Funeral Music* was diffused through 10 loudspeakers placed in key areas throughout the theater. From the platform in front of the orchestra pit—as if suspended in
time and half hidden behind the smoke screen—appeared the phantom
Prince, Princess, and Court ladies, dressed in evening clothes designed by
Jacques Schmidt, of 1920 vintage. They were presented as rich, decadent, and culpable members of the intelligentsia. Their dialogue was
sharp, rapid, provocative, even blasé at times. Was the Prince's act of
holding a convex magnifying mirror to his mistress's face, thus enlarging
her wrinkles, a cruelty? or an example of loving tenderness? Were the
Court ladies the Prince's accomplices and his mistress's jailers? One may
also wonder whether *La Dispute* was the work of Marivaux or of Cho-
derlos de Laclos.

The "dispute" is over the question of whether infidelity is stronger in
man or in woman. The mode of settlement will be observation of the
joyous game of life of two boys and two girls: four young people who
have been raised in complete isolation. To obtain the vantage point to
settle their "dispute," the adult aristocrats walk across a plank leading
from their platform over the insalubrious orchestra pit to the light of the
real stage.

An empty garden at twilight becomes visible as the curtains part.
Upstage, on elevated ground, there appears an impenetrable, seemingly
endless forested area, with real tree branches. An example, perhaps, of
primordial Mother Nature? Also visible are the high walls of a once-
elegant but now dilapidated neoclassical palace. The Prince, arrogant,
distant, and ironic, his hair glued to his head, will observe the unfolding
events, together with his entourage, from the side of the proscenium.

The four adolescents, dressed in white, bounce onto the stage in succession. The innocent girls wear bouffant pants and simple tops, underscoring purity of mind and body. The boys are equally guileless. The young people roll on Mother Earth, thrilled by the contact. Their learning process lasts from dawn to dusk for seven days—the sacred number of the biblical Creation and the time it takes for the adolescents to pass from an extended childhood to puberty. Multiple physical activities, such as fights, clawings, and shouting, as well as alterations of pace and amplitudes of language patterns, reflect the growing-up process. Moods also vary, ranging from delight and insouciance to fear and viciousness.

Destructive traits in each of the children are unearthed from day to day. The need to dominate, narcissism, vanity, egocentricity, jealousy, and envy are all intimately intertwined with a fascination for licentiousness and seduction. Hidden mechanisms make the walls of what audiences are led to believe represent the young people's dwellings move about in space—to the side, but also dangerously close to the center, giving the impression of crushing the children. The pace and direction of these moving walls also mirror the hostility and pain that the children unwittingly generate against themselves and each other. At first their eyes are covered, obliging them to touch each other in the discovery process. Their behavior is marked by fear, but once sight is given to them and they view a landscape of the type that might have been depicted by Bernardin de Saint Pierre, they seem reassured. When Eglé, the first to penetrate into the "real" world, happens to see her face reflected in the "real" water of a pond onstage, she, like Narcissus, falls in love with the image. Thus the body—of which the adolescents have been unaware until now—becomes a tangible force to be probed.

Life in the garden, however, is not Edenic. Rivalries and jealousies become manifest: between Eglé, who loves Azor, and the second lass, Adine, who loves Mesrin. Each one, considering herself more beautiful and therefore worthy of greater admiration than her rival, seeks to dominate the other. Vanity has reared its ugly head as gestures become more violent. Once-melodious voices grow strident, even raucous. That Eglé seduces Mesrin, who is willing to betray his friend Azor, seems to have been "artificially" motivated by her with the purpose of angering Adine. Although Eglé was the first to commit "sin," she cannot deal with Azor's deception with Adine. Tragedy ensues with her suicide.

The Prince and his entourage are powerless to restrain the walls that are literally closing in on the young people, who are trying in vain to reach beyond them in order to escape tragedy. That the entire spectacle to buthed in moonlight, growing brighter and then appears but never opening into daylight, merely into successive dawns, suggests the impossibility of facing the light of consciousness. What, then, should be done? Must one resign oneself to the universality of immorality, and to the instability of relationships, most of which are characterized by cruelty or betrayal?

Edward Bond's vision of *Lear,* mounted by Chéreau in 1975, is that of a violent and ruthless dictator. "Violence shapes and obsesses our society," Bond wrote in his preface, "and if we do not stop being violent, we have no future." Chéreau considered Bond's *Lear* a "terrible, embarrassing, new, totally contemporary play."[3]

The actors' mood swings were expressed gesturally as well as by alterations in their breathing pace as they spoke. Through the concomitant abolition of punctuation—question marks, exclamations, commas, periods—a question could become a certainty, a statement of fact an accusation, and meanings as well as depth of involvement could change (Aslan, 38).

Richard Peduzzi's startling scenography added to the play's disorienting and perverse tone. Upstage, set against a transparent pearl gray sky—a kind of lunar landscape—was a large area of ground embossed with heaps of slag and cranes. Downstage was a garden, where a group of miners or terracers, blackened from coal or mud, were working.

Lear, an old man in high hat and frock coat, sporting a cane, and accompanied by counselors, engineers, officers, and his two middle-aged daughters, Bodice and Fontanelle, inspects the protective wall that he had ordered built long years ago around his kingdom to ward off his enemies. Suddenly, a scream is heard, and a body falls to the ground from the rafters: a man has lost his footing while working on the concrete wall. The old Lear, followed by a bearded man, also dressed in frock coat, makes his way up the hill, to where the accident took place. He must fulfill his obligation as monarch and punish the person responsible for this job-related accident. As there is a victim, so there must be a criminal. He proceeds according to his class-defined understanding of justice. The guilty person, a worker, counts for little. In fact, he is probably a "saboteur." Lear has him tied to the stake and gives the order to shoot him. At this moment his two daughters intervene, attempting to prevent the execution, not for humanitarian reasons but simply because they seek to reign in their father's stead. They declare their father/tyrant/king to be senile—mad. The angry Lear executes the man himself (Temkine, 2: 142).

Lear's daughters reveal themselves to be particularly ignominious in their punishment of Lord Warrington, Lear's faithful counselor. Had his refusal of their advances motivated their anger? To avoid humiliation and to assure that their secret is kept, they cut out his tongue; so that he may never hear again, they pierce his eardrums with knitting needles. The torture they impose on him, the obscenities they speak, and the lascivious gestures accompanying their sadistic frenzy disclose the criminal mind in all of its hysterical madness. The actor playing Warrington was remarkable in his anguished gestures, his stumblings as he tried in vain to evade the brutalities of these harpies.

The old monarch, betrayed by his daughters, and despoiled of all of his possessions, plunges ever more deeply into his own world of folly. Although vanquished, he still has the sense of power he once enjoyed. As he begins reviewing his past, notions of compassion and love emerge, enabling him to a certain extent to avoid complete entrenchment in a world of madness.

The dead husband of Lear's youngest daughter, Cordelia, who treated the old man with understanding and affection, returns as a ghost and becomes the monarch's inseparable companion. Although identified in some ways with Shakespeare's clown in Bond's play, he is a self-sacrificing individual who takes on Lear's suffering. Once freed of his anguish, Lear sees himself with greater clarity and is able to offset denial. His loss of sight endows him with inner lucidity and with the strength, Chéreau wrote, to denounce the Christian notions of confession, expiation, and sermonizing as trickery and deception.[4]

Bond's Cordelia, unlike Shakespeare's, is not only a woman of the people but a revolutionary. With clear conscience, this militant, strong, warmly sensual soldier, now heading the armed forces, encourages rebellion even though she knows that in time revolutionary ideals are always perverted. She orders the rebuilding of the wall—a kind of no-man's-land that Lear himself in his madness had begun to tear down in the hope that barriers between people would no longer be erected (Temkine, 2: 119).

While Chéreau did not consider *Lear* a political piece, associations with the Berlin Wall came to the spectator's mind. Nor could one help thinking—in the scene in which Lear's daughters cold-bloodedly yet joyously perpetrate their ignominious mutilations—of Auschwitz and the sadistic Nazi doctors who carried out their sinister experiments on innocent people. The implicit superimposition of today's martyrs onto Shakespeare's work lent mythical power to this historical fable.

Ibsen's *Peer Gynt*, staged by Chéreau in 1981, a mythical fantasy based on the legendary hero of Norse folklore, was always considered to be unsuitable for the stage because of its length and many scenic changes (stormy seas, precipitous mountains, deserts, the Orient, and other locales). Ibsen's dramatic work, revolving around the adventurous, boastful, irresponsible, and identityless Peer, was performed under Chéreau in its entirety. It ran for seven hours over two evenings. Gérard Desarthe's portrayal of Peer, which took the hero from age 17 to 70 and necessitated his presence onstage at virtually all times, was a tour de force. Thanks to his close collaboration with Chéreau, Desarthe did not play Peer as the fragmented personality he had been in prior productions but as a whole being, an individual forever searching for an answer to existential experience. At odds with his human condition, as well as with himself, he struggles to come to terms with his weaknesses—cowardice, compromise, opportunism, aging—and strives to judge his acts objectively (Aslan, 141).

To a cast of 21 Chéreau added 40 crew members, including technicians who made scenic backdrops representing various stops in Peer's voyages appear and disappear with a flick of a switch. Technical miracles also coordinated sound, light, and sets to conjure up all kinds of weather, noises, and images.

Unlike his well-known predecessors, such as Lugné-Poë, Krauss, Reybaz, Bergman, and Stein, who had produced *Peer Gynt* with great distinction, Chéreau's interpretation was different. It was neither politically nor socially oriented, nor could it be identified culturally with nineteenth-century Norway. It dealt with problems facing people everywhere in the twentieth century. Chéreau followed Ibsen's lead as he understood it: humankind was given free will as a punishment. Liberty to "be oneself, the liberty to be saint or criminal, or to be nothing," imposes an awful burden on the individual. Peer, like his creator, was endowed with a strong will, empowering him to cross from the earthly realm, which includes family and friends, to the land of his dreams, where he spies the trolls—mountain demons in all of their beauty and grotesqueness. The crossing over requires the strength to "adapt to universal cowardice." Throughout Peer's peregrinations he fights hard against the Angel, the Dragon, the Monster within; against "the voice of his own speech"; and, most forcefully, against fear. In his dreams "he reached out to his mother," searching all the while for forgetfulness, amnesia, escape from his own memories." Ibsen wrote, "One possesses for eternity only what one has lost" (Aslan, 141).

Chéreau's sets incarnated Ibsen's secret metaphysical domain: a trap-door opening onto a shadowy abyss summarily swallowed a table and leftover scraps from a banquet; a piece of cloth became water or a water-fall; forests, mountains, and clouds came into view only to vanish moments later; a trailer/lodging, ships, and mobile walls enclosed a life-time of yearnings. Audiences were made privy to episodes involving love and sacrifice as well as cowardice, violence, and opportunism. Other issues addressed were poverty, as peasants scrounged for a morsel, scratching and clawing the earth for food, and license and luxury, in a world where aristocrats and emperors dominated. Peer's coming to moral consciousness occurs after a shipwreck when, to save his own life, he allows another to drown. Thus are disclosed the inner workings of not merely one individual but humanity at large.

Costumes, visible or hidden, were adapted by Jacques Schmidt to the actor's body. Early into rehearsals footwear, wigs, and other accou-trements were worn in order to establish the manner in which these would affect the actors' walking or jumping onstage. A scene of the play takes place in a Cairo mental institution, where the patients' acrobatics reminded Chéreau of the U.S. Marines wading through Vietnam's napalm-polluted swamps. With this in mind, he had the performers stick torn bandages to their legs, and splatter clay over their bodies, thus giving the impression from a distance of blemished or scabby flesh. Because of such touches, the mental institution scene took on the cast of a concentration camp, disquieting to both actor and spectator (Aslan, 62–65).

André Diot's lighting effects were inextricably bound to the mise-en-scène. During the tempest scene, lights were made to work in consort with sound: to replicate the frenzied or legato rhythms of the actors moving about in crablike rotations, or walking in slow or rapid steps. Sound, correlated with light, was rerecorded by André Serre and emanated directly from loudspeakers spread throughout the theater. Because Chéreau considered the music of Grieg's *Peer Gynt Suite* "affect-ed," "castrating," and an impediment to the fleshing out of Ibsen's mul-tidimensional text, it was not used (Aslan, 139).

Chéreau's many stagings of theater and opera in France and abroad—Chekhov's *Platonov* (1987), *Hamlet* (1988), and Berg's *Woyzeck* (1992) among them—were and are fascinating for their startling scenic images, their covert viscerality smoldering in a world of deepening shadows, and their macabre luminosities. His interests expanded to include performing in such films as *Judith Therpauve* (1978), *Danton* (1983), and *The Last of les Médiums* (1991), as well as directing the film *Queen Margot* (1993), based on the novel by Dumas père. Recently he has been directing video shorts and television plays

Although the obsessively mad or fantastic beings Chéreau has brought to life have provoked anger and disgust, they have also elicited great admiration for the authenticity and integrity of his vision. He is a searcher who tries, through art, to make individuals aware of their inner universe, no matter how tarnished it may be. He always questions and always pushes his actors on, perhaps even to the brink, "to do what they have *never* done before" (Aslan, 77).[5]

Chapter Seven

Tropism, Poetics, and Cosmic Theater: Nathalie Sarraute, Andrée Chedid, and Liliane Atlan

Whether used cerebrally or viscerally, words govern the scenic order and the thoughts and emotions of the characters in the plays of Nathalie Sarraute, Andrée Chedid, and Liliane Atlan. Phonemes open up their noncharacters' blocked inner world—domains subject to denial and contradictory impulses. Although the personal visions of Sarraute, Chedid, and Atlan are strikingly different, all three encode their verbal couplings in such a way that the focus falls on identityless types—the hallmark of our contemporary society.

Nathalie Sarraute: A Theater of Tropisms

Sarraute's theater is not absurdist, guerrilla, panic, political, or philosophical; her dramatic pieces are of her own invention. She is the creator of a "theater of tropisms," defining the word *tropisms* as follows:

> They are undefinable movements which glide very rapidly to the limits of consciousness; they are at the root of our gestures, our words, of the feelings we manifest, which we believe we feel and which we can define. They seemed to me and still seem to me to constitute the secret source of our existence.
>
> When these movements are in the process of formation, they remain unexpressed—not one word emerges—not even in the words of an interior monologue; they develop within us and vanish with extreme rapidity, without our ever really perceiving them clearly; they produce within us frequently very intense, but brief, sensations; these can be communicated to the reader only through images, thereby giving them an equivalent and enabling them to feel analogous situations. These movements had to be decomposed and allowed to extend into the reader's conscious mind in the manner of a film in slow motion. Time was no longer experienced in terms of the workaday world, but rather in a distorted and aggrandized present.[1]

Like her novels, Sarraute's plays have minimal plots. They are built around controlled or contrived situations in which silences and conversations hinge on the manner in which certain words are pronounced, and their power to alienate or attract. As the tropisms or visualizations that emerge from the conversations and subconversations interact or clash with one another, they frequently unmask the participants and reveal hidden relationships among them. The mechanism used by Sarraute to set her play in motion is the tropism. The detail buried within it, and referred to by the performer(s) in sparse but rambling dialogue, creates suspense and leads to the play's climax. Spectators must catch the detail and absorb it if they seek to follow the conversations. The tropism provokes tension. It mystifies at first, then delights; later it hurts and may attract or repel, anger or pacify.

Sarraute's characters are not flesh-and-blood creations but faceless beings without identity. They are endowed with neither form nor substance; they are transparencies whose existences are built on ever-altering sequences of images. These presences may be viewed as actual feelings or concrete sensations. They voice their wants in impersonal and detached terms, using nuanced timbres and intonations. In *Le Mensonge* (1967; *The Lie*) the presences have first names. In *Le Silence* (1967; *The Silence*) only Jean-Pierre has a name, and the other noncharacters are Women 1, 2, 3, and 4 and Men 1 and 2. In *Isma* (1970) He and She emerge; the rest of the cast are Men 1, 2, and 3 and Women 1, 2, and 3. In *C'est Beau* (1973; *It's Beautiful*) we are made privy to a mother-father-son triangle in which the One is pitted against the Two in ever-shifting combinations. *Elle est là* (1978; *It Is There*) revolves around an idea buried in someone's head. *Pour un oui ou pour un non* (1984; *At the Drop of a Hat*) calls attention to the fact that H^2 was insulted by the tone used by his friend H^1 in pronouncing a certain phrase.

As in a parlor comedy, Sarraute initiates her viewers slowly, by degrees and with dignity, into a controlled and subtly alluring private world. Once she has enticed her prey into a realm of intrigue, she abandons them there—in a psychologically and spiritually spaceless area where they are left to flounder with a group of unidentifiable beings. Interestingly enough, both audience and dramatist participate in the event as it occurs. Detachment permits an intellectual understanding of the arguments, whereas identification allows the protagonists and audience alike to undergo the anguish, disgust, joy, or hate implicit in the inner landscape. Such sequences of detachment and identification are experienced in a state of constant flux, in a hierarchy of disturbing moods.

That Jacques Lassalle, in his capacity as administrator of the Comédie-Française, chose to produce and direct *Le Silence* and *Elle est là* in 1993 to inaugurate the opening of the newly refurbished Vieux-Colombier Theater was his way of paying tribute to Nathalie Sarraute. *Le Silence* introduces audiences to a mundane group. One man has just finished relating his recent trip to his friends; they are delighted with his narration A single person in the group voices no reaction; the others cannot fathom his silence. Is it a timid, angry, jealous, or insulting silence? The drama revolves around each person's growing desire to break contact with the rest of the group and to seal himself within his own world.

Elle est là features two businessmen in deep discussion. Earlier, the collaborator or associate of one of the men had not offered an opinion on a certain topic that arose during their discussion. Now that she is gone he probes the situation. Although she said nothing he is certain that she did not agree with his idea. As a result, his peace of mind has come to an end. His partner tells him that he must not waste his time thinking about such details, but he cannot help himself. It has become an idée fixe: he wants to know whether she agrees with him or not. He has the silent woman return, with the thought of discovering her conviction. He finds an ally in the audience—who, like him, is intolerant of anyone with a differing opinion. When the single word *intolerance* is uttered onstage it becomes obvious that the insalubrious, shadowy, and silent inner realms in each being are fertile fields for the germination of terrorism, totalitarianism, and violence.

As Sarraute burrows deep inside the protoplasmic beings of her minidramas, she extracts the full import of an experience, each element of which is detected by her infallible antennae and then given from in the dazzling verbal gyrations that are her theater of tropisms.

Andrée Chedid: A Theater of Poetics

The dramas of the Egypto-Lebanese Andrée Chedid, who has lived in Paris since 1946, are a blend of the real and elusive worlds of both the West and the Middle East. Although two civilizations, two ways of life, and two psyches are fused in her verbal distillations, her protagonists emerge from a universal mold. They are eternal in their philosophical and psychological configurations, for they have stepped from the dream into life full-blown. Her dialogue is crisp and stark, embedded with poetic luminosities that crystallize sensation and reveal the most subtle shades of feeling.

violence, shock, and pain are implicit in some of Chedid's hallucinatory lines. Her verbal voice, revealing her concerted rebellion against
injustice, partiality, and inhumanity, never falls silent. When this kind of
raw emotional response emerges from the mouths of the players, it dis-
locates stage happenings, dissociates images, and reveals a willful disorder—and malaise.

Chedid's plays are classical in their simplicity. There is no extraneous
action. Everything onstage emerges directly from the body of the written text. Her protagonists are atemporal, archetypal, arising from the
deepest layers of the unconscious. They do not, however, develop psychologically as in conventional theater. As they move about onstage each
becomes an energy center diffusing its own aura, which either attracts or
repels the others. Her frequently statically paced dialogue gives her plays
a sense of terrifying timelessness. Suspense is maintained not by exaggerated rhythm effects or by plot but by the juxtaposition of images and
words and sounds. Actions and gestures are studied and restrained.
Silences and breathing heighten the apprehension implicit in such plays
as *Bérénice d'Egypte* (1968), *Nombres* (1968), *Le Montreur* (1969; *The
Showman*), *Echec à la reine* (1984; *Guard Queen*).

Bérénice d'Egypte, a three-act play, is innovative in its use of masks,
puppets, and dialogue. The sets are multileveled, the royal palace being
superimposed on a street below. Lighting serves not only to separate different playing areas but also, when necessary, to fuse them, thus increasing or decreasing tension. The setting is in Alexandria; the time, 58–55
B.C.E. Ptolemy XI (Auletes), the illegitimate son of Ptolemy VIII of the
Macedonian dynasty, is the ruler of Egypt. Strabo, the Greek geogra-
pher, wrote of this monarch's reprehensible dissoluteness, his unjust and
violent rule, the corruption and vice he encouraged. Known also for his
fanatical outbursts, Ptolemy has come down in history as the debaser of
the very name of Pharaoh and the denigrator of the status of royalty.

It is night as the play opens. Bérénice, Ptolemy's daughter, is in her
palace, which opens onto a dimly lit balcony. She voices her concern
about her people's misery. She also ponders the fate of the seer
Nechoude, who is alluded to as the old beggar although he never begs;
he only sits in front of the palace walls. Armless and legless, he represents the chorus or the voice of the people. A prophetic figure, his function throughout the play is to disclose undercurrents and rumblings—
those unspoken and as yet unrealized feelings that inhabit the collective
psyche.

Bérénice cannot survive emotionally unless she hears the life-sustaining force of Nechoude's voice. Like a divine emanation, this patriarchal power feeds her and gives her strength to bear her spiritual imprisonment.

Political turmoil ensues between Egypt and Rome. The discontented Alexandrians force Ptolemy to abdicate in favor of Bérénice. Independent and strong, she marries the man she has always loved rather than her father's choice. Three years elapse. She and her husband have created a government in which integrity and honor prevail. The people are jubilant; slaves have been freed and peasants can raise their heads; all is well. Harmony is short-lived, however: Rome has declared war on Egypt. Ptolemy is in the vanguard of the invaders. Bérénice's sister, the famous Cleopatra, welcomes him as he enters the city with Rome's conquering army. Bérénice and her husband, together with the kind of world they represent, are soon incarcerated in contiguous thick-walled cells; they are bound in death for eternity.

Nombres is a two-act play based on the Old Testament's story of Deborah (Judges 4:4–9). Chedid's Deborah longs to be a harbinger of compassion and peace; she seeks, impossibly, to change destiny and cement her ideals of universal love.

In high contrast to Deborah is Barak, the military leader of the Hebrews: vigorous and dazzling in his gold armor, he represents military power and masculine energy. Yet he knows that unless Deborah is beside him in battle, his energy will remain unchanneled and his forces will not triumph. Deborah's poetic encounter with Barak is like the crossing of two cosmic principles.

The various characters weave a series of hieratic emblems, mesmerizing the viewer, forcing him or her into complicity. The oracular pronouncements, the rhythmic interchanges, and the contrapuntal voices are devices used to immerse audiences in the problems and dilemmas exposed in the play. The sets—a hilltop, a palm tree—are visually stark, reminiscent of those used by Beckett in *En attendant Godot*. Chedid's use of triple, vertically placed stages, with action shifting from one area to another, not only stresses the differences in the protagonists' points of view but also takes on the haunting effect of ritual.

Le Montreur is a play in two interludes, with musical accompaniment. Here whimsy is blended with banter, passionate tirades with sequences of dancing and mime in commedia dell'arte style. The Puppeteer, the prime mover, represents consciousness. Ageless and emotionless, his face exhibits the fixity and pallor of ancient masters of ceremonies, priests of old, divine seers and shapers of destiny. He is the precipitator of action, the encourager of divisiveness, the one who empowers the play to move on. This archetypal force, dressed in white, is seen onstage throughout the drama. His gestures are sober, his countenance imperturbable. Of unknown origin and seemingly removed from the happenings onstage, is he real or phantasm? The audience never quite knows. He is "eternal mystery. Eternal presence. Eternal question," Chedid wrote. It is his message that must be understood according to each person's nature and beliefs.

Although the Puppeteer attempts during the course of the play to reveal by gesture, song, and music the secret message that contains the seed and summation of the life experience, only silence, paradoxically, is heard. Exhausted from his travail, this universal force who dwells in each of the human and nonhuman puppets manipulated during the course of the play finally blows out the candles. Only darkness fills the stage.

Echec à la reine, like many legends and myths, tells the story of a Queen and her adoring clown, who in this manifestation is called Jok. Dressed in the usual extravagant manner—pointed booties, a multicolored costume adorned with small bells, a hat with donkey's ears and plumes—he tells the audience of his infinite love for she who mocks him always. But is he really what he purports to be? The Queen remains deaf to his entreaties as well as to his threats; she merely gestures him to silence. Finally, turning his way and doffing her crown and wig, she reveals herself to be old, wrinkled, and dried out. Jok, "moved, troubled by such fragility, offers her, in a tender gesture, his two hands for her to lean on."

In the following scenes the Queen grows increasingly younger, livelier, more attractive and enticing. She joins Jok in a game of knucklebones. The rhythms of song and dance accelerate, as do displacements onstage. With clever repartee and laughter, the *play plays out.* We learn of the Queen's love for her deceased husband and for her son, Slif, who, unwilling to rule, had left the land some seven years ago. Jok's corrosive jealousy of her past—"captive to a buried King; hostage to an absent son"—increases.

Because Jok wants the Queen to live fully and freely, he will free her from her burdensome commitments and rule in her stead. No sooner does he remove his false nose, donning the Queen's crown, scepter, and cape, than life suddenly flows into her: "my body budges, my soul moves."

A year passes. Jok is increasingly loved by his people, as the Queen had been during her reign. Suddenly everything changes. Slif has returned; he repudiates his mother, accusing her of plotting against him and of giving his kingdom away to Jok. Slif then assumes the kingship, wearing Jok's false nose and accessories, but falls into disfavor. The Queen learns that her son's life is in danger; rushing to help him, she is followed by the ever-vigilant Jok, who, accused by Slif as the usurper of the throne, is shot by the mob.

In Pirandellian tradition, relationships in *Echec à la reine* increase in ambiguity. Was Jok really the Queen's clown, or was he the King—or a usurper? Was the Queen his beloved, or was she his mother—or his beloved mother? Was the King really dead? Was his funeral a mascarade, or was it an entertainment—or a game? Why does Slif wear Jok's false nose and don his large hat and accessories? Who are these people who play each other's roles, replace each other, and love/hate each other? What are their realities? What is kingship, governance, legitimacy, nationality, and freedom?

Chedid's poetic theater, made up of significant and problematic situations, provides unique distillations of what she herself has felt most deeply. Language serves as her vehicle—as a passage, an opening, a way of dramatizing a double-edged world replete with premonitions, intuitions, and mystery.

Liliane Atlan: Cosmic Theater

Although rooted in the earthly and the actual, Liliane Atlan's theater is cosmic in dimension and hallucinatory in perception. Embedded in history—in the event, in the moment—her dramas are, to use Beckett's words, "time ridden." *Monsieur Fugue* (1967), *Les Messies* (1969; *The Messiahs*), *La Petite Voiture de flammes et de voix* (1971; *The Little Carriages of Flames and Voices*), *Un Opéra pour Térézin* (1989), and other works are dramatizations of a personal saga. Still, they transcend limitations, each work passing from an individual plane to a collective or mythical realm, singing the song of a soul—hers and ours.

Atlan freely acknowledges the seminal influences on her brand of theater. Artaud's Theater of Cruelty shares with hers a mystical affinity between viscerality and shock value. Like Jean Genet, Atlan confronts two worlds, "the glorification of the image and the Reflection," thereby bringing into focus a terrain as secure as quicksand and as predictable as volcanic eruptions. Her words, like Beckett's, are symbols, embodiments of feelings and sensations as well as of ideas. They are both monstrous and marvelous. They are bone-hard, because they have been pared down to essentials, and they act and react as discrete entities in rhythmically energetic patterns.

Atlan's plays are abrasive; they challenge humanity's beliefs and philsophies as well as its religions. Atlan offers no panaceas for humanity's plight, nor does she appeal to people's nonexistent humanity. Her theater unsettles, provokes, questions.

Monsieur Fugue is based on an unforgettable and excoriating event during World War II—one that could occur at any time and any place. Janosh Korczak, a teacher in the Warsaw ghetto, of his own will accompanied children to the gas chamber in an attempt to ease their final agony.

Monsieur Fugue takes place after the complete destruction of a ghetto. Fires have been burning for a whole week; even rats have vanished; and the people who have attempted to escape the labor camps by fleeing into the forest or hiding in sewers have been caught and sent to Rot-Burg for extermination. Children are forced into a truck by Nazi soldiers; Grol, as the teacher is called in the play, journeys with them to the Valley of the Bones through a thick mist that covers the entire acting space. Grol helps the children to give free play to their creative imaginations: the scene shifts to the back of the truck, to the richest fantasy worlds, where the young ones live out dreams of their entire life, from childhood to old age, despite the fact that they know adolescence and adulthood only through their parents. Enacting onstage what they heard before they were captured, they laugh, joke, and weep. So caught up are they in their game that they no longer distinguish reality from fantasy—except at the end of the journey, when they play out real tragedy and extraordinary heroism as they accept their harrowing fate.

Atlan's words abrade and scorch, yet they overflow with love. Her sensitivity stirs heart and mind, even while also opening audiences up to a sacred sphere in the life experience—the timeless and spaceless domain of subliminal reality.

Les Messies is a theatrical venture of cosmic proportions. It oversteps the boundaries of empirical reality and enters an inexhaustible sphere. The play's action "is lost in the immensity of the cosmos," writes Atlan. Ideally, the stage area should embrace the entire theater and "be fashioned in such a way as to give the impression of being performed within a type of celestial vault." Galaxies and spheres—as if suspended in space—appear before the viewer. The spectators' frame of reference is expanded, plunging them into pleromatic domains—in a new timeless and spaceless realm. Disoriented, unnerved, they experience a vertigo of being.

The play opens on a day in the lives of seven Messiahs lost in the immensities of the cosmos. It is night. They are reciting their liturgy. Tired, because they have done virtually nothing for long stretches of time, they hope and pray for some kind of cataclysmic event—tornado, earthquake, war—anything that would require them to act and make them feel useful, if only to save humanity.

The Messiahs featured in Atlan's play are not stately and awesome or gentle and kind figures as adumbrated in religious literature, music, and art. Rather, they are irreverent and shock-provoking yet pathetic creatures: they are spectacular in the sterility and impotence of their comportment and the ossification of their thoughts. Some have literally developed gangrene. Rather than instigators or creative forces, they are envoys, missionaries, ready to impose their vacuous ideas on others. The banal panaceas offered humanity by these Messiahs in myths and legends throughout history, and enacted during the course of the play, have not succeeded in elevating humanity. Instead, they are designed to keep people in a state of servitude, by spreading the notion that a cure for humanity's ills will come from the outside—when it can only emerge from within.

La Petite Voiture de flammes et de voix also probes and irritates in a poetic way. It focuses on the trauma of a severed human being (Louli-Louise), two aspects of the same person portrayed by two actresses. A prey to inner chaos, Louli-Louise knows bouts of madness in her attempt to find a way back to life—to feel that link she had once known with the sacred, when love and warmth had been hers.

La Petite Voiture is both modern and ancient in that the latest theatrical techniques are used to externalize and reinforce the pain felt by Louli-Louise, while her attempt to heal her fragmented and abraded being is expressed in images found in the tracts of the Merkabah mystics (sixth century B.C.E.), an esoteric sect that focused its doctrine on Ezekiel's vision of the throne-chariot.

Louli-Louise's paths, divided into seven sections (there were seven heavens for the Merkabah mystics), lead onlookers into a world reminiscent of the terrifying visions of Blake, Breughel, and Ensor. As Atlan's protagonist journeys along the first path, a blaze of white lights inundates the stage. The gestures of Louli, a nurse, pushing Louise in a carriage, are mechanical and ritualistic. Here both women have identical wax faces; only Louli's red hands distinguish her from the other. During the course of the play they change both physically and emotionally, as they traverse the seven paths and the seven stages of Creation in

ritualistic manner, arousing in themselves feelings of nostalgia, despondency, pain, and violence of titanic poetic power.
Un Opéra pour Térézin is not only theatrically innovative but monumental in its scope and depth. (Terezin, a World War II concentration camp in Bohemia, was used by the Nazis as a center to gather victims from all over Europe, prior to sending them to Auschwitz for incineration. Five percent of the people brought to the camp survived; 0.62 percent of them were children.)

Un Opera tells the story of European musicians, painters, and writers imprisoned in Terezin. Although Atlan knew of no artistic form suitable to tell the story of their extermination, she declared, "I could not *not* write it." She decided to use as the basis for her drama the Haggadah (a narration of the Jews' exodus from Egypt, celebrated yearly in the Passover dinner), which relates the mythic birth of the Hebrew people. Rather than narrating the founding of a people, however, she tells of their extermination. In so doing she was able to make the past become present and live anew. The strength and power to resist and then face extermination came to the protagonists through their art—and Atlan's art—via the ritual of theater.

Atlan's synopsis of *Un Opéra* reads as follows:

> Only the outlines of two bodies embossed in concrete and the story of the musicians of Terezin remain of a whole population. Although these musicians imprisoned in the ghetto of Therezienstadt were famished, they played their quartets, operas, and Verdi's *Requiem* virtually without instruments. Because of the deportations, the choruses had to be continuously reconstituted—until finally, all were sent to their death, each singing the *Requiem* for him- or herself.
>
> Yearly did their descendants relive their story by celebrating "The Rite of the Opera." They celebrated it in their homes, on the same night, in different parts of the world, connected to each other, as if space no longer separated them. From so many dispersed families, yet able to see each other, to hear each other, to speak with each other, from the multitude of these voices each intoning the same story, in keeping with his or her own rhythms and carried by one to the other, was born an unforeseeable—uncertain—chant, a kind of "Song of Songs."

Un Opéra, perhaps one of the most moving and harrowing testimonies of humanity's criminality, has bypassed empirical reality. The individual participates in a collective act. Atlan describes the ritual for *Un Opéra:*

The ceremony celebrated by families in their homes begins at sundown. Each person knows that the same rite is being celebrated at the same time by other families, in other places, in other languages.

We [the performers] become these musicians at Terezin in the process of composing an Opera for Terezin, despite the fact that the libretto has disappeared.

We become these musicians who went to their death singing the Requiem for themselves.

We become these musicians who saw their brothers die, and are recounting these moments, including names, numbers, statistics.

We infuse these artists—now vanished in smoke throughout the earth—with our breath, once a year, during an entire night, we let truth cry out.

Because we are unable to endow those who have vanished in smoke with new life, we bend over their drawings together—their only remains—drawings found after the war in cracks in the wall where the artists had left them.

Because we are living their story together, we feel the need to see and speak with each other as if space did not separate us.

The interactive image, having become the handmaid of speech, impacts on beings and events, which in time becomes legend.

Un Opéra is the first example of Atlan's new brand of theater, which she calls *La rencontre en Etoile* (*recontre* means "encounter"; *étoile*, "star," the latter indicating the fiberoptic system that makes interactive communication possible). This technique implies the shattering of all traditional theatrical subdivisions, categories, structures, methods, tones, and styles. To decompose or deconstruct, in order to recompose and restructure in a new frame of vision, enabled Atlan to penetrate beyond the visible world and thus reach into the very fabric of C(c)reation. To this end, electronic images were projected on video screens directly and instantaneously in different parts of the theater—and in other theaters in various areas of the globe where the same ritual was being enacted—thus abolishing space and linear time. People in one part of the globe could hear, speak to, and see others in distant lands, inviting dramatic events to be lived out on both physical and imagistic levels. By fusing the disparate, the past, present, and future were lived in an eternal present in the numinous Passover event in *Un Opéra*.

Atlan's plays, like fulgurating hymns or oratorios, reveal a polyphonic writing style in which multiple voices rejoin each other in order to reach what Kabbalists call the Center—the point of Origin, the Beginning.

Chapter Eight

A Theater of Concatenation, Fragmentation, and Mythical Signification: Michel Vinaver

Although the author of such novels as *Lautame* (1950) and *L'Objecteur* (1951), Michel Vinaver (b. 1927) was drawn to writing plays. When, in the 1960s and 1970s, the anti-textual movement dominated theater, he chose to base his stage pieces on solid texts. "I do not write for directors," he said.[1]

Because Vinaver's writings disseminate disorder and perplexity, as well as bring universal problems into focus, we may allude to his theater as one of concatenation, fragmentation, and mythical signification. In keeping with Artaud's dicta, Vinaver seeks to disrupt the status quo and stimulate the emergence of new values and fresh ideas. Rooted in the world of contingencies, his dramas are also, paradoxically, detached from it, bathing in the transpersonal or mythical sphere.

As a dramatist, Vinaver returns to the ancients' use of myth in theater. He seeks to have his audiences experience stage happenings as catharsis, or explosively, so that chaos will be injected into their hearts and psyches. Such inner turbulence will open them up to a new and pertinent understanding of, and reaction to, the myth in question, while also relating it to contemporary times. He hopes to deflate and disrupt rigid concepts, banish exclusionism, and renew thought and feeling patterns. Fresh insights enrich both artist and spectator: both can opt for a fluid, ever-changing, and cohesive yet differentiated outlook on life.

As an interdisciplinary "tool," theater allows Vinaver to employ—to exploit—language as a relational force; speech, for its vocal, tonal, rhythmic, and pictorial elements. Because his plays are mythic in depth, they reveal to the discerning a sphere that exists beyond the textual and intertextual stage reality: "Writing is my way of digging in search of meaning. Each play is a site to be excavated. But I am not searching for ONE meaning (to the world, to life, etc.). I am trying to connect things, with the hope that such work will give birth to small bits of meaning—

and so forth, in a discontinuous and plural manner."[2] Rather than focus on a story line, he chooses to "weave contrapuntal motifs, the general movement being that of a spiral making its way through a structure of 'theme and variations.'"[3]

Because phonemes trigger gestures as well as rhythms, sounds, and images, they give impetus to the creation of connecting principles: sets (a world of objects), accessories, lighting, sound effects, and their coordinates. As Pierre Boulez wrote, "Gesture, like the object, roots the text in a visible reality. When I speak of the object, I am not referring only to the accessory manipulated by the actor, to the smaller object, but to the larger one as well; to sets which define space and movements, coordinates and encounters; to sets which also act and also seem to acquire an autonomous life. Place and object, thanks to these, the text is invested with immediacy of meaning exceeding the singular event."[4]

The different elements in stage life, in keeping with Boulez's statement, are lived both autonomously and tangentially to each other, singly and as a unit. Such linkage or "interlacings," when referring to Vinaver's most "musicalizing play," *La Demande d'emploi* (*Request for Employment*), give rise to a whole world of emerging and vanishing tactile and visual sensations and ideas that are conflictual in their immediacy and harmonious in their cyclical expanse (*Ecrits*, 308).

Space also plays an important role in Vinaver's theater. Georges Braque's thoughts on the subject mirror those of the dramatist:

> There are people who say: "What does your painting represent? . . . What? . . . There is an apple, of course, there is . . . I don't know . . . Ah! a plate; next to. . . ." These people seem to totally ignore the fact that what lies in BETWEEN the apple and the plate is also painted. And, indeed, it seems to me as difficult to paint what lies in between the two as the things themselves. This "in between the two" appears to me as significant as what they call the "object." The point being that the relationship of these objects to each other and [that of] the object to the "in between the two" constitutes the subject.[5]

Distances onstage between one object and another act as catalysts for Vinaver, as they had for Braque. An open space separating the spectator from the proscenium must also be considered as participating in the creation of a whole network of intervals, of unrelated sequences that conjure a sense of mystery in the eye of the beholder as well as in his or her instinctual realm. So powerfully does interspace figure in Vinaver's optic that by diminishing the importance of characters and events in his theater a problematic, changing, and intangible realm comes to the forefront.

For Vinaver, then, theater is based on interweavings or interlacings of a complex of entities—sounds, silences, words, rhythms, steps, objects, spaces—from which a "secret" domain emerges: that of daily, superficially banal, existence. Although the stage is empty or "amorphous" at first, once humans, tonalities, objects, and events people it, ambiguities are activated for spectators to disentangle as best they can.

Vinaver's theater becomes a dialogue between actor, director, scenic designer, sound technician, and audience—on a personal and subjective level, as well as on an impersonal and objective one. All-encompassing, his language depends on the intent and the mood Vinaver seeks to create. His verbal/vocal range is vast: intense, energetic, pliable, questioning, lyrical, meditative, hostile, exclusionary, embracing, disruptive, impotent, domineering, poetic, prosaic. Verbal tapestries scan, span, and scale the many forms of his thought and emotion: in contrapuntal sequences, they serve as detours or contours to open up his characters to visionary experiences or to limit them to an opaque approach to life.

Understandably does Vinaver feel an affinity with Chekhov, whose theater, in his opinion, best reflects Braque's emphasis on the vitality of the interspace "between the two" objects. So, too, does Brecht's concept of distancing, or *Verfremdung,* affect Vinaver: it invites spectators to experience stage happenings via a perpetual interaction between the visceral and the cerebral, between emotion and thought.

The concept of intertextuality also fascinates Vinaver. His admiration for some of the great writers of the past—including Euripides, Aristophanes, Rabelais, and Shakespeare—has inspired him to interweave elements of ancient fables and myths into modern and universal frames of reference. The remarkable structural elements of Aristophanes' theater—Combat, Agon, Counter-Offensive, Banquet, Marriage—are basic to Vinaver's approach to his own ("Auto-Interrogatoire," 47–57).

Vinaver's intertextual notions attracted him to the writings of the mythologist René Dumézil, particularly those dealing with the Scandinavian nature gods—the Ases and Vanes. Myth in general—Greek, Hebrew, Christian—enriched him and permitted him to experience a space/time continuum in which linearity and cyclicality, the finite and the infinite, the one and the many, the existential and the spiritual cohabited. That Vinaver both contrasts and fuses mythical elements with empirical reality adds to the willed complexity, ambiguity, and scope of his drama. The human relations in such plays as *Par-dessus bord*

(*Overboard*) or *Portrait d'une femme* emphasize the multiple worlds of business, politics, and law; differences among classes, groups, and families disappear only to resurface. Each sphere, be it the individual's or the collective's, touches on and becomes enmeshed in another. Questions arise perennially; their answers become increasingly difficult. By offering his viewers one sinkhole after another he encourages them to probe further: What is the meaning of reality, of identity and relationships, in a continuously altering world of mosaics?

Within the myth's limited/unlimited parameters, Vinaver's theater burgeons and explodes. Like other dramatists—Deutsch, Wenzel, Gatti—he fleshes out eternal themes such as war, aggression, murder, rape, theft, deception, exclusionism, but in a different manner. He alludes to these crucial subjects deftly, subtly, by fragmenting them—a technique that enables him to focus on small segments of a huge problem. That he frequently bases the premises of his plays on a reported fact or event does not prevent his commonplace heroes and heroines from rising to mythical spheres. His plays exist in an *eternal present,* divested of duration, each instant existing in and of itself. As in myth, his drama encompasses the theme in its variations.

Inner (Human) Linearity/Outer (Myth) Time/Space Continuum

In his first play, *Les Coréens* (1955), directed by Roger Planchon (1956), Vinaver focuses on the universal and eternal question of an occupation army and the choices offered a soldier in his new habitat. Although the story line is simple, the thoughts involved are of mythical import.

After bombardment and the apparent destruction of a Korean village, Corporal Belair, one of six French soldiers in the U.N. forces, becomes lost in a complex of seemingly endless rice paddies. Five dazed soldiers patrolling the area in search of their lost comrade not only fail to recognize each other but do not seem to even know what they are about. In contrast is Belair's very *real* situation. Because he is far from his native land, cut off from his unit and compatriots, he is overwhelmed by an increasing sense of exile. His solitude is compounded by the painful wound inflicted on him in his genital area. Feelings of loss, disorientation, and displacement intrude upon Belair.

An eight-year-old Korean girl happens by chance upon the wounded soldier; she takes him to her bombed-out village, where his wound is dissolved. Despite the dearth of food, he is fed the soup prepared by the community for their returning soldiers, who do not appear. The soup—the villagers' single defense against famine—plays both a nutritive and mythical role in the drama: representative of a communion of souls, it leads to transformation—a rebirth in both the villagers and the soldier—as new life emerges from the rubble of the war. The little girl asks Belair to join her side—that is, the Korean side. In essence she is asking him to identify with the enemy, to commit treason. Anxiety takes hold of Belair. Up to now passive, he becomes the recipient of an unpremeditated offer that triggers deep inner conflict and, perhaps, in the Sartrean sense, that special "nausea" that comes with commitment to a new life experience. The intense activity generated by the choice he is offered urges him, Vinaver writes, "to move toward a different unimaginable state." Unlike his compatriots, who live out their existences in "meaningless" and robotlike fashion, as attested to by their "anchorless language," mirroring their "projectless" attitudes toward life, Belair, the one suffering soldier, agonizes over the pros and cons of the choice he is compelled to make. After deciding to remain with the villagers until the end of the war, he, unlike the other military men, is, in the Sartrean sense, *the only one who is really alive.* Vinaver suggests that Les Coréens is "the story of a passage"—in mythical parlance, a *rite of passage* from an unconscious to a conscious state, or to "a new time" (Les Voisins, 11–12).

Roland Barthes called Les Coréens "objective" and not political theater. Because of Vinaver's "depoliticization of reality," he succeeded in ushering in "a new use of language" to French theater: a blending of tenderness and warmth with the tragic reality of a wartime situation. "Coexistence," writes Barthes, is "not to be understood in the restrictive international political sense, but in the general view, by recognizing the fact that the contemporary world offers an *immediately* structurable reality, in contradiction with the traditional dogma of Revolution and in its essentially eschatological sense of duration."[6]

Vinaver's heroes, as attested to in Les Coréens and his other plays, are not instigators but the recipients of external events that transcend them but nevertheless are deeply troubling to them. The resulting psychological confusion turns their relatively pat world topsy-turvy, inviting them to discover heretofore hidden values on which to build a new life for themselves. A certain degree of optimism, therefore, is present in what Vinaver terms the "initiatic process": an accidental happening (Belair's encounter with the little Korean girl) followed by a new course in life.

Iphigénie Hôtel (1959), directed by Antoine Vitez (1977), revolves around both a specific historical event and a mythical one: the former, the fall of the Fourth Republic on 13 May 1958 and the advent of the De Gaulle government; the latter, a symbolic reference to the House of Atreus. The locus of the play's action is Mycenae. French tourists are told by their guide that it would be worthwhile to make a slight detour to visit the ruins of the ancient palace where such legendary figures as Agamemnon, Clytemnestra, Aegisthus, Orestes, Electra, and Iphigenia had centuries ago.

Back at the hotel, the tourists are made privy to the takeover of the French government by De Gaulle. They receive the news through outdated telephones and telegraphs that are usually out of order; thus the events are not only falsified but contradictory. While a usurpation of power is occurring on the national scale, a parallel movement is being effected in the hotel by Alain, the valet. As the two spheres of interest are interwoven, feelings of exile and distress erode the pleasure the tourists had hoped to experience. Gradually, their interest begins to shift to mundane matters— the love relationships and power struggles in the hotel.

Unlike the ancient myth of Iphigenia, Vinaver's play is not tragic— and he often uses absurd and dry humor—but a troubling and disorienting atmosphere nevertheless reigns. Has time stood still? Are jealousies, connivings, power struggles, and love and hate as powerful today as they were in ancient eras? An interplay between macrocosm (France) and microcosm (hotel) invites comparisons between mundane matters preoccupying the collective and those obsessing contemporary tourists and hotel personnel. Each sphere of existence considers itself to be involved with nothing less than apocalyptic problems: be it in the retention of jobs, climbing the social and economic ladder, or entering into relationships. Vinaver builds up his powerfully rhythmic and syncopated dialogue via interchanges between thematics involving France/hotel and those focusing on Greece/House of Atreus. Emotions veer from terror to pleasure, from despondency to nostalgia for a country and a past that offered humanity, from a contemporary's vantage point, some hope in the future (*Ecrits*, 231–32).

Vinaver's intermingling of contemporary events occurring in France and in the hotel, identified with the House of Atreus, creates a dual time framework: linear and nonlinear. Such delimited and expanded frames invite audiences to perceive the course of history in terms of an individual's life span—diachronically. Although time, in a mythical context, is

Reversible, it does not imply in Vinaver's view a repetition, but rather a "stilralling of atoms. The wind aphal is key! It implies the onset of an unsolvable dialectical opposition and its perpetual projection into some further spanning or curving process of evolution or devolution.

Themes and Variations

Thirteen years elapsed between the writing of *Iphigénie Hôtel* and Vinaver's next publicly performed play. Whether because of discouragement and bitterness over the political situation in France or for financial reasons, Vinaver stopped writing for production. Or was he perhaps having doubts about his talents? Maybe the time was not ripe for his brand of theater. Had not textual theater been relegated to the background, while nontextual dramas—like the Living Theater's *Paradise Now* or Robert Wilson's *Deafman's Glance*—were in demand? Ronconi, Mnouchkine, happenings, and collective creations, along with Planchon's and Chéreau's revolutionary stagings of classics, were playing to filled houses. Vinaver was "passionately" interested in the new nontextual theater—but only as spectator. As an artist, he was committed to plays with a text. Vinaver the playwright was transformed into Vinaver the successful businessman. The frenetic, exciting, and frequently dramatic world of business melded with that of theater. He was ready to change course. In time he would return to the stage to reveal all that was revealable.

The revelations eventually arrived in the form of *Par-dessus bord* (1972), directed by Roger Planchon in 1973. The piece differed from Vinaver's previous plays. Not only did it run for eight hours, but the individuals involved in the drama were silhouettes and caricatures rather than flesh-and-blood beings. The protagonist was "inhuman"—a business enterprise.

The complexity of *Par-dessus bord*'s internal structure is made that much more evident by Vinaver's use of the *interspace* and by his decision to eliminate all punctuation except for the question mark. The lack of directions for stage sets and the frequent use of what may be alluded to as Sarrautean tropisms—gratuitous dialogues spoken without identifying the speaker/subject—leave spectators frequently in a quandary. The impersonality of the dialogue and the variety of the detached points of view enunciated, however, lend not only a choral effect to the interludes but invite home and workplace happenings to penetrate each other. For example, interrogations revolving around an individual's loyalty to the firm may also apply to family situations, as does employees' anger over the manner in which others overstep the limits of decency in their aggressiveness.

Remarking that the individual's daily activities in the workplace set off "the double helix of digestion and excretion," Vinaver's protagonist is a firm that manufactures toilet paper, the implication being that not only does the country's economic system function according to "digestion and excretion" but this same formula is also applicable to individuals' interrelationships (*Les Voisins*, 42).

The directors of the business enterprise in *Par-dessus bord* seek to transform their product—with, one might add, typical Jarryesque allusions to the anus—from hard to "soft strength" and their business techniques from refined practices to aggressive American marketing techniques. Owing to the rapidity of events and situations resulting from the firm's aggressive business practices, a new language is born. Speech patterns alter, reflecting a character's function as well as his/her social level: the stage resounds with office slang, suave selling lingo, academically conditioned phonemes, mechanically manipulative media style, the jargon of high finance. A slow divestiture of traditionally elegant vocabulary parallels a concomitant change of values.

The plot line is relatively simple: with the sudden demise of Dehaze, the firm's head, Olivier, his successor, is cast out. As in the case of many myths and legends, it is not the "good" Olivier but the "bad" brother, Benoît, who takes over the family firm. Passemar, Vinaver's double and the most interesting figure in the drama, is the spokesperson both for management and for the playwright he seeks to become. As he dramatizes the difficulties involved in running a firm, addressing commercial problems and business practices in a relatively objective manner, audiences begin to realize that the regulations governing trade practices apply equally to theater. Passemar, seemingly well educated, having gleaned his information from Monsieur Onde (René Dumézil), professor at the Collège de France, whose lectures he attended, paraphrases them at times, creating humorous contrapuntal blendings of myth and economics. Monsieur Onde intervenes now and then, and when predicting the future, he states, "After the disaster the earth will emerge from the sea beautiful and green and without seeds grain will grow there the sons of dead gods will return to the enclosure of the Ases [Scandinavian gods] all will speak in friendly tones of the past and of the future and the gold tables which had belonged to the Ases will again be found again on the lawn."[7]

Moments later, in the midst of inquiries and meetings with future buyers in which the many uses of toilet paper are emphasized, the anal humor becomes sidesplitting. Incredible fantasy figures then appear onstage: three masked dancers dressed as Vestal Virgins question some spectators on various subjects connected with toilet tissue. While Passemar peers at them, they begin surrounding him, insinuating their way into his fictional theatrical reality. He muses, then decides that because such interludes "interrupt the flow of the [play's] action," he will eliminate them (*Par-dessus bord*, 109).

Moments later, as Passemar again ponders his text, the masked dancers reappear, now dressed as Scandinavian gods. They base their choreographed mimed body movements on the myriad and inexplicable wars fomented by the deities. To increase the irony and hilarity of the seemingly incongruous happenings, by replicating mimetically the god-created wars, the dancers relate them to the firm's aggressive business practices.

Par-dessus bord is vertically structured: the highest and most nebulous category in the play alludes to a virtually divine sphere, a transcendent level: that of the collective business enterprise. Involving quasi-mystical international laws, the category is believed to be beyond human understanding—as is deity. Immediately below such abstract regions exist the firm's top-level executives; they function in the world of reality. Included in this group are the members of the ruling Dehaze family: company directors and those whose lives are devoted to the well-being of the establishment. The lower categories in this hierarchical structure include workers who are dependent on and associated with the business enterprise: Lubin, the firm's spokesperson, his daughter, and his son-in-law, the latter miraculously saved from slaughter in Auschwitz.

The mythic element, as was and will be implicit in Vinaver's theater in general, is strong in *Par-dessus bord*. Although its context is modern—it dramatizes a worldwide economic war—its thematics and variations, according to Vinaver, take on the epic qualities of the *Iliad*. Because the participants in this giant enterprise/play live on both a collective and personal level, they resemble Homer's heroes: they are not a prey to fear of death, of the past, or of the future. On the contrary, "a jubilation in the accomplishment of the present instant exists from peripeteia to peripeteia . . . every instant peaks and crests" (*Les Voisins*, 44).

Like a cubist canvas or sculpture, *Par-dessus bord* is open-ended. Marked by discontinuity, contradiction, and incoherence, it allows for a variety of interpretations. Any categorization of Vinaver's gigantic farce, which is leveled at society, business, theater, and the performing arts in general, is impossible. Thus we can only speculate on Vinaver's views regarding the comportment or ethics of individuals or groups.

So colossal and unwieldy was the text of *Par-dessus bord* that Planchon asked Vinaver for permission to rewrite it for the stage production. The author granted it, but regretted having done so. Planchon's tightening not only diminished the thrust of the author's satire and his complex system of interlocking thematics but also did away with the piece's epic and mythic dimension. Although Planchon successfully called into play a variety of stage techniques—including musical comedy—designed to enliven the stage happenings, Vinaver's innovative language techniques were lost in the exchange. Indeed, the whole polyphonic and explosive verbal structure, its textured patternings, even its "intelligibility" became problematic.[8]

Starkly different from the grandiosity of *Par-dessus bord* is the leanness of *La Demande d'emploi,* produced in 1973 with a *mise-en-espace* by J.-P. Dougnac. With a relatively small cast (four characters onstage at all times), this piece, which focuses on searching for a job, is understandably dear to the author, since he wrote it after having lost his own.

Regarding *La Demande d'emploi,* Vinaver noted, "It's the first play that I have written in which no one knows time-wise what is taking place. Time has been lost." Chronology is absent better to accentuate the willed confusion of rhythms, thematics, and dialogue. Because one character can talk to another in different time schemes, it is impossible to relate events and situations to each other in chronological sequences. Because of Vinaver's nonlinear procedures, each of the 30 tableaux, or staged "instants," proceeds in a "spiral movement." Each of the "instants" starts unexpectedly and concludes just as "abruptly," without anything really having happened (*Les Voisins,* 49).

Vinaver's dramatic composition, based on repetition—a "return to" as well as an advancement toward some unpredetermined experience—is comparable to a musical composition with its theme and variations. In Marguerite Duras's *Moderato Cantabile* sections of a Diabelli sonata were played over and over again, and Vinaver had in mind (although he did not actually use onstage) Beethoven's *Variations on a Theme of Diabelli.* Indeed, he called *La Demande d'emploi* his most "musicalizing" play, because its themes and variations were written into the very fabric of the dialogue (*Ecrits,* 308).

La Demande d'emploi introduces a recently unemployed 50-year-old sales director who is seeking a job. The other characters are his preserving wife, who finally obtains employment, his irresponsible 16-year-old daughter, a product of the 1968 leftist movement who, to her delight, has been impregnated by a black man; and an interviewer/inquisitor, a recruiting director for a large firm. Wife and daughter push the father figure out of the contest. Does he commit suicide? Or move on elsewhere? No one knows. Is the father weak? Passive? Are the women powerful *vagina dentata* types? Whatever the answer, clearly he has been emasculated, reduced to the status of a nonperson by his wife, who, having earned economic security by acquiring a job, no longer needs him, and by his daughter, who revels in sexual freedom.

The achronological sequences are deviations from the initial job-severance and job-seeking situations. The speakers, whose words seem unrelated to one another in terms of time, place, and context, deconstruct the story line or dramatic situation. Everything changes precipitously; nothing seems stable; all is continuously altering, diachronically, without apparent rhyme or reason. Vinaver's use of objective and subjective, distant and familiar language, veering from innocence to brutality in the contrapuntal interviewing technique, produces mood swings ranging from comedy to tragedy.

Some critics considered the play pessimistic. It is also remarkably innovative, albeit confusing. Vinaver discerns its ambiguity: both sad and comic, it is the "gap existing between what he [protagonist] expects of himself and the situation in which he finds himself. It seems to me to be a banana peel play." Since, for Vinaver, life offers no security, even the comedy in his play is bound to be distressing, despite the fact that it serves to relieve the progressively intense feelings conjured up by the play of the text. There are moments of "drolery, but this drolery is so deeply linked to the very disquietude that provokes laughter, that is also creates opposition" (*Les Voisins*, 51, 53).

Chamber Theater

Sensitive, touching, and deftly powerful, Vinaver's miniature dramas with their limited casts, grouped under the rubric of "Chamber Theater" (from chamber music), are small gems. Dialogue is interspersed with silences; banal situations are interlaced with harmonious or dissonant themes and variations thereof. Each of these chamber theater pieces reaches out, writes Vinaver, to "enormous, infinite, fascinating" domains that invite "unending exploration."[9] Structured around such simply subjects as love, the renewal of confidence, or increasing disgust and hatred, each drama in this category is memorable. The lightness of the vocabulary and the bantering in Vinaver's simple dialogue frequently reveal universal emotions.

Dissident, Il va sans dire (Dissident, It Goes without Saying), directed by Jacques Lassalle in 1978, features only two characters: a divorced mother, Hélène, and her 17-year-old son, Philippe. They live out their love-hate relationship in brief and fractured dialogue. Silence becomes overt in their attempts to avoid confrontation as Philippe tries to win psychological independence from his mother and she, although relenting, inadvertently tightens her apron strings.

Rejecting his father's social rank and prominence, Philippe has taken an assembly-line job with Renault. He tells his mother one day that a strike has been called, and that to show his solidarity with his fellow workers he must leave his employment. Neither the audience nor the mother have any way of knowing whether his statement is true or not. If false, could it be his way of expressing hostility toward his mother? In any case, confusion is injected into the scene when the mother later asks if he has gone to look for another job; his affirmative answer does not remove a nagging doubt implanted in the minds of mother and spectator. Yet she remains amiable. In time, however, she begins to wonder about his friends. They are not her son's type, she muses. She finds them rather offensive. Still repressing her reactions, she senses that something is brewing. What does she really know of her son's activities? No more than does the audience. Does she suspect that he has been trafficking in drugs? This to pay for his habit he has been stealing from pharmacies? That turns out to be the case, and he is caught. Prior to his arrest, Philippe returns to his mother for a final love duet—as if nothing had happened to mar their "harmonious" relationship. Will he be released on good behavior? Will the mother see him again? There is no way of knowing. Hope, nevertheless, is still a factor.

The subtle power play in Vinaver's tightly textured drama creates fascinating contrapuntal rhythmic effects, like the fluctuations in a musical composition. The interlacing voices of mother and son not only make for the play's dense and prismatic qualities but also for its ambiguities. As in the Oedipus myth, the intense love bond that mother and son enjoy yet try to break on a conscious level is underscored by the seeming openness of their conversations. What is visible is frequently a smoke screen— Vinaver's attempt to divert attention from a morbid and miasmic inner personality. Called into question, then, is the truth of what is uttered. Although banalities are the mediants via which everything may be said, the "non said," the world of silence, as previously mentioned, is equally vocal, disclosing an unrealized or unconscious dimension, like Cézanne's "blank spaces": although "untouched," they are nevertheless present and implicit (*Les Voisins*, 57).

Nina, c'est autre chose (1976; *Nina, That's Another Thing*), directed by Jacques Lassalle in 1978, focuses on a love triangle. Breaks in the story line have no apparent ties to the topic previously discussed by the characters. Vinaver's technique of mirroring a madly independent, crazily cut-up empirical world in his symbolically vague dialogue adds ambiguity and mystification to the work.

Charles, a 40-year-old hairdresser, invites his lover, a young shampooist, Nina, to move into the apartment he shares with his 42-year-old brother, Sebastien. His home has become a "sanctuary" devoted to honoring his deceased mother: he unceasingly thinks and talks about his dearly departed. Daily he cooks her favorite foods, thereby renewing her presence in the home. Once Nina enters the closed precinct, she disrupts the all-powerful matriarchal presence by enticing Sebastien to be her lover. Now she services both men.

Conversations revolve around a multitude of topics: jobs, clients, foreign accents, race, and so on. What remains unforgettable in this context is the unusual manner in which the protagonists address each other, as if they were talking at cross purposes: pauses between statements, interruptions, and discontinuity create a solipsistic climate. The protagonists live in their own worlds and seem oblivious to what the others are saying. Their dialogues—or, better still, monologues to which only they are privy—create crazy-quilt impressions and verbal patterns that add to the work's ambiguity and ribald humor. The omission of punctuation produces run-on sentences, adding further to the confusion in thought patterns and thus increasing the farcical elements implicit to the situation.

Nina finally leaves the brothers because she is unwilling to spend the rest of her days playing mother to two *old* adolescents. Prior to her departure, however, she succeeds in opening them up to the joys of the empirical world. She was the catalytic factor that brought renewal into a world where death had once reigned. As for Nina, she will try to realize her desires with a man closer to her age. Will she succeed? If so, for how long?

Les Travaux et les jours (1977; *Works and Days*), directed by Alain Françon in 1979, was inspired by the Hesiod work of the same name. It consists of moral maxims and precepts about farming, which he dedicated to his wastrel brother. Unlike *Par-dessus board,* where many facets of a business enterprise were dramatized, only after-sale problems are focused on in *Les Travaux et les jours*. Moreover, instead of toilet paper, in Vinaver's new theater piece the old-fashioned family business concentrates on coffee grinders. Nor is the cast unwieldy, limited as it is to five characters: three receptionists who answer phone calls from irate customers seeking repairs for their grinders; a worker, Guillermo, who repairs urgent or simple malfunctionings on the spot; and, Jaudouard, the manager.

The uniqueness of *Les Travaux* lies in the daily conversations of the receptionists, who, between calls from the firm's customers—or sometimes during them, when they interrupt the conversation to speak their minds to their co-workers—interweave their personal problems, involving love ties and family situations, into their job-related activities. Thus are spectators made privy to an enterprise in which up-to-date technical facilities supposedly were to have improved communication with customers as well as between the employees. Nothing of the kind occurs.

The suspenseful and nonsuspenseful trite little stories peppering Vinaver's dialogue are so atomized as to give the impression of tense and conflicting situations among the personnel and the clients. At cross-purposes or in bits and pieces, the conversations resemble multiple crossword puzzles, webs of thoughts and disclosures, locked in equivocacy, inconsistency, and uncertainty. Important as well is the fact that the fractured—or "explosive"—dialogue discloses various levels of reality: a bewildering subliminal world, via a Vinaverian kind of stream of consciousness. It is an indistinct and truncated world in which each character talks at cross-purposes or turns a seemingly deaf ear to the interlocutor. The receptionists are certainly involved in their jobs and in the lives of their co-workers, but they live in frustrating and disjointed worlds. While the three women vie for the attention of the two men, it becomes evident as well that their dependency on home and workplace, rather than bringing them fulfillment, further damages their atomized psyches.

As is the case in other Vinaver plays, dialogue produces rhythmic and tonal effects that heighten interest in the action, even while increasing their unintelligibility. The protagonists' multifunctional vocabulary creates a whole range of visceral and affective movements: enmeshed in one another, they become inseparable and usher in a floating world made up of intangibles and abstractions. The operators' half-sentences, questions, and reactions create a chaos of desire, love, jealousy, adultery, integrity, or the lack of these in business practices or family matters. Some of the protagonists give the impression of wanting to break out of their constricting bureaucratic world by seeking to disregard the firm's laws and demands, others simply embed themselves still further in the dream they keep constructing and reconstructing for themselves. Because audiences hear only the conversations of the secretaries and not those of the customers, they find themselves continuously reassessing what they believe to be the truth of the situation. Impressions may be false because customers frequently call not merely to have their coffee grinders serviced, but to talk to a human being to alleviate their solitude.

What actually is happening during the medley of uncertain and conflicting situations? We learn eventually that the firm is not doing well, that it has been sold, that the after-sale department has been abolished, that two of the operators have been fired, and that the youngest has been retained only because she ogles her boss in a certain way. The 64 personal computers that have been installed will print out letters to the customers in answer to their queries. Thus has the human element been replaced by the machine and the notion of security destabilized.

A la renverse (1980; *It Bowls You Over*), directed by Jacques Lassalle in 1980, is one of Vinaver's most explosive pieces. Again he turns to the problems of a business enterprise: a suntan-lotion manufacturer's business community is threatened because the media insists that exposure to sun causes skin cancer. Television screens highlight the heroic but futile battle with skin cancer of the Princess Bourbon-Beaugency, who had once loved to sit in the sun, faithfully using cream blockers to protect her from lethal rays. The princess's role is to persuade her audience not to follow her example. The company's promotional policy, which tries to refute the media's negative impact on its business, is unsuccessful.

Confusion over the message Vinaver was trying to convey earned the play poor reviews. Was it a metaphor prognosticating the future decline of capitalism? Or because it showed that the number of television viewers was increasing, was he implying that television was killing theater? Critics also noted that too many machines cluttered the stage, adding confusion and detracting from the human element.

Les Voisins (1984; *The Neighbors*), directed by Alain Françon in 1986, is rich in psychology, mythological allusions, and linguistic interplay between its four characters. Like Musset or Sarraute, Vinaver probes the human psyche unsparingly yet with finesse and sensitivity.

Les Voisins focuses on two widowers, Blason and Laheu, who occupy identical adjoining houses but share a balcony. The real goal of the play, reminiscent of the myths of old, is to attempt to probe the meaning of *friendship* under difficult circumstances. Veneers, masks, barriers, and denial are slowly shorn until human nature is visible in the raw. Whatever superior feelings the protagonists might have enjoyed at the outset of the play, their baser natures in time emerge.

Blason, who works for an insurance company, has a working daughter, Alice. His neighbor Laheu, service chief in the Universal Biscuit Company, has a working son, Ulysses. The two children are in love. Allusion is made early in the play to Elisa, Ulysses's beloved dog, whom the young people have just buried. Although dead, this animal plays an increasingly important role in mirroring the ups and downs of their relationship. At times Alice conveys her feelings of love and admiration by remarking that Ulysses is "handsome like a dog." At other times she is hurt because Ulysses has shown greater affection for his canine than for her, and she asks him to fondle her as he used to fondle the animal. Nor does Alice fail to commemorate the anniversary of Elisa's death with a fine meal. She expresses her true feelings for the dearly departed canine, however, by serving cold chicken—her relationship with Ulysses also having iced up.

Laheu is a spendthrift; Blason, a perennial miser. Despite the fact that he buries his gold under his terrace, Blason is markedly different from his forerunners—Molière's or Balzac's miser—because of the lightness of his dialogue. When his gold is stolen, his suspicions fall on Laheu, the only one who knew where the gold was hidden. The former good relationship between the two widowers founders. The dialogue, now studded with subtle recriminations and mood swings, is pregnant with repressed anger. Then, refusing to take the blame for a theft he did not commit, Laheu viciously refutes his attacker. So destructive and unpleasant do the personalities of the neighbors become that both men lose their jobs.

The crime, the audience learns, was premeditated on Blason's part, planned by him and Daphné—a character audiences never see: Blason's "sordid" woman friend, according to Leheu. Or was it? Like Genet, Vinaver accentuates the mystery revolving around this fascinating person, who moves incomprehensibly throughout the piece like a goddess, affecting the lives of the protagonists. The widowers begin to play despicable tricks on each other; each tempts the other into confessing.

Blame, however, is not limited to these two. The field expands as Blason accuses the naïve Ulysses of theft and asserts that it was he who told Daphné about the hidden treasure. Charge upon charge is leveled at young and old until the police discover that Daphné, along with an unnamed partner, was the culprit. A question remains unanswered. Could the adolescent Ulysses have entered into complicity with Daphné? Or might it be that he had such a profound distaste, at least unconsciously, for what gold symbolized that he got rid of it? A young man whose tastes were simple, whose manner was forthright, might have wanted his Alice to approach life and people as he did—simply.

Food plays an important role in this and such other Vinaver plays as *Les Coréens,* implying a variety of notions. It may symbolize the agape, where food is shared in communion and in joy; or it may be identified with the (eating, devouring) power principle; or it may be seen as a status symbol. Each of the three meals served in *Les Voisins* mirrors an interplay of human relationships. The first dinner takes place when friendship, experienced on the highest of levels, has not yet been tested. The luxurious menu prepared by Blason includes the finest of caviars and champagnes, served on beautiful Sèvres china and in equally fine crystal goblets. (Although ostentatious, Blason is no spendthrift. His miserliness is disclosed by the small portions each of the guests is given.) The second meal, offered after the theft of Blason's gold, is less plentiful. The third and final repast is served not inside the home, but on the terrace. Cold chicken, Elisa's favorite food, is offered. The relationship of the two men has grown virtually untenable by this time, with Blason suspecting Laheu of having stolen his gold. The cold chicken symbolizes the frozen relationship between the former friends.

Seemingly, all turns out well. Together the fathers decide to go into the secondhand furniture business. By chance they discover a sizable bar of gold in a secret compartment of an antique piece of furniture they have just purchased. Should they keep it or return it to the old lady from whom they bought the piece? Legally they have the right to keep the gold ingot, but Blason decides to return it to its owner, who resides in a rest home.

As for the children, rather than acquire the fancy restaurant they dreamed of at the outset of the play, they open a small fast-food stand hawking French fried potatoes and sausage. Their down-to-earth attitude is their way of coping with reality. Although far from elegant, their stand will feed them and, if need be, their fathers. Ulysses, learning about the reappearance of cursed gold, is so horrified that he stabs himself. He fails, however, to kill himself. As the curtains ring down, audiences see Alice carrying the bloodied Ulysses on her shoulder. A dog barks—the new one they have just adopted. Will history repeat itself? In what manner? The play leaves this and other questions unanswered.

What about an obsessive interest in gold or money? What is the meaning of true friendship? Societies are invited, Vinaver implies, to work out their own answers and differences on both a personal and collective scale—a necessity for survival in the world of the twentieth century. More and more do we find Vinaver's protagonists clutching at straws in order to define themselves in an increasingly disparate and dehumanized world. Questions of ethics—particularly in connection with the judicial system—are examined in *Portrait d'une femme* (1984; *Portrait of a Woman*) and *L'Emission de télévision* (1988; *Television Broadcast*).

Portrait d'une femme, based on a murder case reported in *Le Monde* in 1952, was achronologically recounted by Vinaver in his 1986 reading. The events that provoked Sophie Auzanneau, accused of having killed her former lover, conclude with her failed suicide attempt. Sophie's trial is a mythical court proceeding, since it has neither beginning nor end but pursues its course through a "spiraling" eternity. Interwoven into Vinaver's "splintered" dialogue are problems of identity and of judicial procedure and integrity. The play is seen without intermission in order to increase the level of concentration.

Because the sets were considered important in creating a sense of movement and fragmentation throughout the work, a stagehand remained on the proscenium at all times. Two distinct types of furniture were used: the "monochrome, undifferentiated, expressionless, interchangeable" objects such as tables, beds, chairs, and doors, identified with their functions, and the "hyperrealistic" pieces used during the court sequences to create an ambiguous atmosphere. Although the human element—guards, jury, photographers, journalists, audience—never left the stage, "their configurations [were] forever modified, giving the impression of perpetual movement."[10]

Vinaver's focus on the judicial proceedings was intended not only to involve audiences but also to underscore the "ordinariness" of such a crime. Anyone—even people in the audience—could have committed the same act with sufficient provocation. What factors had been instrumental in compelling Sophie to murder? Vinaver dramatizes Sophie's 1953 trial retrospectively: family, landlady, teachers, friends, and lovers are called on to testify in frequently unrelated sequences. Their multiple interpretations of events at different junctures in Sophie's life and in a variety of places—a café in Lille, the outskirts of Dunkirk, a brasserie in Paris—serve to alter continuously the spectators' impression of her. It is impossible to glean a firm understanding of the inner workings of Sophie's altering personality, forever in the process of evolution or devolution.

Certainly a satire of the judicial process is implicit in the clever yet abstruse mélange of repartees The acceleration and slackening of momentum in the questioning process and the vocal highs and lows of the dialogue add to the play's suspense. Vinaver compares the multiple views, variations, and vocalizations to the themes and orchestrations of a musical composition.

Sophie's reactions to World War II, to the behavior of the Germans, to her brother's death in a submarine during the hostilities, to another brother's demise a few months later in a plane crash, are all detailed by the judges and lawyers whose trade is to outwit each other. What emerges from the various testimonies, confessions, and arguments is pathos: Sophie's failure to realize a great love, leaving her unfulfilled, unloved. These are the major factors, according to the consensus, motivating her murderous act.

Psychologically, Sophie may be alluded to as a *medium* woman: a composite of others' attempts to impose their views and their ways on her, thereby divesting her of whatever identity she might have had. Who is she? A passive recipient of the personalities making up her entourage, her *one act* serves to transform her into a rebellious individual struggling against crushing feelings of inadequacy. Is her act a reaction to a male-dominated society? Is she merely—in Sartrian or Pirandellian terms—the product of what others believe her to be?

Although a recorded voice informs the audience that Sophie was sentenced to hard labor for the rest of her life, no one ever knows what provoked Sophie's murderous gesture. Save for pointing to the inadequacies of the legal system, the author is in no way judgmental. What he offers his viewers is an incomplete image of segments of reality, one sequence on a par with the next, but without cause or effect. Vinaver seeks neither cohesion nor any kind of rational imprint in his play. The stage happenings are merely projections of discontinuous facets within the personality of a being or beings.

L'Emission de télévision, directed by Jacques Lassalle (1990), is considered one of Vinaver's most *Molièresque* works. It presents a triple inquiry into the nature of truth. A judge, Phélypeaux, investigating a murder case in his office, is interviewing various witnesses. The stage happenings are expanded to include participation in the judicial process by the spectators in the office (and, by extension, the audience of the play), who are provoked into reacting to the fractured stage happenings as if they were actually witnessing the taking of depositions. The judge meanwhile has the witnesses' multiple and sometimes contradictory statements typed out and signed by them, asking each the rote question, "Do you recognize these to be your words?" Whether or not they agree, they are helpless to redress the perversion of truth. Humor, always a powerful instrument in Vinaver's constructs, is introduced by, among others, Estelle Belot, the court clerk. She believes that her dreams give her access to past and future, thus allowing her to recognize, without any doubt, the real criminal—to the judge's annoyance. A third factor is the television reporting of the case and the zeal with which two aggressive young women reporters accomplish their goal—with perhaps disastrous results. Confrontational, even brutal realities, as well as delicate and sensitive reactions, work on the mind and psyche of those involved in the progressively industrialized and impersonal world of television. How much of what the public sees on television is manipulated by the producer, the reporter, the actors, and advertisers?

Words, sentences, and sequences of phrases with or without a subject add to the impact and to the confusion of the hearers. Emotions range from compassion to rejection, love to hate, understanding to a lack thereof. Irony, satire, and humor are prevalent in the play's continuous discourse. As each character tries to create some kind of design or purpose out of the verbal cut-ups, he or she becomes increasingly enmeshed in a cause-and-effect puzzle that defies explanation.

Not only do Vinaver's texts intermingle drama with farce, tragedy with comedy, but his poetics, replete with alliterations, sonorities, unfinished clauses, unspoken feelings, and silences, are manipulated by him with fearsome exactitude, thereby creating a climate of uncertainty, confusion, and suspense. Underlying his dialogic techniques and mental gyrations is the mood of disquietude in those who know that fate, along with an increasingly powerful technocracy and bureaucracy, dictates our destiny.

Ironically, Vinaver warns his audiences and critics not to seek in his plays any kind of answer to existential problems or even to try to probe their depths. To do so would be to misinterpret his intent. Because his dialogue is straightforward, he claims, he asserts that he says what he means. His words, therefore, must be taken for what they are and in no way linked to what he repudiates: the critic-created "subtext" (*Les Voisins*, 58). There are therefore no endings, no conclusions to his dramas. Only the *incipit,* followed by active relationships, exists in a world in which spiraling uncertainties in personal and impersonal domains pursue their courses indefinitely.

Chapter Nine

"Head Plays": Valère Novarina

The stage pieces of Valère Novarina (b. 1942)—dramatist, novelist, essayist, painter, director—although highly corporeal, have been called "theater novels," "mental theater," or "head plays." They are initiatic journeys, religious rituals, trajectories into into language, instinct, and feeling. They do battle with such thematics as "chaos," "voice," "word," "language," "orality," and time." To categorize these works would be to limit their metaphysical, philosophical, and philological import.

Like Beckett's, Novarina's writings are highly cerebral, spanning dimensions during their forays into mind. Devoid of flesh and blood, Novarina's characters exist as Names, and the actors incarnating them are "soloists" who enter into contact with a text. Actors are dual: they *act,* and thus are aggressors, and they are also spectators, passive recipients of their own dramatic interpretations. They observe, feel, experience the *Name* in the tension of the "linguistic event."

Metaphysical anguish, although corrosive, is relieved at times by explosive breakthroughs into *ekstasis* that manifest themselves in the poetics of Novarina's psycholinguistic monologues. Word, for Novarina, is sign and symbol. Its reification of thought appears in his playful punning, rhyming, homonymy embossed with tragedy. Ludic sequences come to the fore when Novarina juggles neologisms, archaisms, foreign and invented words, slang, and patois. Assonances and alliterations, although seemingly unintelligible conglomerations of sounds and letters, are in fact tightly structured. Such devices are crucial for the author: they liberate him, momentarily at least, from the crushing burden of life.

Lettre aux acteurs

Novarina's *Lettre aux acteurs* (1989; *Letter to the Actors*), like Antonin Artaud's *The Theater and Its Double,* is metaphysical in dimension. Like Artaud, he focuses on the notion of *breath* as the source of creation.

"Breath kindles life, sets it afire in its own substance," Artaud wrote; it empowers the actor to bring forth a *being* (his double).[1] Although similar ideas are implicit in many religious texts, Artaud was one of the earliest Westerners to use "breath" as part of acting technique. In the Bible we read that God breathed "into his [Adam's] nostrils the breath of life and man became a living soul (Genesis 2: 7). Chantings and invocations by the Hindu *brahman* (reciter of prayer) follow complex breathing patterns, identifying "breath" with such deities as Vayu ("Wind" or "Air"). Thus breath is linked to a *universal principle* and is endowed with the power to evoke God.[2] Buddhists believe in the all-pervading Breath, the Essence of the Mind, the One—from which all life emerges and into which it again dissolves.

Breathing, for Novarina also, takes on spiritual as well as earthly dimensions. It does not imply merely a displacement of air, but a meticulously studied geography of the body/mind complex: "to have a true respiratory economy, to use all the air that you take in, to consume it all before breathing in again, to become breathless, till the constriction of the period's final asphyxiation, the sentence's period like the gut clenched after the race."[3]

In that breath penetrates the body via orifices, its rhythms, Novarina insists, must be carefully regulated by the actor's mental system and also his muscular system. Such discipline is possible, for, as Artaud had noted, the actor who *knows* his body *knows* the location of each emotion and is able to reach directly into the "skein of vibrations" to activate each in its own way.[4] Novarina suggests that since an actor's body is a repository for unknown powers, it is these entities that must be probed, exercised, and called forth when needed.

The auricular factor in theater is crucial for Novarina. "I write with my ears," he states, so that even a blind spectator can hear a text being "eaten." "What are they eating [onstage]?" he may ask. "They are eating themselves?" Linguistic cannibalism allows the Novarina actor to assimilate and absorb into himself the outer/innermost essence of the word. The dismemberment and eating of words, which the actor must indulge in to perfection, may be associated with the religious ceremonies of *sparagmos* (dismemberment) and *omophagia* (eating of the flesh), two rituals considered instrumental in preserving human life. To swallow or to chew the words or bodies of divinities, whether symbolically or physically, is to celebrate a sacramental meal: the host as body and the wine as blood (Matthew 26: 26). Acting, for Novarina, is just that—a sacramental meal.

Had not Jean Genet also alluded to theater as communion when he stated, in his *Homeward to The Maids*, that the Mass was theater at its highest perfection?

> Beneath the most familiar of appearances—a crust of bread—a god is devoured. I know nothing more theatrically effective than the elevation of the host . . . perhaps it is God himself or a simple white pellet that he holds at the tip of his four fingers—or that other moment in the Mass when the priest, having broken the host on the paten in order to show it to the faithful, puts it together again and eats it. The host crackles in the priest's mouth![5]

The actor, as dismemberer and eater, is an impersonal, aggressive force—an "Employee," as Novarina calls him, in need of nourishment in order to become a receptor of energetic pulsating rhythms. The disciplining of these will enable him to regulate his verbal discharges. Nor is the actor "an interpreter because the body is not an instrument." He is an entity filled with liquids, solids, muscles, nerves, organs, whose function is to *speak*. To do so, he must penetrate himself. His work does not entail the "composition of a character, but the decomposition of the person, the decomposition of the man who appears on the boards," one who wears a white "empty death mask."

As Employee, the actor is a "medium," with neither body, breath, nor words of his own; he is a being used by powers emanating from some place—a "manipulator" who disappears as he talks, an observer who watches himself die. Thus may it be said that "the theater is a rich dungheap." Nor is acting "representation"; it is "expenditure," and performance is "duration," an excoriation. "Kill, extenuate your first body to find the other one—another body, another respiration, another economy—which must act."

The actor is androgynous—a complex of opposites, as are the unmanifested creator gods of Judaism, Christianity, Hinduism, Buddhism. Upon choosing his form, he makes it come into being. Theater is manifestation. Acting is not merely a recital of texts. "The text," wrote Novarina, "is nothing but footprints on the ground left by a dancer who has disappeared."

What of the dramatist? The "avid" author hungers to see his play on the boards. Like the actor who "devours" his words, the author "devours" the actor with his eyes, ingesting and digesting energies that stir inner substances and topographies. Like the creator god Shiva, he, too, begins his dance within, activating, rhythmifying, and pulverizing the word.

Entrée dans le théâtre des oreilles
(1989; Entry into the Theater of the Ears)

The auricular aspect of Novarina's theater implies the hearing of primal undifferentiated matter by both author and actor. A descent into Self—a reservoir of cosmic forces—is required. Taoists believe such an inner storage space existed prior to the foundation of the world; ancient Egyptians alluded to it as an unlimited inner ocean from which the sun god Ra emerged; Judeo-Christians call it the *void* abiding prior to Creation.

Entrée dans le théâtre des oreilles (1989; *Entry into the Theater of the Ears*) demands a descent into the inner void, or penetration of one's underworld, paralleling to some extent the ancient Orphic death, dismemberment, and rebirth ritual. Psychologically, such a trajectory may be viewed as a descent into one's collective unconscious.

Each step in the Orphic transformatory process is lived out in accordance with cosmic flux. For the writer, this means an ascent/descent (mystic space is nondimensional) into paths leading to his undifferentiated sphere, or void. Within this uncreated, unformed space, the writer is all *ear,* as he listens intently to the soundings of extinct languages, words lost long ago after differentiation had set in (the Tower of Babel myth).[6] The writer hears remnants of an *original* language, or what Baudelaire called "confused" words, in his poem "Correspondances."

During cataclysmic instants in cyclical or mythical time, dichotomies vanish and the writer *knows* the *oneness* of word and thought. His ear hears the inaudible: "He hears his worldless language. He dances for what is not there. He dances in space that is not there. He sings mutely, in a language without words, through an immobile dance."[7]

Theater being an exchange, the actor and spectator exchange breath—never visibly, never representationally, but inwardly. Tension, anguish, pain, and ecstasy are experienced as breath is exhaled/inhaled, as words are mouthed and munched, each word battling the other for entry, for incorporation onto the written page or in the spoken line. What remains after such contention? A battlefield of dead phonemes awaiting resurrection. Because the creative act is violence, is a cruelty— "behind each word there is a crime." It is "a struggle of tongues in space." As the writer explains his foragings, his sentience dilates: "I descend into languages. I have invented nothing. I hear a litany of names. In all languages . . . I make them all speak" (*Entrée*, 77).

The writer relates the malaise and dizziness that took hold of him as he reached into the void—the land of the dead or unmanifested—when he began his initial struggle to revivify the dimensionless in spacelessness. Unwilling to circumvent obstacles, he fell into despair. He knows now that to gain is to lose: to destroy oneself means to concentrate one's energies on hearing that inner voice more deeply and thus "to let my head keep quiet, to let my mouth keep quiet, to let my hand speak, to redo the same thing a hundred six thousand times."

The writer confesses that his 304 pages of broken syntax were written by what might be called an automatic hand. His "incomprehensible" work, a "lesson in emptiness," enabled him to communicate with elements beyond the two known hemispheres of the brain, giving him access into other organic and inorganic domains.

The author knows that he is "made of words": "Burrow into deep matter until you find the void within. Descend, descend so deep that you reach an aerial hole, fall in levitation, rise to the aerial hole. Listen to the languages so that you hear the silence within" (*Entrée*, 80).

Vous qui habitez le temps

Novarina's works generally take many years to formulate. *Vous qui habitez le temps* (1989; *You Who Inhabit Time*) is an exception: he completed in less than one year five expository scenes and eight conclusionary ones, writing eight hours a day from July 1988 to April 1989. Significant as well was his decision to accept theatrical conventions: a cast of eight characters, but existing as Names only. Each Name manifests his or her own behavioral patterns, language, and manner of entering and exiting the stage space.[8]

The Dantesque journey dramatized in *Vous qui habitez le temps* can be viewed both as a descent into timeless spheres and as a linear sojourn into empirical domains. The action consists of sequential and interrelated paradoxes: contradictions whose contraries cannot be asserted. The Names, "enclosed" in "limitless" space, see and are seen by Redonesque eyes that penetrate the core of being. Pain *is* as Names circulate around "preceding seasons." They are "present" and know the future. Thought, flesh, and being rotate and disintegrate during the drama. Facets of existence cohabit with nonexistence, to be done and undone in keeping with the intensity of the verbal drama indulged in by the inhabiters of time.

The Names given to the substanceless characters in *Vous qui habitez le temps* are also antinomic: they are outer trappings of inner resonances that individualize as they deindividualize. As a Name is uttered or listened to inwardly, it reifies a place, time, or condition; it also animates what has never been. To "name" is to "call" into being, as happens when a tone is sung or a high-frequency sound wave is released in the atmosphere. Names intone, as in prayer and feats of magic; they actualize, as in fetishistic séances.

The opening voice in *Vous qui habitez le temps* is that of The Watchman (Le Veilleur), whose function is to watch over and guard people. He must also awaken the somnolent to the "silence" of the inaudible word heard in an invisible and unseen "inner theater."

As the play begins, the Watchman ascends to the top of the city (Paris) better to "see himself." Unlike Hugo's view from the heights of Notre Dame, or Balzac's Rastignac atop Montmartre, the Watchman's elevation suggests, as in the cases of Adam and Eve, Chronos, or Daedalus/Icarus, that great heights anticipate steep falls. As the Watchman calls out the hours nonconsecutively, linear time schemes are introduced, implying for the rationalist that his mind works as does a malfunctioning clock. The same is true of his verbal associations: between digits, objects (Renault, bicycle, truck, etc.), and abstractions, "the future prepares the past."

The Watchman realizes, paradoxically, that "more and more he is the only one to think as everyone does." As he speaks, rhythms alter, sounds dilate, time vacillates as fusion and diffusion pepper a text inhabited by phonemic time schemes somewhat reminiscent of Beckettian discourse: "waiting, today, formerly, never, every morning." (Numbers in the text are generally written out in full rather than printed as Arabic numerals.) Such a change increases tension and adds as well to the possible religious allusions in an ever-continuing round of integrating/disintegrating wholeness.

The Woman of Numbers (La Femme aux Chiffres) stands for both rational and logical order; she is also a sign conjuring up unknown factors. Recall that Pythagoras considered numbers the basis of reality: that is, awareness of reality was expressed via number. Each number, then, was not only significant in itself but corresponded as well to a whole series of visible and invisible entities in the universe.[9]

A mediatrix between the worlds of finite and infinite Ideas and sensations, the Woman of Numbers may be viewed as an accumulator of rational and nonrational knowledge. As such, she is capable of explaining hitherto incomprehensible levels of being to those who live in the world of three-dimensional time. As a bridge between the amorphous and the world of appearances, she invites the timed to be timeless: "to precede everything that follows."

The Parietal Children (inhabitants of the head) are not to be considered symbols of innocence, purity, or a return to an embryonic state. When they ask whether or not their bodies are theirs, they are talking in Pythagorean terms. Accordingly, reference is made to the horrific dismemberment and eating of the god Dionysus, and to Zeus' resurrection of him as Dionysus-Zagreus. The punishment for such a murderous deed (referred to as the Fall) was the unification of soul (mind) with body (matter). Only after death (if purification was achieved during the earthly sojourn), could the soul be liberated from entombment in successive reincarnations within the body.

Because the Parietal Children do not receive an answer that satisfies them, they peer inside their bodies, where blackness reigns, paralleling Plato's "Allegory of the Cave": the soul (light) is penetrating the darkened realm of body (matter). Like doctors, the Parietal Children examine every segment of audible speech within their bodies, going as far as to peer into their "tubes of reason," and their "tongue" (meaning also language) while listening to the nothingness of silence.

When another presence, the Child of Cinders, enters the stage space, he babbles what might be labeled baby talk. It might also be some preexistent tongue or blend of real and imagined words, utterances occurring frequently in ecstatic and somnambulistic states. The word *cinders* in the Child's name suggests suffering and renunciation for Jews and Christians; for alchemists, it is a state of purity that comes into being after all detritus has been burned off. Chuang-tze associates cinders with the heart of the wise person, following the extinguishing of all mental activity. In the Maya-Quichés' Popol-Vuh, twin heroes are transformed into cinders prior to their resurrection. Like Balzac's Louis Lambert, the Child of Cinders sees beyond the rational world into the very essence of languages and philosophy. He recognizes the tracings left by the history of the world in its timed timelessness.

The Watchman asks the Child of Cinders to look within him: to the hidden geological folds lying beneath his eyes and mouth. What is human history, he asks, if not "the story of disappearances"? Life is loss.

Secreted as well is the Name—Jean Veto—inscribed within the layerings in his eyes. "His real name must remain silent." That a name is not to be disclosed may refer to ancient Egyptian belief that a name envelops an individual's essential dimensions and if another person has knowledge of it that person is given power over him. Indeed, it was said that the Creation came about when Ra (Sun) uttered his sacred/secret name. Among animists, knowledge of a name is the equivalent of dominion over the being or the object to which the name refers. For the Hebrews, God's name which is unknown (and were it known is unpronounceable), is hidden within the letters YHWH (the Tetragrammaton). God's other names designate his divine attributes. Similar is the enumeration of the 99 attributes of God in Islam and the recitations of the Nembutsu in the Japanese temples.

The Watchman's palavers—revolving around love, friendship, names, noncommunication, misfortune, birth-death, and animism—have literary, philosophical, religious, mathematical, and linguistic referents. For example, after he asks the sun, "Whose light is not the real one, to course and enlighten the people of the night?," it rains, preluding the Flood. The multiple blacks and whites used throughout the text, counter-colors, imply polarities in the manifest world—dawn and dusk, drought and flood, life and death—and the in-between potentials, as attested to by the Watchman's "I thus hoped to finish prior to for once really seeing the end of things." Understandable, then, is the presence on stage of the Tomb of the World.

The many tropes enunciated during the course of the drama/anamnesis bombard listeners and readers, as do puns, neologisms, and contradictions, repetitions. Although sometimes heartrending, the witticisms and caricatural elements elicit laughter, as do Rabelais's giants who end each of their journeys with the mysterious word *Trink*. Similarly, the Novarinan toast is "To life and to all that follows! to my cirrhosis! to the victory of my thirst over other things!"

Verbal gyrations also succeed in destroying barriers between objects and species, as well as among the geological, vegetal, and human worlds. Novarina writes contradictory combinations, such as *aujourd'hier* ("today yesterday"); visual antitheses, such as "at night I suddenly looked into the preceding morning suddenly exceeded, in front of me, outside of the house. . . . I awaited staring outside the arrival of the interior present"; and borrowed homonyms, such as *mêmerie* (English, "memory"; French, *même* [same] and *rie,* in the subjunctive of the verb *rire* ["to laugh"]). Each entry adds to the richness of an ambiguous world.

Responding to the Watchman's request to look into him, the Child of Cinders's gaze is flayed as he looks into "another." Yet he retains his faith in God, although he will commit suicide in order to reveal the meaning of "serenity" to "humanity." Like Beckett's Child in *Waiting for Godot*, the Child of Cinders waits for his future in death, and his rebirth into past, which is also a future in the hopeless/hopeful round of being and nonbeing implicit in the manifest world.

The Child of Cinders, in whom *polarities* and *potentials* exist, knows the answers, yet he questions, "Do we call things so they will come? Do we call things so they will be?" He also knows that with each Creation, or Manifestation, Death also comes into play. Within the oneness of the uncreated sphere exists the seed of fecundity/aridity, growth/disintegration. "The world is recalled by us," he says, "only because of its disappearance." Life yields perennial loss.

A dancer enters the stage space. Like Shiva, he incarnates energy in performance, evocative of Rimbaud's "dance, dance, dance, dance" in *A Season in Hell*. Just as Shiva's arms gather time/space unto himself in evolution, Novarina's performer mimes as metamorphosis takes place.

L'Inquiétude

Unlike *Vous qui habitez le temps, L'Inquiétude* (1993), a stage adaptation of *Discours aux animaux* (1987; *Discourse to Animals*), has no Names as characters. A single actor concentrates on expelling his "long metaphysical wailing."[10] Novarina remarked that in *L'Inquiétude* he tried to sound out the emotional ramifications of intense "solitude": that of "facing objects, God, nothing." He was also intent on revealing language in a state of expansion as it reaches into the mineral, vegetal, and animal worlds. Because words are filled with myriad values, sonorities, feelings, and ideas, they contain the mystery of the unexpressed—an enigma that haunts Novarina. He wonders whether his anguish can be allayed by praying "to God or to animals." He calls out to grass, stones, twigs, dust, scales, all forms of existence, to receive his offering "from my hands my mouth and my word." He speaks to all things in whatever way available to him: "I crunched, drilled, cried, groaned, cawed, raucoused, crushed, nodded, ululated, creaked."

Novarina seeks to dilate the scope of language just as Orpheus, the archetypal poet, did through music. The goal of the writer is to communicate with stones, birds, and animals, rendering language, then, a sort of palimpsest. Like the archaeologist, Novarina would remove layers that conceal languages and, in so doing, would reveal traces of primordial forms dating back to cosmogonical origins.

The opening lines of *L'Inquiétude* refer to Orpheus, not by name but by intent: "Then I sat down and I said to the stones: Action is cursed." Just as the sounds emanating from Orpheus' lyre mesmerized animals and minerals by the beauty of their modulations, so the actor and/or writer must have the faculty of charming the impulses and instincts inhabiting the word. He or she does so by activating unknown and amorphous forces, which release accompanying tonal waves into the atmosphere in an endlessly resounding orchestration of harmonies and cacophonies.

Like the incantatory disciplines practiced by Orphics, so the exorcistic verbal recitations and patternings of *L'Inquiétude* are intended to take readers/initiates into the infinite world of the uncreated *(void)*. From such a vantage point they would experience the most perfected work of art in its unmanifested state.

The opening lines of *L'Inquiétude,* as previously mentioned, suggest an Orphic descent during which the performer breaks through the crust of outside matter and reaches preexistent spheres of being where he seizes his vision, his creation. There, words exist as burning coals; blocks of light spread throughout the blackness of his vaulted world (cranium). Is the actor, then, a prophet? a revealer who attains atemporality through the word? Is he a *nabi* (to use Martin Buber's expression), who bears God's message, becomes God's mouth, and reveals his hidden mysteries through the *inaudible speech of inwardness?*[11] The numinosity of this spiritual exploration leads to a reawakening of the soul on a deeper level and its resurrection in the spoken word.

Novarina's actor begins his Orphic descent in the shelter (the closed region of his cranium) he has constructed for himself 18 years before. He will set out from within on his personal and collective anamnesis—or cosmogonic adventure. As he listens to his word/speech, he follows its dicta: he passes through space/time regions fraught with terror/serenity, going back, perhaps, even to the world's origin. During his trajectory he *knows* the dismemberment of language: the aggressive, violent, and hostile intent of words, as well as their expression of the anguished need of love.

Like Prometheus chained on the rocky montain peak in the Caucasus, or Christ nailed to the Cross at Golgotha, the performer exists, as if suspended in space, in his own uncertainty. Midway between heaven and earth, he feels himself to be a mediator, belonging to neither immortal nor mortal spheres, and indicating that his attitude has not yet been rooted.

Within the actor's inner wasteland of imbalance and vertigo, he experiences an "immense feeling of thirst." Spurred on by hurt and rage, he leaves the city where "his barely formed mother had deformed him," where he had won the title of "Superior in Incapacities," where he had been condemned because he "thinks without things." Lack of communication with his family ordained him not to speak, only to write: "Jean lived without a childhood until the day before his birth." Later, animals surrounded him and told him how to "amass" his days; what to do with that *one* thought revealed to him yearly, which he then set into scrimshaw. The doctors called to heal him were ineffective. He journeyed to Algiers. He received Holy Communion. And "a year later," new sensations were triggered after he perceived something "engraved in capitals under a palm tree with a kriss" (an Indonesian dagger in the form of a crescent, endowed with supernatural powers). The word *kriss*, combining the notion of dismemberment (cutting) and transcendence (crescent), triggered the numinosum "God blessed me; he loved me; he ate me."

His parents' attempts to impose on him reason, logic, and order—or Cartesianism—left him dissatisfied. He was sent to a "Gynaeceum for Boys of La Flèche." Recall that Descartes had been sent to that same school, and it was there that his bouts with lung disease had obliged him to spend many days in his room, which earned him the name of "Le Chambriste."

Like Descartes, the young Jean lived increasingly in his enclosed world (by extension that of the performer and writer). Unlike the seventeenth-century philosopher/mathematician, his memory blurred; words/objects/names atomized; contexts disappeared amid orchestrations of mysterious tongues. He accepted the fact that he who had traversed all "latitudes" and heard all "platitudes" suffered enslavement to hostile inner dichotomies. To steady himself against the growing tide of rage within him, he recited numbers. "I counted. . . . While counting, I repeated to myself: 'Don't even count any more.'"

In that numbers arouse energy, they foment dynamism: they are "idea forces"—solidifications of spatial possibilities. They also lend order to what might otherwise be considered chaotic, thus giving a sense of security to those in need of it, and in this way they are considered archetypal foundations of the psyche. Understandably, an entire book in the Bible was called Numbers because within its pages were enclosed generations of souls leading back to the beginning of time, thus giving historical continuity to the Jewish people. The tracing of Christ's lineage back to

David is likewise an attempt on humanity's part to experience its ancestral soul in its original form.

As in Rimbaud's "Drunken Ship" and Paul Claudel's *Break of Noon,* constellations sway; their lights fall around the actor like billions of extinguished animals—Dog Star, Horse (Pegasus), and others. Regressing throughout his anamnesis, he sees himself at five years of age, whereupon he again reifies his thoughts, rubbing them together, so to speak, to produce the spark to "be," paralleling God's "Let there be light; and there was light" (Genesis 1: 3). Like Orpheus, he orders "the stones and pebbles" to rise "in speech" so that he may experience their souls. He hears wolves, animals, fish, each responding to his intonations in its own language/sign. Nothing is left, neither note nor word. Because he "falls" each minute more deeply into "absolute joy and without reason," the doctors inject chemical substances into him to bring him back to life. Only now does he realize "that life makes for sickness . . . and not the contrary as the ill are assured."

He calls to Jean-Jacques Rousseau, author of *Confessions,* of *Dialogues,* of *Rêveries,* who had encountered his double (mind/body) in nature and animals. He, like Rousseau, has eyes to weep. In a deeply moving apostrophe, he implores, "Divine hand, remove yourself from me, uproot this ceiling from me!" Living in Name, as inner absence, God "did not create, he extended his limits outside the worlds. . . . If God withdrew from here, it's only to let us alone to speak in his image." In silence, he hears his inner "voice once again teaching him how to speak." As in an apocalypse, numinosity reaches into him as he glories in the flesh and "glories in the spirit within!" He has "divided the reunited."

That Novarina used the word *withdrew* in referring to God, who he believed lived within him as "absence," brings to mind the astonishing view of the Divine Creation of the world as formulated by the sixteenth-century Hebrew Kabbalist Isaac Luria. Unlike the traditional theologian's view of the cosmic drama of Creation as a *creation ex nihilo,* Luria viewed creation out of nothingness as a result of God's exile or withdrawal into himself. His act of withdrawal, contraction, or concentration into himself—his essence becoming increasingly hidden in the process—led to the liberation of primordial or pneumatic space, from which the manifest world came into being.[12]

As the dazzled and dazed performer begins his dance and intones his "Salute to an unknown God!" he speaks in tongues. His bodily rhythms become frenzied; most of his words, beginning with "in," couple and

sever in rhymed and assonanced patterns like living creatures. The mysterious overtones that had blocked his view within are now purred for an
epiphany, the invisible and inaudible primordial experience manifests
itself within the performer's being. Like Nietzsche's dancer in *Thus Spake
Zarathustra,* the performer's body quivers in attunement with animate
and inanimate forces in the universe. A sense of belonging descends
upon him during his verbal and bodily throbbings, dispelling his flaying
sense of alienation as he withdraws into his Creation.

Although only Names, Novarina's beings are like novitiates in the
world's religious communities who practice prayers, recitations, invocations, mantras. Unlike these worshipers, however, Novarina's creatures
do not experience the condition of primordial unity and reintegration
into the godhead. Although they have stepped over the boundary from
Something to Nothingness, they are still stuck midway, fighting, struggling, agonizing somewhere within their "tube" mind or "tube" body. A
play on two Hebrew words may explain the bridge that must be crossed
for Oneness to be experienced: the transposition of one letter in the word
ain, meaning "nothing," produces *ani,* meaning "I" (Being). The passage
from Nothingness to Being thus takes place.[13]

Novarina's Names/characters have glimpsed, albeit fleetingly, "the
abyss of Nothingness" *(ain)* via speech, after which they are cast back
into the differentiated world as something *(ani),* only to repeat the
process over again. Sorrow *is* because vitality has been retained.

Novarina's ritualistic use of language restores to theatre its ancient
function, when emerging in its beginnings from deity: as from Bharata
(India), Amaterasu (Japan), Dionysus (Greece), Christ (France). Like
Mallarmé's theater and that of Villiers de l'Isle Adam, Artaud, and
Beckett, Novarina's dramas exist in their orality, visualizations, and
metaphysical concepts within the lobes of the mind. His understanding
of the *Name* called up in the *Word,* without uttering its unutterable
essence, invites the body/mind complex to follow mesmerizing sonorities
into rapture or trance. Energy can then be channeled to an inner and
subjective rather than an outward and objective world by way of a *via
contemplativa* and a *via illuminativa.*

Appendix:
Plays, Production Dates, and Directors

Philippe Adrien

Adrien, *La Baye* (1969): Antoine Bourseiller
Adrien, *Albert 1* (1969): Georges Peyrou (France-Culture)

Liliane Atlan

Atlan, *Monsieur Fugue* (1967): Roland Monod
Atlan, *Les Messies* (1969): Roland Monod
Atlan, *La Petite Voiture de flammes et de voix* (1975): Michel Hermon
Atlan, *Un opéra pour Térézin* (1989): Christine Bernard-Sugy (France-Culture)

Corinne Atlas

Atlas, *Le Coin d'ombre* (1983): France-Culture

Bruno Bayen

Frank Wedekind, *Dance Macabre* (1974): Bayen
Goethe, *Torquato Tasso* (1976): Bayen
Bayen, *Hernando Colòn* (1992): Bayen

André Benedetto

Benedetto, *Emballage* (1970): Benedetto
Benedetto, *La Madonne des Ordures* (1973): Benedetto

Andrée Chedid

Chedid, *Bérénice d'Egypte* (1964): Alain Barroux (France-Culture)
Chedid, *Nombres* (1966): Henry Soubeyran (France-Culture)
Chedid, *Le Montreur* (1971): Yves Gasc
Chedid, *Echec à la reine* (1984): Jean-Daniel Laval

François Chéreau

Jakob Lenz, *Soldats* (1967). Chéreau
Kuan Han-Ching, *La Neige au milieu de l'été et Le Voleur de femmes* (1967): Chéreau
Molière, *Dom Juan* (1969): Chéreau
Shakespeare, *Richard II* (1970): Chéreau
Marivaux, *La Dispute* (1973): Chéreau
Edward Bond, *Lear* (1975): Chéreau
Ibsen, *Peer Gynt* (1981): Chéreau
Chekhov, *Platonov* (1987): Chéreau
Shakespeare, *Hamlet* (1988): Chéreau
Alban Berg, *Woyzeck* (1992): Chéreau

Enzo Cormann

Cormann, *Takiya! Tokaya!* (1992)

Michel Deutsch

Deutsch, *Dimanche* (1976): Dominique Muller
Deutsch, *La Bonne Vie* (1977): Jean-Pierre Vincent
Deutsch, *L'Entrainement du champion avant la course* (1978): Philippe Sireuil
Deutsch, *Convoi* (1980): Jean-Pierre Vincent

Eugène Durif

Durif, *L'Arbre de Jonas* (1990): François Coupat and Daniel Pouthier
Durif, *Conversations sur la montagne* (1992): Patrick Pineau
Durif, *Les Petites Heures* (1992): Jean-Pierre Colas (France-Culture)
Durif, *Croisements, Divagations* (1993): Joël Jouhanneau

Colette Fayard

Fayard, *Effacement* (1989): Dominique Bluzet

Serge Ganzl

Ganzl, *Le Coeur battant* (1989): Anne Petit

Victor Garcìa

Valle-Inclán, *La Rose de papier* (1964): Garcìa
Genet, *Les Bonnes* (1970): Garcìa
Lorca, *Yerma* (1973): Garcìa
Valle-Inclán, *Divines paroles* (1976): Garcìa

Armand Gatti

Gatti, *La Vie imaginaire de l'éboueur Auguste Geai* (1962): Jacques Rosner
Gatti, *La Passion du Général Franco* (1968): Gatti
Gatti, *Les Treize Soleils de la rue Saint-Blaise* (1968): Guy Rétoré
Gatti, *L'Arche d'Adelin* (1973): Gatti
Gatti, *La Colonne Durruti* (1974): Gatti
Gatti, *Le Chant d'amour des alphabets d'Auschwitz* (1988): Gatti
Gatti, *Ces Empereurs aux ombrelles trouées* (1991): Gatti
Gatti, *Marseille: Adam quoi?* (1993): Gatti

Gérard Gelas

Gelas, *Opération* (1970): Gelas
Arrabal, *Pucelle pour un gorille* (1992): Gelas

Jean-Claude Grumberg

Grumberg, *Dreyfus* (1974): Jacques Rosner
Grumberg, *En r'venant d'l'Expo* (1975): Jean-Pierre Vincent

Victor Haïm

Haïm, *La Peau d'un fruit sur un arbre pourri* (1971): Jean-Paul Roussillon

Jean Jourdheuil

Vigny, *Chatterton* (1976): Jourdheuil
Jourdheuil and Chartreux, *Mazimilien Robespierre* (1976): Jourdheuil
Jourdheuil and Chartreaux, *Jean-Jacques Rousseau* (1978): Jourdheuil

Jean Jourdheuil and Jean-Pierre Vincent

Brecht, *La Noce chez les petits-bourgeois* (1968): Jourdheuil and Vincent
Büchner, *Woyzeck* (1973): Jourdheuil and Vincent

René Kalisky

Kalisky, *Sur les ruines de Carthage* (1979): Jean Pierre Miquel

Bernard-Marie Koltès

Koltès, *Combat de Nègre et de chiens* (1983): Chéreau
Koltès, *Dans la solitude des champs de coton* (1987): Chéreau
Koltès, *Roberto Zucco* (1990): Peter Stein

Madeleine Laïk

Laïk, *Double Commande* (1982)

Georges Lassalle

Sarraute, *Elle est là* (1993): Lassalle

Georges Lavaudant

Lavaudant, *La Mémoire de l'iceberg* (1974): Lavaudant
Bourgeade, *Palazzo Mentale* (1976): Lavaudant
Shakespeare, *Richard III* (1984): Lavaudant
Brecht, *Baal* (1988): Lavaudant
Lavaudant, *Terra incognita* (1992): Lavaudant

Jorge Lavelli

Arrabal, *L'Architecte et l'Empereur d'Assyrie* (1967): Lavelli
Lorca, *Le Public* (1988): Lavelli
Gombrowicz, *Opérette* (1989): Lavelli

Pierre Léaud

Léaud, *Fugue en mineur (e)* (1978): Pierre Romans
Léaud, *Passé composé* (1986): Claudine Dalmas
Léaud, *Les Murs n'ont pas d'oreilles* (1987): Thierry Bourcier

Daniel Lemahieu

Lemahieu, *Usinage* (1984): Claude Yersin
Lemahieu, *Entre chien et loup* (1981): Pierre-Etienne Heymann (reading)
Lemahieu, *L'Idéal* (1990): Lemahieu

Armando Llamas

Llamas, *Image de Mussolini en hiver* (1986): Stéphane Loïk

Eduardo Manet

Manet, *Les Nonnes* (1969): Roger Blin
Manet, *Les Chiennes* (1987): France-Culture

Marcel Maréchal

Audiberti, *Le Cavalier seul* (1963): Maréchal
Vauthier, *Capitaine Bada* (1966): Maréchal (first production in 1952, directed by André Reybaz)

Daniel Mesguich

Shakespeare, *Hamlet* (1977): Mesguich
Shakespeare, *Titus Andronicus* (1989): Mesguich

Philippe Minyana

Minyana, *Laura dans l'olivette* (1980)
Minyana, *Le diner de Lina* (1983): Stéphane Loïk
Minyana, *Fin d'été à Baccarat* (1985): Carlos Wittig

Ariane Mnouchkine

Arnold Wesker, *The Kitchen* (1967): Mnouchkine
Shakespeare, *A Midsummer Night's Dream* (1968): Mnouchkine
Soleil, *Les Clowns* (1969): Mnouchkine
Soleil, *1789* (1970): Mnouchkine
Soleil, *1793* (1972): Mnouchkine
Soleil, *L'Age d'or* (1975): Mnouchkine
Klaus Mann, *Mephisto* (1979): Mnouchkine
Shakespeare, *Richard II* (1981): Mnouchkine
Shakespeare, *Twelfth Night* (1982): Mnouchkine
Shakespeare, *Henry IV* (Part 1) (1984): Mnouchkine
Cixous, *L'Histoire terrible mais inachevée de Nodorom Sihanouk* (1985): Mnouchkine
Cixous, *L'Indiade ou L'Inde de leurs rêves* (1987): Mnouchkine
Les Atrides (1990): Mnouchkine

Valère Novarina

Novarina, *Lettre aux acteurs* (1989): Novarina
Novarina, *Entrée dans le théâtre des oreilles* (1989). France-Culture
Novarina, *Vous qui habitez le temps* (1989): Novarina
Novarina, *L'Inquiétude* (1992): Marc Blezinger

Eric Pelsy-Johann

Pelsy-Johann, *L'Homme égaré* (1985): Marie Stockmort

Roger Planchon

Molière, *Le Tartuffe* (1962): Planchon
Planchon, *La Contestation et la mise en pièce de la plus illustre des tragédies françaises "Le Cid"* (1969): Planchon
Planchon, *L'Infâme* (1969): Planchon

Noëlle Renaude

Renaude, *Blanche Aurore Céleste* (1991): Claude Guerre (France-Culture)
Renaude, *Petits Rôles* (1992)

Serge Rezvani

Rezvani, *Le Palais d'hiver* (1976): Daniel Mesguich

Nathalie Sarraute

Sarraute, *Le Mensonge* (1967): Jean-Louis Barrault
Sarraute, *Le Silence* (1967): Jean-Louis Barrault
Sarraute, *Isma* (1970): Claude Roland-Manuel (France-Culture)
Sarraute, *C'est beau* (1973): Claude Régy
Sarraute, *Elle est là* (1978): Claude Régy
Sattaute, *Pour un oui ou pour un non* (1993): Jacques Lassalle

Jérome Savary

Savary, *Le Radeau de la Méduse* (1968): Savary
Savary, *Robinson Crusoé* (1972): Savary
Molière, *Le Bourgeois Gentilhomme* (1980): Savary

Bernard Sobel

Brecht, *Homme pour homme* (1970): Sobel
Brecht, *Têtes rondes et têtes pointues* (1973): Sobel
Lenz, *Le Précepteur* (1975): Sobel
Marlowe, *Le Juif de Malte* (1976): Sobel

José Valverde

Bosquet, *Kafka/Auschwitz* (1993): Valverde

Michel Vinaver

Vinaver, *Les Coréens* (1956): Roger Planchon
Vinaver, *La Demande d'emploi* (1973): Jean Pierre Dougnac
Vinaver, *Par-dessus bord* (1973): Roger Planchon
Vinaver, *Iphigénie Hôtel* (1977): Antoine Vitez
Vinaver, *Dissident, il va sans dire* (1978): Jacques Lassalle
Vinaver, *Nina, c'est autre chose* (1978): Jacques Lassalle
Vinaver, *Les Travaux et les jours* (1979): Alain Françon
Vinaver, *A la renverse* (1980): Jacques Lassalle
Vinaver, *Les Voisins* (1986): Alain Françon
Vinaver, *Portrait d'une femme* (1986): reading by Vinaver
Vinaver, *L'Emission de télévision* (1990): Jacques Lassalle

Jean-Pierre Vincent

Chartreaux and Deutsch, *Germinal* (1975): Vincent
Molière, *Le Misanthrope* (1977): Vincent
Chartreux, *Violences à Vichy* (1980): Vincent

Antoine Vitez

Vitez, *Le Procès d'Emile Henry* (1967): Vitez
Racine, *Andromaque* (1971): Vitez
Aragon, *Catherine* (1975/6): Vitez
Racine, *Britannicus* (1981): Vitez
Racine, *Bérénice* (1980): Vitez

Jean-Paul Wenzel

Wenzel, *Loin d'Hagondange* (1977): Chéreau
Wenzel, *Claudine Marianne attend le mariage* (1978): Claudine Fiévet

Wenzel, *Les Incertains* (1979): Alain Mergnat
Wenzel and Bloch, *Haïr Laurel* (1983). Wenzel

Jeanine Worms

Worms, *Un chat est un chat* (1968): Jacques Legré
Worms, *La Boutique* (1971): Alain Scoff
Worms, *Le Goûter* (1972): Jacques Echantillon

Notes and References

Chapter One

1. Colette Godard, *Le Théâtre depuis 1968* (Paris: Lattès, 1980), 145; hereafter cited in text. Raymonde Temkine, *Mettre en scène au présent*, vol. 2 (Lausanne: La Cité-L'Age d'Homme, 1979), 53.
2. Bettina L. Knapp, unpublished interview with Jean-Pierre Vincent and Jean Jourdheuil, 1972.
3. J.-P. Vincent, *Violences à Vichy* (Paris: Stock/Théâtre Ouvert, 1980), 168.
4. Jean Jourdheuil, *L'Artiste, la politique, la production* (Paris: 10/18, 1976), 196. See *Le Théâtre, l'artiste, l'état* (Paris: Hachette, 1979).
5. Quoted in Bettina Knapp, *Off-Stage Voices* (Troy, N.Y.: Whitston Press, 1975), 50.
6. Yvette Daoust, *Roger Planchon: Director and Playwright* (Cambridge: Cambridge University Press, 1981), 192.
7. Odette Aslan, *Les Voies de la création théâtrale*, vol. 1 (Paris: Editions du Centre National de la Recherche Scientifique, 1970), 315; hereafter cited in text.
8. Daniel Mesguich, *L'Eternel éphémère* (Paris: Seuil, 1991), 38; hereafter cited in text.
9. Leonora Champagne, *French Theatre Experiment since 1968* (Ann Arbor, Mich.: UMI Research Press, 1984), 87; hereafter cited in text.
10. Georges Baal, "*Titus Andronicus*, Directed by Daniel Mesquich: The Other Stage beyond Misery," *Theater Research International* 16 (1991): 112; hereafter cited in text.
11. *Platonov*, Théâtre National Populaire, 2–22 August 1990.
12. Quoted in Marion Thébaud, *Le Figaro,* 20 July 1992.
13. Patrick Ferla, *Conversation avec Marcel Maréchal* (Lausanne: Pierre-Marcel Fabre, 1983), 35.
14. Giles Sandier, *Théâtre et combat* (Paris: Stock, 1970), 33; hereafter cited in text.
15. Yannic Mancel, quoted in Jacques Lassalle, *Pauses* (Paris: Actes Sud, 1991), 14–18; hereafter cited in text.
16. See also Jacques Lassalle, "L'Heureuse dépendance," *Bulletin de l'Association Goldoni* 2 (1992): 23–24.
17. See Jacques Lassalle, "En un obscur commencement," *Program* (March 1993): 12–14.
18. José Valverde (Paris: Théâtre Essaïon, 1993).
19. Eric Pelsy-Johann, letter to the author, 17 June 1993.

10. Lilt Poly-Julian, letter to the author, 17 June 1993

21. Quoted in Fabienne Pascaud, with Emmanuel Bouchez, "La Nouvelle vague," *Théâtre*, 4 March 1992, 9–11.

Chapter Two

1. Jean-Pierre Sarrazac, *L'Avenir du drame* (Lausanne: L'Aire Théâtrale, 1981), 68; hereafter cited in text.
2. Michel Deutsch, "Interview," *Ecritures* 11 (1980): 5–7.
3. Marc Quaghebeur, "Le Resserrement tragique chez Kalisky," in *Sur les ruines de Carthage* (Reims: La Revue de la Compagnie Jean-Pierre Miquel, 1980), 98.
4. Odile Quirot, "Le Radicalisme et le doute," *Théâtre Ouvert* (March 1990): 4–5.
5. Quoted in Monique Le Roux, "La Course vers la mort," *La Quinzaine Littéraire* 10 (1992): 28–29.

Chapter Three

1. The Théâtre de l'Aquarium, also housed at the Cartoucherie at Vincennes, was originally founded by Jacques Nichet for a university troupe (the Ecole Normale Supérieur) in 1963. Nichet was known for his critical, imaginative, and frequently collective improvisations. His sensitivity and in-depth style enabled him to integrate creative theatrical methods with political satire. In 1986 he became director of the Centre Dramatique Nationaux (CDN) in Montpellier, offering such innovative productions as Diderot's *D'Alembert's Dream* (in 1987), García Lorca's *La Savetière prodigieuse* (in 1988), and Marivaux's *Le Triomphe de l'amour* (in 1989).
2. Judith Graves Miller, *Theater and Revolution in France since 1968* (Lexington, Ky.: French Forum Publishers, 1977), 61.
3. Colette Godard, "Théâtre," *Le Monde,* 12 February 1946.
4. Gilles Sandier, "Théâtre," *Le Matin,* 19 November 1981.
5. Sandier 1981 and Pierre Macabru, *Le Point,* 21 November 1981.
6. Denis Salter, "Hand Eye Mind Soul: Théâtre du Soleil's *Les Atrides,*" *Théâtre* 1 (1993): 59–65.

Chapter Four

1. Anna Dizier, *Antoine Vitez* (Paris: Solins, 1982), 5; hereafter cited in text.
2. Jean-Pierre Sarrazac, *Antoine Vitez: Toutes les mises en scène* (Paris: Jean-Cyrille Godefroy, 1981), 90; hereafter cited in text.
3. Jean-Pierre Althaus, *Voyage dans le théâtre* (Paris: Pierre Marcel Favre, 1984), 18.
4. Recall Artaud's portrayal of Charlemagne in Alexandre Arnoux's

Huon de Bordeaux. When Charles Dullin saw him in rehearsal bedecked with a long, curly beard and advancing toward the throne on all fours, he tried to dissuade him from this interpretation. Whereupon Artaud shot up, brandishing his arms, and in a commanding tone stated flatly, "Oh! When you work in truth! Then! . . ." (Jean Hort, *Antonin Artaud* [Geneva: Editions Connaître, 1960], 69).
    5. Vitez had been Aragon's secretary.
    6. Danièle Sallenave, quoted in Dizier, 181–84.

Chapter Five

    1. Armand Gatti, "Au commencement était le verbe," videotape, Marseilles, 16 July 1990.
    2. Armand Gatti, *Armand Gatti: Revue de Presse* (Avignon, 1991). These are albums put together in scrapbook style.

Chapter Six

    1. Odette Aslan, *Les Voies de la création théâtrale*, vol. 14, Patrice Chéreau (Paris: Editions du Centre National de la Recherche Scientifique, 1986), 35; hereafter cited in text.
    2. Georges Banu, *Le Théâtre, sorties de secours* (Paris: Aubier, 1984), 78–82.
    3. Patrice Chéreau, *Programme de "Lear" de Bond,* 1975.
    4. Nicolas Treatt, *Chéreau,* unpublished manuscript, 1984.
    5. Chéreau became codirector of the TNP in 1971; he was appointed codirector of the Théâtre des Amandiers at Nanterre in 1982; he has been freelancing since 1990.

Chapter Seven

    1. Nathalie Sarraute, *Tropisms and the Age of Suspicion,* trans. Maria Jolas (London: John Calder, 1963), 8.

Chapter Eight

    1. Evelyne Ertel, "L'Eloge du fragment," *Théâtre Public* 97 (1991): 40.
    2. Michel Vinaver, "Auto-Interrogatoire," *Travail Théâtral* 30 (1978): 48; hereafter cited in text.
    3. Michel Vinaver, *Ecrits sur le théâtre* (Lausanne: Editions de l'Aire, 1982), 308; hereafter cited in text.
    4. Michel Vinaver, *Les Voisins* (Saint-Imier: Canevas Editeur, 1988), 80; hereafter cited in text.
    5. Michel Vinaver, Preface to *Iphigénie Hôtel* (Paris: Gallimard, 1963), 9.
    6. Roland Barthes, "Notes sur *Aujourd'hui,*" *Travail Théâtral* 30 (1978): 58–60.

1. Michel Vinaver, *Par-dessus bord* (Paris: L'Arche, 1972), 89.

8. Jean-Pierre Sarrazac, "Le corps à corps des écritures de Michel Vinaver," *Travail* *Théâtral* 30 (1978): 62.

9. Michel Vinaver, "Théâtre de chambre," *Travail Théâtral* 30 (1978): 70.

10. Michel Vinaver, *Portrait d'une femme*, in *Théâtre complète* (Paris: Actes Sud, 1986), 501.

Chapter Nine

1. Antonin Artaud, *The Theatre and Its Double*, trans. Caroline Richards (New York: Grove Press, 1958), 135.

2. William Theodore de Bary, ed., *Sources of Indian Tradition* (New York: Columbia University Press, 1958), 1: 3.

3. Valère Novarina, "Lettre aux acteurs," in *Le Théâtre des paroles* (Paris: POL, 1989), 9. Translations by Allan Weiss of "Letter to the Actors" and "The Drama of Life" are in *Drama Review* 37, no. 2 (1993): 95–104.

4. Bettina L. Knapp, *Antonin Artaud: Man of Vision* (Athens: University of Ohio Press, 1981), 113.

5. Jean Genet, Foreword to *The Maids*, trans. Bernard Frechtman *Tulane Drama Review* (Spring 1963).

6. Mircea Eliade, "Mysteries and Spiritual Regeneration in Extra-European Religions," in *Eranos Yearbook* (New York: Pantheon, 1964), 5: 17–24.

7. Valère Novarina, *Entrée dans le théâtre des oreilles*, in *Le Théâtre des paroles* (Paris: POL, 1989), 80. Translation by Allan Weiss, "Entry into a Theater of the Ears," *Alea* 3 (1993): 149.

8. Noëlle Renaude, "Le Théâtre doit nous sortir du sommeil matérial-iste," *théâtre/public* (June 1989): 72.

9. Marie-Louise von Franz, *Number and Time* (Evanston, Ill.: Northwestern University Press, 1974), 11; Edouard Schuré, *The Great Initiates* (New York: St. George Books, 1962), 305, 311.

10. Noëlle Renaude, "Le Désir de vertige," *théâtre/public* (June 1986): 7–9.

11. Aryeh Kaplan, *Meditation and the Bible* (New York: Samuel Weiser, 1978), 156.

12. Gershom Scholem, *Kabbalah and Its Symbolism* (New York: Schocken Books, 1973), 110.

13. Gershom Scholem, *Major Trends in Jewish Mysticism* (New York: Schocken Books, 1965), 218.

Selected Bibliography

Althaus, Jean-Pierre. *Voyage dans le théâtre.* Paris: Editions Pierre-Marcel Favre, 1984.

Antoine Vitez: Toutes les mises en scène. Paris: Jean-Cyrille Godefroy, 1981. Contains articles by Anne-Françoise Benhamou, Emmanuel Decaux, Danièle Sallenave, Jean-Pierre Sarrazac, and Olivier-René Veillon. With the participation of Claudine Amiard-Chevrel and François Regnault.

Artaud, Antonin. *The Theater and Its Double.* Translated by Caroline Richards. New York: Grove Press, 1958.

Aslan, Odette. *Les Voies de la création théâtrale.* Vol. 1. Paris: Editions du Centre National de la Recherche Scientifique, 1970.

———*Les Voies de la création théâtrale.* Vol. 14: "Patrice Chéreau." Paris: Editions du Centre National de la Recherche Scientifique, 1986.

Attoun, Lucien. "Théâtre Ouvert." *théâtre/public* 2 (1974).

——— "Vingt et un ans de théâtre d'essai et de création." *Théâtre* (1991–92): 247–51.

——— "Un théâtre ouvert sur le monde." *Revue des Deux Mondes* (February 1992): 20–23.

Baal, Georges. "*Titus Andronicus,* Directed by Daniel Mesguich: The Other Stage beyond Misery." Translated by Brian Singleton. *Theater Research International* 16 (1991): 112–15.

Banu, Georges. *Le Théâtre, sorties de secours.* Paris: Aubier, 1984.

Barthes, Roland. "Notes sur *Aujourd'hui.*" *Travail théâtral* 30 (1978): 58–60.

Bradby, David. *Modern French Drama 1940–1990.* Cambridge: Cambridge University Press, 1991.

Champagne, Leonora. *French Theater Experiment since 1968.* Ann Arbor, Mich.: UMI Research Press, 1984.

Cixous, Hélène. "Théâtre enfoui." *Europe* 726 (1989): 72–76.

Daoust, Yvette. *Roger Planchon: Director and Playwright.* Cambridge: Cambridge University Press, 1981.

Deshoulières, Christophe. *Le Théâtre au XXe siècle.* Paris: Bordas, 1989.

Deutsch, Michel. "D'un théâtre l'autre." *Ecritures* 11 (1980): 6.

Di Meo, Philippe. "Une mère lointaine." *théâtre/public,* 14 July 1986, 16–21.

Dizier, Anna. *Antoine Vitez.* Paris: Solins, 1982.

Durif, Eugène. "Depuis *Le Petit Bois.*" *Ecritures* 1 (1992): 2–3.

Ertel, Evelyne. "L'Eloge du fragment." *Théâtre Public* 97 (1991): 36–40.

——— "Une fête pour la création." *Théâtre Public* 82–83 (1988): 73–75.

Ferla, Patrick. *Conversation avec Marcel Maréchal.* Lausanne: Pierre-Marcel Favre, 1983.

Gatti, Armand. *Revue de Presse* Avignon, 1991.

———. *Dossier. Le Chant d'amour des alphabets à Auschwitz.* 1993.

———. *Oeuvres théâtrales* Vols. 1–3. Lagrasse: Verdier, 1991.

———. *The Imaginary Life of the Street Cleaner Auguste G.* Translated by Alba Amoia. In *The Contemporary French Theater.* New York: Avon Books, 1973.

———. *Marseille: Adam quoi? Revue de Presse.* 1993.

Gavart-Perret, Jean-Paul. "Valère Novarina ou le dernier poète de la modernité. *Java* 8 (1992): 34–40.

Genet, Jean. Foreword to *The Maids.* Translated by Bernard Frechtman. *Tulane Drama Review* (Spring 1963).

Godard, Colette. *Le Théâtre depuis 1968.* Paris: Lattès, 1980.

———. *Théâtre.* Vol. 1. Paris: Christian Bourgois, 1971.

———. "Théâtre." *Le Monde,* 14 December 1981.

Gozlan, Gérard, and Jean-Louis Pays. *Gatti aujourd'hui.* Paris: Seuil, 1970.

Grande, Maurizio. "L'Insomnie des noms." *Java* 8 (1992): 14–20.

Haïm, Victor. "Gestation et devéloppement de 'Belle Famille.'" In *Auteurs dramatiques français d'aujourd'hui.* Paris: Trois Cailloux, 1984.

Hort, Jean. *Antonin Artaud.* Geneva: Editions Connaître, 1960.

José Valverde. Paris: Théâtre Essaïon, 1993.

Jourdheuil, Jean. *L'Artiste, la politique, la production.* Paris: 10/18, 1976.

———. *Le Théâtre, l'artiste, l'état.* Paris: Hachette, 1979.

Kalisky, René. *Sur les ruines de Carthage.* Reims: Revue de la Compagnie Jean-Pierre Miquel, 1980.

Koltès, Bernard-Marie. "Des lieux privilégés." In *Auteurs dramatiques français d'aujourd'hui.* Paris: Trois Cailloux, 1984.

Knapp, Bettina L. *Off-Stage Voices.* Troy, N.Y.: Whitston Press, 1975.

———. *Antonin Artaud: Man of Vision.* Athens: University of Ohio Press, 1981.

———. "Nathalie Sarraute." In *European Writers: The Twentieth Century.* Vol. 12. New York: Charles Scribner's Sons, 1990, 2333–59.

Knowles, Dorothy. *Armand Gatti in the Theater: Wild Duck against the Wind.* London: Athlone Press, 1989.

Laurent, Michèle. *Les Atrides.* Paris: Théâtre du Soleil, 1992.

Lassalle, Jacques. *Pauses.* Paris: Actes Sud, 1991.

———. "L'Heureuse dépendance." *Bulletin de l'Association Goldoni Européen* 2 (November 1992): 23–24.

———. "En un obscur commencement." *Programme* (March 1993): 12–14.

Lavaudant, Georges. *Terra incognita.* Preface by Michel Bataillon. Paris: Christian Bourgois, 1992.

———. "Le Lieu de tous les temps." Interview with Didier Méreuze. *Le Théâtre: Art Press* (1980–90): 142–47.

Lemahieu, Daniel. "Comment ça parle aujourd'hui." In *Auteurs dramatiques français d'aujourd'hui.* Paris: Trois Cailloux, 1984.

Lerrant, Jean-Jacques. *La Criée.* Marseilles: Editions Jeanne Laffitte, 1992.

Le Roux, Monique. "La Course vers la mort." *La Quinzaine Littéraire* 10 (1992): 28–29.

──────. *Richard II: Le Théâtre*. Paris: Bordas, 1992.

McCarthy, Gerry. "Théâtre Ouvert: A Theatre for Writers in France." *Theater Quarterly* 32 (1979): 73–75.

Macabru, Pierre. "Théâtre." *Le Figaro*, 14 December 1981.

Marivaux, Pierre de. *La Fausse Suivante*. Preface by Jean Goldzink. Notes by Jacques Lassalle. Paris: Imprimerie Nationale, 1991.

Mesguich, Daniel. *L'Eternel éphémère*. Paris: Seuil, 1991.

Miller, Judith Graves. *Theater and Revolution in France since 1968*. Lexington, Ky.: French Forum Publishers, 1977.

Mnouchkine, Ariane. "Le Choix et la nécéssité." In *Théâtre, 1991–1992*, 47–53. Paris: Hachette, 1992.

──────. "Lettres/arts." *Le Matin de Paris*, 10 December 1991.

──────. "Le Masque: Une discipline de base au Théâtre du Soleil." In *Le Masque: Du Rite au Théâtre*, 231–34. Paris: Editions du Centre National de la Recherche Scientifique, 1985.

──────. "Théâtre." *Témoignage chrétien*, 14 December 1981.

Moscoso, Sophie. "Notes de répétitions." In *Le Théâtre du Soleil*, part 2, *Shakespeare*. Paris: SNEP, 1984.

Nattiez, Jean-Jacques. *Tétralogies: Wagner, Boulez, Chéreau*. Paris: Christian Bourgois, 1983.

Nicole, Eugène. "Les Rôles du nom dans le théâtre de Valère Novarina." *Java* 8 (1992): 28–33.

Nores, Dominique, and Colette Godard. *Jorge Lavelli*. Paris: Christian Bourgois, 1971.

Novarina, Valère. "Valère Novarina enveloppé de langues comme d'un vêtement de joie." Interview with Hadrien Laroche. *Java* 8 (1992): 41–70.

──────. *L'Inquiétude*. Paris: POL, 1992.

──────. *Vous qui habitez le temps*. Paris: POL, 1989.

──────. *Le Théâtre des paroles*. Paris: POL, 1989. Contains *Lettre aux acteurs* and *Entrée dans le théâtre des oreilles*.

Pascaud, Fabienne, with Emmanuel Bouchez. "Nouvelle vague." *Théâtre*, 4 March 1992.

Quirot, Odile. "Le Radicalisme et le doute." *Théâtre Ouvert* (March 1990): 4–5.

Quaghebeur, Marc. "Le Resserrement tragique chez Kalisky." *In Sur les ruines de Carthage*, 95–102. Reims: La Revue de la Compagnie Jean-Pierre Miquel, 1980.

Renaude, Noëlle. "Le Désir de vertige." *théâtre/public* (June 1986): 7–9.

──────. "Le Théâtre doit nous sortir du sommeil matérialiste." *théâtre/public* (June 1989): 67–73.

──────. "Novarina: L'Ecriture de livre et de la scène." *théâtre/public* (May 1991): 9–16.

──────. "Six jours au Jardin d'Hiver." *théâtre/public* 82–83 (1988): 75–76.

Rockwell, John. "Behind the Mask of a Moralist." New York Times 27 September 1992.

Rousseau, Nita. Marcel Maréchal. Paris: Actes Sud, 1992. Interviews.

Roy, Claude. "Ariane Soleil." In Le Théâtre du Soleil, part 2, Shakespeare. Paris: SNEP, 1982.

Salter, Denis. "Hands Eye Mind Soul: Théâtre du Soleil's Les Atrides." Théâtre 1 (1993): 59–65.

Sandier, Gilles. Théâtre et combat. Paris: Stock, 1970.

———. "Théâtre." Le Matin, 19 December 1981.

Sarraute, Nathalie. Tropisms and the Age of Suspicion. Translated by Maria Jolas. London: John Calder, 1963.

Sarrazac, Jean-Pierre. L'Avenir du drame. Lausanne: L'Aire Théâtrale, 1981.

Satgé, Alain, and Jorge Lavelli. Lavelli Opéra et mise à mort. Paris: Fayard, 1979.

Schuré, Edouard. The Great Initiates. New York: St. George Books, 1962.

Séonnet, Michel. "Le Théâtre des exclus." Le Magazine Littéraire (July–August 1991): 98–104.

Simon, Alfred. "Les Pouvoirs mystérieux de la tragédie." In Théâtre, 1991–92. Paris: Hachette, 1992.

Stricker, Jean-Marc. "Jérôme Savary: De la provocation à la séduction." L'Avant-Scène 775 (1985).

Temkine, Raymonde. Mettre en scène au présent. Vol. 1. Lausanne: La Cité–L'Age d'Homme, 1971.

———. Mettre en scène au présent. Vol. 2. Lausanne: La Cité–L'Age d'Homme, 1979.

———. "Shakespeare en représentations." In Théâtre du Soleil, part 2, Shakespeare. Paris: SNEP, 1984.

———. Le Théâtre en l'état. Paris: Editions Théâtrales, 1992.

Théâtre du Soleil. L'Age d'or. Paris: Stock/Théâtre Ouvert, 1970.

Théâtre du Soleil. 1789/1793. Paris: L'Avant-Scène, 1973.

Théâtre Ouvert. A Livre Ouvert. Catalog. 1971–88.

Théâtre Ouvert. Les Activités de Théâtre Ouvert. Catalog. 1988–91.

Théâtre Ouvert. Catalog. 1992–93.

Ubersfeld, Anne. Vinaver dramaturge. Paris: Librairie Théâtrale, 1989.

Vinaver, Michel. "Auto-interrogatoire." Travail Théâtral 30 (1978): 47–57.

———. Le Compte-rendu d'Avignon. Paris: Actes Sud, 1987.

———. Ecrits sur le théâtre. Lausanne: Editions de l'Aire, 1982.

———. Iphigénie Hôtel. Paris: Gallimard, 1963.

———. Les Coréens. Paris: Actes Sud, 1986.

———. L'Emission de télévision. Paris: Actes Sud, 1990.

———. L'Ordinaire. Dijon: Editions de l'Aire, 1992.

———. Par-dessus bord. Paris: L'Arche, 1972.

———. Théâtre complète. Vols. 1 and 2. Paris: Actes Sud, 1986.

———. "Théâtre de chambre." Travail Théâtral 30 (1978): 70.

Vincent, J.-P. Violences à Vichy. Paris: Stock/Théâtre Ouvert, 1980.

Weiss, Allen S. "Radiophonic Art: The Voice of the Impossible Body." *Discourse* 14, no. 2 (1992): 188–99.

————. "Le Théâtre de la possession." *Java* 8 (1992): 21–26.

————. "Mouths of Disquietude." *Drama Review* 37, no. 2 (1993).

————. Translations of "Letter to the Actors" and *The Drama of Life*. *Drama Review* (Summer 1993): 95–104.

————. Translations of "Entry into a Theater of the Ears." *Alea* 3 (1993): 146–56.

Wenzel, Jean-Paul. "Auprès de ses doutes." In *Auteurs dramatiques français d'aujourdh'hui*. Paris: Trois Cailloux, 1984.

Index

194

The Author

Bettina L. Knapp is professor of French and comparative literature at Hunter College and the Graduate Center of the City University of New York. She has received a Presidential Award from Hunter in the area of scholarship/creative activity, as well as a Guggenheim Fellowship and a grant from the American Philosophical Society. She is the author of *Antonin Artaud: Man of Vision*; *Theater, and Alchemy*; *Louis Jouvet: Man of the Theatre*; *Jean Racine: Mythos and Renewal in Modern Theatre*; *Off-Stage Voices*; *French Theatre 1918–1939*; *The Reign of the Theatrical Director*; *Archetype, Dance, and the Writer*; *That Was Yvette*; *Aristide Bruand*; *Women in Twentieth-Century Literature*; *Anaïs Nin*; *Emily Dickinson*; and *The Brontës*. She is also the author of *Jean Genet, Fernand Crommelynck, Georges Duhamel, Jean Cocteau, Maurice Maeterlinck,* and *Sacha Guitry* in this series.

GAYLORD F